# NORTH KOREA
# ON THE BRINK

November 2007

Catherine,

many thanks

# North Korea on the Brink

## Struggle for Survival

## Glyn Ford
### with Soyoung Kwon

## Foreword by Gareth Evans

Pluto Press
London • Ann Arbor, MI

First published 2008 by Pluto Press
345 Archway Road, London N6 5AA
and 839 Greene Street, Ann Arbor, MI 48106

www.plutobooks.com

British Library Cataloguing in Publication Data
A catalogue record for this book is available from the British Library

ISBN 978 0 7453 2599 6 hardback
ISBN 978 0 7453 2598 9 paperback

Library of Congress Cataloging in Publication Data applied for

10  9  8  7  6  5  4  3  2  1

Designed and produced for Pluto Press by Curran Publishing
Services, Norwich

Printed and bound in the European Union by
Antony Rowe Ltd, Chippenham and Eastbourne, England

# Contents

*List of figures, tables and maps*                          *viii*
*List of abbreviations*                                       *ix*
*Note on Korean names and words*                             *xi*
*Foreword by Gareth Evans*                                   *xii*
*Preamble*                                                    *xv*

**1.  North Korea in context**                                **1**
    Introduction                                               1
    Northern exposure                                          1
    Hypocrisy and democracy                                    5
    Regional perspectives                                      8
    European voice                                             9
    Going North                                               12

**2.  Drawing the Iron Curtain**                             **16**
    Introduction                                              16
    Geography                                                 16
    The Yanks arrive                                          18
    Revolts, riots and invasion                               20
    Annexation and resistance                                 20
    Rising nationalism                                        21
    Kim enters stage left                                     22
    Colonial consequences                                     23
    The Soviets come and go                                   26
    Gerrymandered elections                                   28
    Pre-war war                                               29
    Stalin says yes                                           31
    Mao concurs                                               32
    Who kicked off?                                           33
    Civil war to cold war conflict                            33
    The process                                               37
    Going for a draw                                          39
    POWs                                                      41
    The end                                                   42
    Hangover                                                  44
    Winners and losers                                        46

**3.  Kim's Korea**                                          **48**
    Introduction                                              48
    Divide and rule                                           49
    Kim under threat                                          50
    Then there was one                                        52
    Leaving Marx                                              54

Economy takes off     56
Heroes of labour     58
Economic turbulence     60
Economic autarky     60
Economy in reverse     62
Welfare state     63
Alone abroad     66
Switching partners     68
Alternative to the Soviet bloc     69
Friends and foes     70
Reunification of the Fatherland     73
Kim's legacy     76

4. **A life in Wonderland**     **79**
Introduction     79
Building the nation     79
Shaping the nation     84
Controlling the nation     88
*Juche* culture     93
*Manga* mania     95
Bread and circuses     96
Games people play     100
National health     103
Equal opportunities     105
Crime and punishment     107
Coming out?     110

5. **Food, famine and fugitives**     **112**
Introduction     112
Food and famine     113
Korea's cry for help     114
Calling on the EU     115
Aid at what cost?     118
EU aid     121
Solving its own problems     121
Reform's rhetoric     125
In our own style     125
Factions     129
Reading the signs     131
Kim 3     132
Flood of refugees?     132
Defectors' world tour     137
North Korean Human Rights Act     140
EU talks about human rights     141
Things can only get better     143
Same country, two pictures     144

6.  **WMD paranoia rules**                       **145**
    Introduction                                 145
    Team America                                 145
    Military perception                          146
    WMD                                          147
    Nukes                                        148
    Framing an agreement                         151
    Nukes II                                     154
    Nuclear club                                 157
    Missiles' reality                            158
    Born on the fourth of July                   160
    Star Wars                                    161
    Comrades-in-arms                             165
    Security perception or reality               168

7.  **Negotiating its place**                    **169**
    Introduction                                 169
    Traditional allies                           169
    Inter-Korea relations                        172
    Sleeping with the enemy                      176
    Broken promises                              180
    KEDO                                         183
    Six-party talks                              186
    Back to square one                           190
    New partner for dialogue                     193

8.  **Changing regime or regime change?**        **199**
    Introduction                                 199
    Kim's regime                                 200
    Nuclear crisis I                             201
    Nuclear crisis II                            202
    Reform rules                                 203
    Reading the signs                            205
    EU: payer or player                          209
    Diverging interests                          210
    Possible solutions                           214

    *Notes*                                      *219*
    *Recommended reading and viewing*            *230*
    *Index*                                      *233*

Unless otherwise indicated all photographs are the authors' own.

# Figures, tables and maps

## Figures

5.1   Change in rhetoric in North Korea 1980–2006        129
5.2   The number of North Korean defectors               137

## Tables

3.1   Economic assistance from the Communist countries    58
3.2   Political classification system in North Korea by
      social origin                                        64
5.1   The number of North Korean defectors arriving
      in South Korea                                      136
7.1   Timetable of diplomatic relations between
      EU member states and the DPRK                       196

## Maps

North Korea                                                xx
Korea's surroundings                                      xxi

# Abbreviations

| | |
|---|---|
| ACF | Action Contra La Faim |
| APTN | Associated Press Television News |
| ASEAN | Association of Southeast Asian Nations |
| AWACS | Airborne Warning and Control System |
| BAT | British American Tobacco |
| BBC | British Broadcasting Corporation |
| BTWC | Biological and Toxins Weapons Convention |
| CARE | Cooperative for Assistance and Relief Everywhere |
| CFSP | Common Foreign and Security Policy |
| CIA | Central Intelligence Agency |
| COMECON | Council for Mutual Economic Assistance |
| CPSU | Communist Party of the Soviet Union |
| CPV | Chinese People's Volunteers |
| CVID | Complete Verifiable Irreversible Dismantlement |
| DMZ | Demilitarised Zone |
| DPRK | Democratic People's Republic of Korea |
| EBA | European Business Association |
| EU | European Union |
| FAO | Food and Agriculture Organisation |
| GDP | Gross Domestic Product |
| GNP | Gross National Product |
| HEU | Highly Enriched Uranium |
| HFO | Heavy Fuel Oil |
| IAEA | International Atomic Energy Agency |
| ICBM | Intercontinental Ballistic Missile |
| IOC | International Olympic Committee |
| IT | Information Technology |
| KAL | Korean Air Line |
| KCIA | Korean Central Intelligence Agency |
| KCNA | Korean Central News Agency |
| KCP | Korean Communist Party |
| KEDO | Korean-Peninsula Energy Development Organisation |
| KEPCO | Korea Electric Power Corporation |
| KGB | Russian-language abbreviation for Committee for State Security |
| KMT | Kuomintang |
| KPA | Korean People's Army |
| KWP | Korean Workers' Party |
| LWR | Light Water Reactor |
| MAC | Military Armistice Commission |

| | |
|---|---|
| MDM | Médecins Du Monde |
| MIRV | Multiple Independently Targetable Re-entry Vehicle |
| MPS | Ministry of People's Security |
| MSF | Médecins Sans Frontières |
| NAM | Non-Aligned Movement |
| NATO | North Atlantic Treaty Organisation |
| NDC | National Defence Commission |
| NGO | Non Governmental Organisation |
| NKWP | North Korean Workers' Party |
| NMD | National Missile Defence |
| NPT | Non-Proliferation Treaty |
| OTA | Office of Technology Assessment |
| PATRIOT | Phased Array Tracking to Intercept Of Target |
| PBS | Pyongyang Business School |
| PDS | Public Distribution System |
| PLO | Palestine Liberation Organisation |
| POUM | Partido Obrero de Unificación Marxista (Party of Marxist Unification) |
| POW | Prisoner of War |
| PVOC | Private Voluntary Organisation Consortium |
| RMB | Renminbi (Chinese currency) |
| ROK | Republic of Korea |
| ROKA | Republic of Korea Army |
| SEZ | Special Economic Zones |
| SKWP | South Korean Workers' Party |
| SI | Socialist International |
| SPA | Supreme People's Assembly |
| SSD | State Security Department |
| THAAD | Terminal High Altitude Area Defence |
| TMD | Theatre Missile Defence |
| UN | United Nations |
| UNC | United Nations Command |
| UNCHR | United Nations Commission on Human Rights |
| UNDP | United Nation Development Programme |
| UNICEF | United Nations Children's Fund |
| US | United States |
| USS | United States' Ship |
| USSR | Union of Soviet Socialist Republics |
| WFP | World Food Programme |
| WHO | World Health Organisation |
| WMD | Weapons of Mass Destruction |
| WTO | World Trade Organization |

# Note on Korean names and words

With introduction of a spelling reform in South Korea in 2000, new forms for some very common words transformed Pyongyang into Pyeongyang, Kumgang to Geumgang, and Kaesong to Gaesong. Some sources have moved to the new spelling, but the North Korean press and the international media generally have stayed with the old spelling. This book uses the forms most familiar to the English-speaking reader except for the words in quotations. Therefore, mostly the old version for the name of places is used. Most of the Korean terms are used following the North Korean style, for instance, Juche instead of Chu'che or Rodong instead of Nodong.

For Korean names, we followed the style of North Korea with the family names followed by first names and without hyphen in the first names. Examples are: Kim Il Sung, Kim Jong Il, Kim Dae Jung, etc. Some names are given in a different form or order if they are already established in common usage such as Syngman Rhee. For the Chinese names, the standardised pinyin transliteration is used. Mao Zedong rather than Mao Tse-tung or Beijing instead of Peking. Japanese names are, however, likely to invert the name order (e.g. Junichiro Koizumi, Vladmir Putin).

# Foreword

North Korea remains one of the most stubborn problems for the international community. Over the past 60 years it has defied regular predictions of its imminent collapse, survived the end of the Soviet Union, endured the death of its all-powerful leader Kim Il Sung and gained a outsized place among global concerns because of its pursuit of nuclear weapons. Even as its last few communist allies opened their economies and prospered, it has remained resolutely closed off to the world, a dark and little understood nation at the heart of northeast Asia. Its problems go back to its origins at the end of the Second World War when the Korean peninsula was split by Stalin and Truman. The legacies of that war persist in the region; a dead weight of history has blocked progress towards real peace and security.

Isolation has prompted decades of speculation about North Korea's government, its intentions and the lives of its people. This has often taken on the most lurid tones: as an unknown quantity, it has always been possible for analysts to project their darkest fears onto the country. For decades, North and South Korea traded insults, lied about each other and stirred up the worst fears in their people. North Korea remains one of the most isolated nations in the world. Only a handful of flights leave its airspace each month, it trades only a tiny amount compared with it neighbours, and few of its people ever travel abroad. But since 1995, an increasing number of people have gained access to North Korea, visiting as officials, diplomats, aid workers and tourists. Even when closely chaperoned, as all visitors are, it is possible to see for oneself what Glyn Ford describes as the 'normal, abnormal and absurd' in daily life.

There can be no doubt that North Koreans live some of the most grimly controlled lives anywhere and that their government has one of the most troubling histories of human rights abuses in the past half century, including its failure to tackle a famine that may have cost millions of lives. It has remained on a permanent war footing since the Korean War almost wiped out the country in the 1950s. A mindset of conflict and paranoia has been stoked by the hostility of the United States and the division of the Korean peninsula. Even when agreements have been reached, such as the 1994 Agreed Framework that froze the country's nuclear program, both sides have tended to act in bad faith, with the North constantly pressing more demands and the United States delaying implementation in the hope that the regime in Pyongyang will collapse.

Collapse is unlikely and wishful thinking is not a good basis for policy. The North Korean regime is obsessed by its survival and maintains a security apparatus to ensure it. It has played a deft diplomatic game to divide its opponents and keep them off balance. Pyongyang has been skilled at dragging out the six-party talks in Beijing, only making small concessions when it suited them. But negotiations have succeeded in getting international inspectors back into Pyongyang's nuclear facilities and have cooled the temperature on the Korean peninsula. What is needed now is a sustained effort to bring North Korea into the fold. This will require a lengthy and complex series of discussions and considerable patience, a commodity that is often lacking.

Each new administration in Washington DC has reviewed its policies on the Korean peninsula; when President George W. Bush did this in 2001, he blithely discarded the progress that had been made in the last weeks of the Clinton administration. That has proved to be a terrible error, as was the inclusion of Pyongyang in the 'Axis of Evil'. The invasion of Iraq only stoked North Korea's fear of regime change and made it that much more difficult to deal with the issues of proliferation. Now there is a new opportunity to talk to North Korea. It is a chance that should not be missed.

This makes Glyn Ford's work on North Korea even more critical. As a prominent and effective member of the European Parliament, he has been a pioneer in developing relations between the European Union and North Korea. He first visited Pyongyang in October 1997 when North Korean diplomats approached him for help in responding to the famine that was destroying the country. His work with the European Commission led to one of the EU's largest humanitarian responses ever, with some €340 million channelled through the United Nations World Food Program and NGOs operating in North Korea. This aid also started a political dialogue with Pyongyang which was encouraged by the South Korean government of Kim Dae Jung when he launched his 'Sunshine Policy' of openness to the North.

That dialogue has been interrupted by the failures of the Agreed Framework and North Korea's nuclear test in 2006 but it may now be resuscitated if the six-party talks make more progress. Ford makes a compelling case for a greater European role on the Korean peninsula. Up to now it has mostly been a 'payer, not a player', footing the bill for energy shipments but having little say in the deals made among the regional powers. Now that the EU includes many nations that have been through the often painful transition from centralised to market economies, it has considerable expertise in managing these changes. Germany brings both experience of long-term engagement with its Ostpolitik and knowledge of the huge challenges of reunification of divergent states. Europe puts human rights at the heart of its values.

A full but critical engagement with North Korea on these issues could start the process of change that is so desperately needed.

As Ford notes, engagement is a long-term strategy, but it is one that has worked elsewhere in the past. There are no other realistic options on the Korean peninsula but to hope that North Korea can be drawn out and brought into the wider world. This is a view that is now held across the political spectrum in South Korea, the country with the most to lose if war were to break out again. Ending Pyongyang's isolation may reduce the security threat it presents and improve the lives of its 20 million people. It is a process that could take decades but it will start when more policy makers follow Ford's example and no longer regard the country as a closed book. It may be difficult to understand North Korea with its opaque history and its politics. But understanding it, in the way this timely book so well helps us to do, is the first step towards ending a conflict that has gone on for far too long.

Gareth Evans
President and CEO of the International Crisis Group since 2000
Foreign Minister of Australia 1988–96

# Preamble

North Korea 1 Italy 0 (Pak Doo Ik, 41).

It was during the 1966 World Cup that I first discovered the Democratic People's Republic of Korea (DPRK). Since then I have bored my friends and acquaintances with questions, and often no answers, about North Korea.

When I got elected to the European Parliament in 1984, one of my first interventions was to table a resolution on EU–North Korea trade relations. The External Economic Relations Committee prepared a report which basically concluded that there were neither relations nor trade. Over the last decade the situation has changed dramatically but not entirely for the better. Few people today interested in international affairs can be unaware of the country that seemingly threatens the world with its bombs and missiles, but no longer with its ideology. The EU is taking an increasingly important role in international affairs and is no longer prepared to be cast in its recent role of payer not player on the Korean Peninsula. As an MEP interested in this region, I believe the future participation of the EU is vital to global security and to help ensure a permanent settlement is arrived at on the peninsula that protects the rights of the peoples of North and South.

I decided to write this book because the only books I read on North Korea painted it either entirely black or totally white. It was either socialist utopia or part of the Axis of Evil. For me the North is neither. I wanted to write as a European and portray the North correctly in shades of grey rather than black or white, a product as much of its enemies as it is of its friends and itself.

Actually it is a poor beleaguered country run by an unpleasant regime that has served its people ill. However the alternatives proffered by its enemies would serve the Koreans worse. Do we really think that the changed regime in China that has since Deng Xiao Ping taken out of poverty more people than live in the EU is worse than the crony capitalism of the former Soviet Union that has seen life expectancy fall by ten years and has driven tens of thousands into poverty for each mafia millionaire it has created? Do we really think that for ordinary Cubans the Miami diaspora offers more than the Castro regime did or the reforming successor might? Do ordinary Iraqis feel better placed now in the midst of an interlocking set of bloody civil wars than they did under the brutal regime of Saddam Hussein?

I want to do two things with this book. First, to provide an appreciation and understanding of North Korea's history, politics and economics that takes into account the way the North went from feudalism to colony to Communism with no democratic detour or interregnum. Rightly a deeply unloved regime, save at home, it is as much a product of outside forces as it is of its own internal dynamic. Second, to advocate the application of 'soft' rather than 'hard' power. The book argues for 'critical engagement' not 'regime change' to provide 'the greatest good for the greatest number'.

It has taken much longer than anticipated to actually write this third-way view from Europe. But clearly the fact that you are reading this means it was finally finished.

My first acknowledgement has to be to my staff, former and present, for their support. In particular Soyoung Kwon, who provided vital input from the point of view of someone who has studied the North using material only available in Korean and with an academic knowledge only a native Korean speaker could have. Elodie Sellar, who helped draft the earlier chapters. Mark Layward, Stuart Emmerson, Cherry Burrow and Rajnish Singh who have completed the course along with Sarika Salmaria, who was my assistant while in Aceh as Chief Election Observer for the EU and who typed drafts as the historic elections of 2005 and 2006 took place around us. My thanks go as well to Kanoko Kojima and Megumi Yoshi for their help while in my office. I want to give particular thanks to my Head of Office Isabel Owen who inspired me to write the book in the first place, who has assisted me from muddle to middle and indeed drafted much more than she will take credit for.

I also have to thank the East–West Centre at the University of Hawaii for awarding me a POSCO fellowship in 2006 that gave me the breathing space needed to finish the penultimate draft, and in particular Dr Lee Jay Cho and Dr Kim Choong Nam who were supportive and helpful in the extreme.

The quality of the book was improved by the time and patience of those involved in the North Korean negotiations process in the Chinese and DPRK Foreign Ministries, the Japanese and South Korean Ministries of Foreign Affairs and the US State Department. But also of course those working in the European Council, Commission and Parliament: Laurens Brinkhorst, Patrick Costello, Jas Gawronski, Thierry Jacob, Clive Needle, Rosemary Opacic, Julian Priestley, Jacques Santer, David Thomas, Leo Tindemans and Michael Wood. Others I would particularly like to pick out are John Attard-Montalto, Nick Bonner, Bram Brands, Maria Castillo, Kent Harstedt, Charles Kartman, Kim Dae Jung, Kim Sang Woo, Jean-Pierre Leng, Alan Maxwell, Taro Nakayama, Lynda Price, Dorian Prince, John Sagar, Mark Seddon, David Slinn, Hajime Takahashi, Robert Templer and Jonathan Watt.

I would also like to thank the many North Korean officials and friends who have talked to me in a way and provided insights in a manner most commentators claim is impossible for a North Korean. I'm delighted to say that is not true. I know they will be disappointed in how I see their country. The only thing I can say in mitigation is that it offers a plea that they be helped and assisted in finding their own solutions for the future rather than one imposed from outside.

Some of the thinking and ideas in this book appeared in articles published in a variety of newspaper and magazines including the *Forest Clarion*, *Frontline (India)*, *Guardian*, *Il Manifesto*, *Japan Times*, *Korea Herald*, *Morning Star*, *New Scientist*, *New Statesman*, *Soundings* and *Tribune*. They also found expression in conferences and seminars organised in and by the International Institute for Strategic Studies (London), the East–West Centre (Honolulu), the European Institute for Asian Studies (Brussels), the Friedrich Neumann Foundation (Pyongyang), the Italian Foreign Ministry (Lake Como, Italy), KEDO (New York), the National Human Rights Commission of Korea (Seoul), Stanford University (Stanford, USA), the Friedrich Ebert Foundation (Berlin), the Kyonggi Cultural Foundation and the Universitat Autònoma de Barcelona Foundation (Barcelona), The Royal Institute of International Affairs (London) and North Korea International Action (Geneva).

The opinions expressed in this book are entirely my own responsibility. All of the people acknowledged will disagree with some of what I have written, many will disagree with most. In particular as I said above my North Korean interlocutors will be disappointed that I see the North through different eyes from their own. All I hope is that they recognise that I do this from the best of motives in the best attempt to present their country in a different light from the one in which it is normally seen in the West.

## Structure of the book

The book consists of eight chapters. Chapter 1 sets the context within which North Korea is framed, and outlines contemporary developments and its continued isolation. Chapter 2 explains how the emerging North Korean regime evolved and developed from the onset of Japanese colonialism to liberation, a process crucial to understanding the legitimacy and rationale behind the DPRK today. The end of the Pacific War was a crucial point in Korean history, not only because of the division that followed, which substituted two occupiers for one and led to the current conflict, but because it signalled the end of six centuries of serial subordination to its larger neighbours, China, Japan and Russia.

Kim Il Sung, an anti-Japanese guerrilla fighter, handpicked by the Soviets to fill the political void when their troops occupied the North, was initially a loyal Stalinist. He sought Stalin's – and Mao's – permission to invade the South, supposedly to conclude a conflict that had already been going on for several years, driven by the determination of the leaders of both North and South Korea to reunify the peninsula under their leadership. There had been sporadic and growing clashes between the US-supported South and Soviet North prior to the formal outbreak of the war. The North launched its attack on 25 June 1950 and the civil war was swiftly internationalised. The war expanded to involve the United States, the UN and China. Nearly three years of military to and fro ended in 1953 with an armistice which still, nearly 55 years on, has not been turned into a peace treaty. North Korea and the United States are still at war. The legacy of the conflict colours and shapes North Korean daily life, politics and foreign policy.

Chapter 3 looks at the post-war political, ideological, economic and social developments under Kim Il Sung, and at how Kim eliminated the opposition, real and potential, and consolidated his power. The failure of Kim's Korean War put his leadership in question, but astute political manoeuvring allowed him to hang on to power. Khrushchev's 1956 denunciation of Stalin posed a new threat to Kim. Dividing and conquering, he acted swiftly to secure his position with a successive step-by-step elimination of the remaining factions, leaving himself and his former guerrilla fighters in undisputed control. To legitimate and maintain his increasingly monolithic leadership, an intense personality cult developed, with autarky in economy and politics driven by Kim's notion of *Juche* (self-reliance). Alongside this political revolution, the North Korean economy, founded on heavy industry, experienced remarkable growth, enabling the country to quickly recover from its 1953 year zero to leap-frog over and race away from a listless and laggard Southern economy. This surge did not last. The workforce became exhausted with the endless production drives while an over-emphasis on heavy industry distorted production, and the cannibalisation of resources to strengthen the military brought North Korea full-circle. By Kim Il Sung's death in 1994, the economy was in such a fragile state that all it required was a series of natural disasters to push it into collapse.

The total state Kim created, with *Juche*, cult and Communism all focused on him and later to encompass his son, proved a powerful tool of control. *Juche* said 'neither Beijing nor Moscow' and it was sold using Stalinist techniques of mass mobilisation learnt from Moscow and the Red Army. At the same time, Kim mixed in elements of Korea's deep-seated Confucian culture, which accepted strict hierarchical order and absolute devotion to the leader, to reinforce his position. *Juche* trumped any sense of intellectual or ideological inferiority in relation to the North's two Communist neighbours. Over time, heresy metamorphosed into cult and *Juche* was put to the test in the 1990s with economic collapse and famine. It failed. *Juche* had its limits and had been found wanting. Not that anyone in the North was going to admit it.

The fourth chapter describes daily life in North Korea, a mixture of normal, abnormal and absurd, all maintained by isolation, socialisation and control, leading to a collective mentality similar in many ways to that of Japan in the 1930s. A Japanese proverb 'the nail that sticks out is beaten down' is a celebration of collective thought rather than a cry against oppression. North Koreans would feel comfortable with that.

Things began to change in the mid-1990s. The famine left millions dead and the lives of millions more devastated. Refugees fled across the border into China, while the influx of international aid organisations and their staff into the country began to have an impact on the society. Chapter 5 details the contemporary context within which the North's people struggle to survive and the North Korea of Kim Jong Il.

The last three chapters deal with today's foreign relations, security issues, human rights and economic reform. These take Europe seriously. With Europe now a global player with the best relations with Pyongyang, apart from China, it has a responsibility to engage with the international community to help resolve the outstanding issues on the peninsula.

Chapter 6 challenges head on the US arguments as to the security threat posed by North Korea. It assesses the limited threat coming from North Korea's nuclear programme, chemical and biological weapons, its missile capacity and its conventional arms. At the same time, it also looks at how the United States reneged on the Agreed Framework, its uncompromising and stubborn stance during the six-party talks, and its use of North Korea as an excuse to develop and deploy Star Wars. The post 9/11 doctrine of pre-emptive deterrence, Bush's 'Axis of Evil' speech and the invasion of Iraq have understandably led Pyongyang to the conclusion that the problem was not having weapons of mass destruction, but rather not having them. Now a nuclear weapons state, the North is putting that proposition to the test.

Chapter 7 explores the North's relations with the South, the United States, Japan, China and the EU, and the attempt to resolve the crisis through the six-party talks. These talks revealed sharply diverging interests amongst those supposedly ranged on the same side against the North's nuclear adventurism, with a particularly sharp and widening gap between Seoul and Washington and an emerging rejectionist Japan. The final chapter assesses the extent of North Korea's economic reform and its impact, and concludes that a 'changing regime' rather than forced 'regime change' is the only way to avoid the potential disaster of a war on the peninsula that would make Iraq look like a minor skirmish.

Glyn Ford
Cinderford
20 July 2007

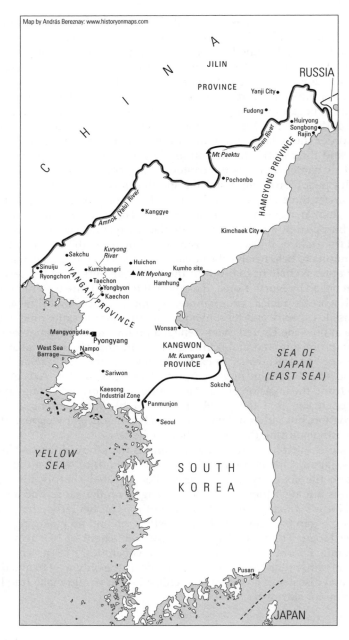

Map by András Bereznay: www.historyonmaps.com

CHINA

JILIN

PROVINCE

RUSSIA

Yanji City ●

Fudong ●

● Huiryong
Songbong ●
Rajin ●

▲ Mt Paektu

*Tumen River*

HAMGYONG PROVINCE

● Pochonbo

*Amnok (Yalu) River*

● Kanggye

Kimchaek City ●

*Kuryong
River*

● Sakchu

● Kumchangri     ● Huichon

Kumho site ●

● Sinuiju
● Ryongchon

▲ Mt Myohang

● Taechon     Hamhung ●
● Yongbyon
● Kaechon

PYANGAN PROVINCE

Wonsan ●

Mangyongdae ●

KANGWON

■ Pyongyang

*Mt. Kumgang* ▲

West Sea
Barrage     ● Nampo

PROVINCE

● Sariwon

Sokcho ●

*SEA OF
JAPAN
(EAST SEA)*

Kaesong
Industrial Zone     ● Panmunjon

● Seoul

*YELLOW
SEA*

SOUTH

KOREA

● Pusan

JAPAN

North Korea

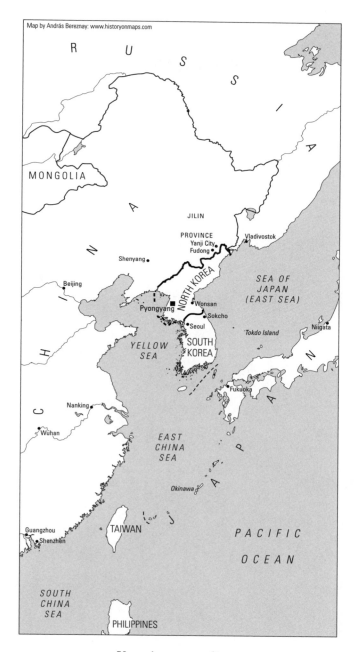

RUSSIA

MONGOLIA

JILIN
PROVINCE

Vladivostok

Yanji City
Fudong

Shenyang

NORTH KOREA

SEA OF
JAPAN
(EAST SEA)

Pyongyang

Wonsan

Sokcho

Seoul

Beijing

Tokdo Island

Niigata

YELLOW
SEA

SOUTH
KOREA

CHINA

Fukuoka

Nanking

EAST
CHINA
SEA

Wuhan

JAPAN

Okinawa

Guangzhou

TAIWAN

PACIFIC

Shenzhen

OCEAN

SOUTH
CHINA
SEA

PHILIPPINES

Korea's surroundings

For Elise and Allessandro

# 1 North Korea in context

## Introduction

Why is so much attention being paid to North Korea (Democratic People's Republic of Korea – DPRK), virtually the last state remnant of an ideological cul-de-sac that came and went in less than a century? Why is it so important not only to the neighbouring countries and the region, but also to the United States (US) and European Union (EU)? In the midst of serial nuclear crises – three to date – the Korean Peninsula is the last threat of the cold war turning hot. If the crisis on the Korean Peninsula is mishandled or miscalculated by either side, it could trigger a war. Even without the use of nuclear weapons, there would be a million dead, a trillion dollars in damage (€140 for every person in the world) and global recession. Escalation to the level of nuclear exchanges would make it, at the least, an order of magnitude worse.

The problem is a tendency to stereotype. North Korea is neither a Stalinist relic with a mad leader, nor a deadly security threat to the world. It is a country run by rational actors whose biggest concern is 'regime survival' and 'regime security' while they are still technically at war with the United States.

From a North Korean perspective, its actions are logical consequences of its struggle for survival. For those who can't or won't see this, North Korea becomes a dangerous enigma where the normal political levers of cause and effect have been taken away.

## Northern exposure

No one should be under any illusions that North Korea and its leadership are not deeply unpleasant. Nevertheless, the country's regime is as much a product of its enemies as of its friends and itself. It may be paranoid, but that doesn't mean that there aren't those out to get it.

After the end of the Pacific War, when Korea was divided by an arbitrary line drawn on a map between Soviet and American zones, both North and South wanted to fight. The South aimed for 'national unification' and the North for 'national liberation'. The outcome was a civil war that turned into a surrogate conflict between the world's two superpowers and a crusade against Communism by a United States in the throes of McCarthyism. After the end of the Korean War, North and South Korea continued to infiltrate informers, spies and terrorists across the demilitarised zone (DMZ) to undermine their

Looking in – the DMZ

alter-egos, but minus their cold-war partners they were only a threat to each other.

North Korea had no history of democracy to fall back on and was initially constructed in the classic 'people's democracy' model of the Soviet empire. It was this that directed its development in the aftermath of the Korean War. Following Khrushchev's denunciation of Stalin and Stalinism in 1956, North Korea's leader Kim Il Sung was under threat. He got his retaliation in first, purging the Party of all that opposed him or might oppose him, and ran the country with his fellow partisans, shifting the country's focus from Stalinism to autarkic nationalism with *Juche* (self-reliance) as his leitmotif.

Courted concurrently by the Soviet Union and Mao's China, North

Korea's post-war economy, based on heavy industry, initially boomed. For a period the North was a global success story. It was a desert blooming. By the late 1960s, however, the economic motor was beginning to stutter as the transposition to light industry and the production of consumer goods failed to materialise. Kim borrowed billions from the West in the early 1970s, but the turnkey projects he bought failed as the 1973 oil crisis threatened the global economy. Even at the beginning of the 1980s North Korea was the world's 34th largest economy, but by the middle of the decade the economy had stalled. The collapse of the Soviet Union only made things worse. Aid from the Soviets stopped and from China slowed, while the Soviet nuclear umbrella over North Korea was furled. Abandoned, the North looked to develop its own nuclear deterrent, the economy went into a tailspin and the population went hungry. Kim and millions died. For Kim the cause was just biology, but the rest died as the consequence of failed policies at home and abroad, combined with floods and drought. They became nameless victims in the worst humanitarian disaster in the last quarter of the twentieth century. The United States knew of the famine, but there was no Bob Geldof or *Live Aid* to put their plight on the world's TV screens. They starved slowly in a conspiracy of silence.

After a three-year hiatus Kim was succeeded by his son Kim Jong Il, who retained his father's distrust of political reform but who was forced to recognise that his regime's survival depended on kick-starting a stagnant economy. The only option was economic reform in the framework of a one-party state. This had been done elsewhere with varying degrees of success. China and Vietnam have taken off, while Laos and Cuba have limped. Kim's genuine but only partially successful attempts at reform have either been ignored completely, or written off as window dressing. Some of the changes behind the scenes have been detailed by the *Financial Times'* Anna Fifield. Yet while you see kiosk capitalists on the streets, Pyongyang is also encouraging the emergence of multi-sectoral conglomerates that helped Japan and the South to take off, in the former case with the *Zaibatsu* and the latter the *Chaebol*. In Pyongyang state-run shops are advertising medicines and motorbikes made by groups such as Pugang, Daesong, Sungri and Rungra 88. Jon Sung Hun, President of Pugang which has an annual turnover of $150 million (€125 million), wants to open up markets in South Korea and China. Already Pugang's mineral water Hwangchiryong is a big seller in the latter. The United States claims Pugang is part of the Korean Ryonbong General Corporation which has been involved in nuclear proliferation. That may well have been true once in some of the corporation's seven divisions – mining, electronics, pharmaceutical, coins, glassware, machinery and drinking water – but now its focus is on moving into the civilian economy where the money seems to be.[1]

South Korea is becoming nervous. Its investment is limited to the two special zones, with most new money going into the Kaesong industrial complex on the border. This has over 10,000 North Koreans working there every day, a workforce expected to rise to 300,000 by 2012. Future plans include light industry, semiconductors and bioengineering, while for fun there will be a theme park and three golf courses in the tourism zone plus an illuminated statue of Kim Il Sung.[2]

Yet Chinese investment in the North is growing exponentially, admittedly from a very low base. It was $1 million in 2003, $50 million in 2004 and $90 million in 2005. In the past three years 150 Chinese companies have begun operating; 80 per cent of the consumer goods in the North's markets are from China, and the $1.5 billion of bilateral trade comprises 50 per cent of the North's total foreign trade.[3] The South Korean government worries about China's economic incorporation of the North into China's north-eastern provinces with their large Korean-speaking minorities.

The North's ambitions extend to the WTO, where it has expressed some interest in obtaining observer status, as post-Saddam Iraq did in 2004 and Iran in 2005 (even though in 2004 North Korea's trade volume of $2.85 billion was 167 times smaller than South Korea's). North Korea

Kaesong Industrial Park in July 2005

has been unable to get the world to take seriously its attempts to reform its domestic economy and take a Chinese-style path to market Leninism. This hidden story is brought out with the regime's attempts at reform and engagement with the international community, all while coping with a genuine fear of US pre-emptive attack – not entirely irrational after Iraq.

Reforms have been hampered by the ongoing political crises related to plutonium and uranium, missiles and bombs. For the United States, the 1994 Agreed Framework with North Korea that supposedly aimed to resolve the nuclear crisis was not intended to be a blueprint for a solution but to buy time for North Korea to collapse. Its promises were never intended to be delivered. The United States even reneged on its interim commitments. What Clinton did out of expediency, Bush did with joy. In a country that produces nothing anyone wishes to buy save military technology – and then only if you're desperate – and with the rhetoric of regime change growing louder in Washington and the West, Kim Jong Il had good reasons to continue with his missile and nuclear weapons programmes.

Regime change, triggered by military intervention, as stated above would cost a million dead and a trillion dollars, making Iraq look like a minor skirmish. Meanwhile, economic collapse threatens to set 10 million refugees on the road to Seoul. A negotiated solution is needed to allow economic reform to continue and the world to feel safe from a second war on the Korean Peninsula. This will only be achieved if South Korea, China and the EU can persuade Japan and, more importantly, the United States that the interested parties in the political and military-industrial complex that seek to prolong the dispute are playing with fire. Any solution must provide North Korea with a new indigenous energy supply and development aid.

## Hypocrisy and democracy

North Korea has been a 'country of concern' for over 50 years. Initially it was one of many within world Communism, now it is the worst of five. Since 9/11 and the ensuing 'war on terror'. US foreign policy has taken on a hard unilateral edge. North Korea has become a part of the President's 'Axis of Evil', a 'rogue state', and an 'outpost of tyranny', branded by the administration as a real and present danger to world peace. Yet it is not necessarily North Korea which poses the real problem but rather those who, for their own purposes, are determined to drive it into a corner.

Even though its last terrorist act was in the 1980s, North Korea is still classified by the United States as a state sponsor of terrorism. The Rangoon bombing in 1983, the bombing of Korean Air flight KAL 858 in 1987 and the harbouring of members of the Japanese Red Army faction have all been used to label Pyongyang a 'terror state'. But generous double standards are at play. North Korea was a victim of airline terrorism long before the United States. Given the nod from Langley, a CIA-funded Cuban exile group blew up Cuban flight CU455 from Barbados to Cuba via Jamaica on 6 October 1976, killing five senior North Korean government officials including the Vice-Chair of North Korea's Foreign Relations Committee. There were no survivors from the explosion and 73 people died. George Bush Senior was the Director of the CIA at the time. After he became president his son, Jeb Bush, successfully lobbied for the release of one of the two ringleaders of the plot, Orlando Bosch, who now lives unmolested in Miami. The other ringleader, Luis Posada, was under arrest in El Paso, but for entering the United States illegally. All charges were dismissed on 8 May 2007. To quote Jeb's older brother after 9/11: 'we've got to say to people who are willing to harbour a terrorist or feed a terrorist: "you are just as guilty as the terrorist."'

Following the United States' abandonment of the 1994 agreement, the North reactivated its Yongbyon nuclear plant, produced enough plutonium for at least half a dozen nuclear weapons, declared itself a nuclear power and conducted its first – albeit only partially successful – underground nuclear test in October 2006. This test was a 'fizzle' not a bang, with the assembled plutonium breaking apart too early for an optimum result. It produced a blast equivalent to 1000 tonnes of TNT or 1 kilotonne. The United States' active nuclear arsenal has a capacity of 2330 megatonnes (1 megatonne is the equivalent of 10 million tonnes of TNT). If the North's five remaining bombs were to operate at the 4-kilotonne design capacity, the United States would have more than eleven and a half million times the North's nuclear power. Actually the US figure is down on what it was. In 1960 it had 100 million times what the North has today. The United States' threat of 'first use' of nuclear weapons against the North during the Korean War and after was exactly what drove the Chinese nuclear programme forward in the mid-1950s. Its new doctrine of pre-emptive deterrence is seen in the North as an adequate reason for developing a nuclear capacity as a matter of necessity. Washington makes self-righteous pronouncements about the perils of nuclear weapons while sitting on piles of them. For the United States, one aspect of the Non-Proliferation Treaty (NPT) is vital: the aspect that stops proliferation. The other face, which promises nuclear disarmament, is just rhetoric. Moreover, North Korea's half dozen nuclear weapons are branded a threat to both the non-proliferation regime and global security, while Israel's hundreds and Pakistan's and India's scores are not.

North Korea's arms exports destabilise global security, but the 400-times larger exports from the United States do not. North Korea's military expenditure is a threat to South Korea, even though it spends less than a quarter of the South's military budget. North Korea's rapprochement with Japan is indefinitely on hold until it fully accounts for the 18 Japanese abductees to Japanese Prime Minister Shinzo Abe, who in September 2006 appointed a minister to deal solely with the issue. Meanwhile Japan has yet to apologise for the almost 900,000 Koreans abducted to Japan during the Pacific War, including the tens of thousands used as sex-slaves (comfort women) by the Japanese army. The bitterness of this has not been soothed by Abe's recent claims that they were volunteers. None of this excuses North Korea's own bad behaviour and worse, but it provides a context. North Korea would be its own worst enemy, if it wasn't for the United States and Japan.

Conservative forces in Japan and the United States have an agenda. One is tempted to say that if they didn't have North Korea they would have to invent it. But in a sense that is exactly what they have done. They have dressed up as the twenty-first century's answer to the Soviet Union at its most aggressive a deeply – and deservedly – unloved fragment of world Communism that is a failed state. They need North Korea as a scapegoat for their political projects. In Japan, the post-war generation, represented by Koizumi and now Abe, has taken over. They are self-confident nationalists who want Japan to become a 'normal country' by ripping up the US-imposed Peace Constitution. Public opinion polls demonstrate a majority in favour of retaining Article 9 and preventing further Japanese militarisation, so the conservatives need to transform people's hearts and minds before the required referendum is held. North Korea is the perfect catalyst, with its 'failed' satellite launch over Japan on 31 August 1998 and its failed Taepodong firing on 5 July 2006, Kim Jong Il's admission in September in 2002 that 'rogue elements' had abducted 13 Japanese – not the 18 that Japan claims – in the 1970s and early 1980s, and its nuclear test on 9 October 2006. Japan can fire its rockets from its launch site on Tanegashima with impunity to demonstrate its potential offensive missile technology and talk about the need to become a stronger military power when it is already the world's fifth largest military spender, while North Korea is beyond the pale.

US attitudes are also driven by an American domestic agenda that requires an enemy in the colours North Korea is painted. Taliban terrorism and Iraqi insurgency fail to provide a motor for 'big defence', for military research and development. To justify the National Missile Defence (NMD) or Star Wars, ICBMs and nuclear weapons are a necessary minimum requirement, even if the numbers are hundreds of times smaller and the quality so poor that neither missile test has worked.

North Korea's efforts almost make the Star Wars tests look a success. The regional arms race, and the collapse of Communism, has driven North Korea to devote a higher and higher percentage of its shrinking income to military spending at the expense of neglecting the civilian economy. Subsequently, North Korea was driven to the nuclear option by example and economics to provide a credible deterrent. The United States forced the North Korean economy to live a lie as 'military-first' policies were imposed by the threat from south of the DMZ and the civilian economy starved. Yet, when Pyongyang concludes that nuclear weapons are a cheap alternative to maintaining conventional forces levels which put the economy at breaking point, it is a step too far and a threat to global security.

## Regional perspectives

Views on North Korea vary amongst its neighbours depending on their own national interests. China sees North Korea as a traditional ally – even if the relationship was put under severe strain by the nuclear test – stuck in an ideological rut that 'on the spot learning' is beginning to shift with Kim Jong Il's serial visits to the key monuments of China's economic miracle. Russia, or rather the Soviet Union, saw the North as an unruly ally. Towards the end, economics leapfrogged over history and Seoul took precedence over Pyongyang. More recently Russia has seen that totally sidelining the North meant it missed political and industrial opportunities. Now while Seoul is the centre of its focus on the peninsula, enough interest is maintained in the North to ensure Moscow does not miss out again. Japan, unwilling to acknowledge its contribution to the burden of the past and the shaping of the present, sees a vengeful North obsessed with a deliberately distorted vision of Japanese colonialism. The North's failure to come clean on the abductions of Japanese citizens makes bad relations worse. Pyongyang provides an excuse for Japanese politicians to manipulate the Japanese population. South Korea views the prospect of early forced re-unification with horror, preferring a 'soft' to a 'hard' landing, but ideally no landing at all. Historically North and South have been Siamese twins with a love–hate relationship. Each needs the other to measure itself against, to test itself, to justify its existence. You can't have one without the other. US fundamentalist approaches that are willing to force regime change even if it means millions of non-Americans might die are both callous and careless.

A different voice has to make itself heard. The issues are too important to be left to the neo-cons who gave us Iraq and politicians with their own personnel hotline to the Almighty. The dossiers on the

North's capabilities are as dodgy as those produced to back up the case for war in Iraq. As Ron Suskind wrote in *The One Per Cent Doctrine*, 'intelligence no longer serves to decide policy, but is used to affirm it,' with the United States screaming at every word torture victims say or defectors allege. For the President it's personal. For Dick Cheney, if there is a one in a hundred chance of a threat, the United States should act as if it is true. Europe in contrast sees the North as a country trying, albeit with limited success, to reform its economy in the direction of market Leninism or cult capitalism, willing to give up its nuclear arsenal and long-range missiles in exchange for peaceful coexistence and security guarantees.

## European voice

The global order is changing fast in this post-cold-war world. Traditional notions of power politics based on military might are less relevant than in the past. Considering the rise of China and emergence of the EU as major global players in the new world order, assertions of US hegemony are a little overdone, unless the sole measure is military might. Recent decades have seen the creation of a single market and single currency in Europe. With the Economic and Monetary Union and 27 member states, Europe is now significantly bigger and richer than the United States; it is the world's biggest trade partner and donor of more than 50 per cent of the world's development aid. The euro is challenging the dollar's dominance of the financial markets. The EU's role on the world stage has been understated, but it will surely start to exercise its new influence. Converging industrial, economic security interests of its member states will inevitably overrule history and force the EU to speak and act with a single voice.

The cutting edge of political debate within the EU now centres on its emerging Common Foreign and Security Policy (CFSP). The French and Dutch rejection of the Constitution, which proposed the appointment of a European Foreign Minister, has not halted the forward march of the CFSP – merely imposed a pause, with the new European Union Reform Treaty being passed in June 2007. The CFSP is no longer a mere adjunct to the foreign policies of individual member states, but will enable the EU to play a role on the world political stage. The legacy of the past will continue to have its influence on individual member states, whether it be France's historical role in Africa, Spain's in Latin America, Germany's in Central and Eastern Europe, or Britain's dependent relationship with the United States.

Yet for every difference there are more commonalities. Europe's distinctive voice on foreign affairs reflects its common interests. The EU now speaks increasingly with a single distinct voice on energy policy and on Africa, Israel and Palestine, Iran and North Korea. One test of the CFSP will be how Europe responds to US demands for a European version of theatre missile defence (TMD) that can do for Iran and Russia what the US–Japan TMD system is doing for North Korea and China. Allowing the deployment in the east of the Union of this offensive technology will encourage rather then deter an Islamic bomb and will undermine EU–Russian relations and any prospects of cooperation on energy policy. The EU is no longer just a spectator: it is starting to play. The Union has created a 60,000 strong 'Rapid Reaction Force' available for military intervention, and has already deployed policing and peacekeeping missions in the Balkans, Afghanistan and the Democratic Republic of the Congo. In 2005, for the first time, the EU went into Asia with its Aceh Monitoring Mission (AMM) in Indonesia, working jointly with the Association of South East Asian Nations (ASEAN) as a part of the Aceh peace process that successfully ended a 30-year long civil war between the government of Indonesia and the rebels fighting for independence. Europe is told it will never match the United States as a military power. That is true, but Europe is not trying to emulate the US. Europe wants to be capable of intervening in its own near-abroad without being dependent on Washington, and to have as an adjunct to its economic and industrial influence the ability to project power against second-division states. Peacekeeping in the Democratic Republic of Congo needed special forces not Trident submarines.

The EU's Asia policy is directed towards sustainable development, security, stability and democracy through institutional dialogue and economic and financial cooperation. Within these broad objectives, policy towards Korea reflects the EU's commitment to the inter-Korean reconciliation process and to increased non-humanitarian assistance to the DPRK. It aims to assist the North in addressing concerns on nonproliferation and security issues, structural reform of the economy and social development. Though these had been on hold to an extent after the 2002 crisis, a mission travelled to Pyongyang from the Commission within weeks of the settlement of February 2007.

The EU's new and growing involvement with the DPRK from the mid to late 1990s brought constructive dialogue with Pyongyang. Diplomatic relations between the EU itself and the DPRK were established in May 2001 following the high-level EU visit led by Göran Persson, the Prime Minister of Sweden and, at the time, President in Office of the European Council. During the visit it was also simultaneously agreed to establish a Human Rights Dialogue between the EU and DPRK similar in format to the long-standing dialogue with China. From 2001 to 2003, there were three rounds of meetings. The dialogue, suspended after the EU sponsored a UN resolution condemning the North, looked as though it would re-start after the February settlement. In September 2004 and

October 2005, seminars on 'economic reform and the development of economic relations between the EU and the DPRK' were held in Pyongyang, aiming to provide European expertise on managing and reforming the economy. Another seminar is scheduled for autumn 2007. In 2004, the European Parliament established a permanent standing delegation for relations with the Korean Peninsula. The Parliamentary delegation travelled to North Korea in July 2005 and June 2007, with a return visit from the North in 2006. Currently 26 out of the 27 member states have diplomatic relations with North Korea and there are six EU embassies (UK, Poland, Romania, Bulgaria Sweden and Germany) in Pyongyang. The EU's financial contribution amounted to almost half a billion euros. With no vital strategic interest in the region and little historical baggage, in contrast to the United States, Europe is in a position to act as an honest broker and use its 'soft power' to help shape events in northeast Asia.

This is all fairly new. After North Korea ended up in deep debt to European banks in the 1970s there was a reluctance to trade with or invest in the country by European industry. At that time, political relations were almost non existent. This remained the case until the humanitarian crisis in the mid-1990s. Since 1997, the EU has provided a large proportion of the humanitarian assistance received by the North, as well as cooperation and assistance with rehabilitation of the energy sector and market economy training. It has probably provided more assistance to the North than anyone save South Korea and China. The EU's relative success in building a relationship with the DPRK is because it is neither the United States nor Japan. Europe, a new global player, is taking stances distinct from those of the United States, Iraq being the clearest example. A political gap has opened across the Atlantic, even if the United States used the North's nuclear and missile tests to rein in the EU.

In the past the United States has seen the EU as payer rather than player. The EU had no role in the negotiation of the 1994 Agreed Framework, yet Europe's cheque book was in demand when the United States refused to pick up any significant share of the subsequent bill. Europe got off comparatively lightly. Japan paid more, while South Korea was stuck with the majority of the costs. Any final solution will involve billions to rehabilitate North Korea. The United States won't pay, can't pay. Japan, which owes the North compensation for its colonial crimes (it paid the South in 1965), will not pay until it gets its constitutional revision and final satisfaction over the abductees or at least the most prominent, Megumi Yokota. Even then it will deduct a hefty amount to repay debts and accumulated interest on its contribution to the Korean Peninsula Energy Development Organisation (KEDO), which was supposed to build two light water reactors for the North as a quid pro quo for abandoning its suspect civil nuclear programme. KEDO was initially suspended and then terminated at US insistence because of the Korean's supposed highly enriched uranium (HEU) nuclear weapons programme. The Republic of Korea (ROK) will contribute as much as it can to avoid a shotgun re-unification. Yet recently the EU Parliament and Commission have indicated a distinct lack of enthusiasm to continue as cash cows for Congress with a rhetorically robust position of 'no say, no pay'. Whether the United States will pay attention, or the EU will hold the line, only time will tell.

## Going North

Information on North Korea's daily life is limited and unreliable, although the situation has improved with increased international access following the famine. In the late 1990s in towns and cities outside of Pyongyang, many a visiting European was the first non-Communist foreigner seen since the Korean War. Until then North Korea was tightly closed and completely isolated from all but Marxist-Leninist tourists from the Soviet Union and its empire and Western Communist Parties. They still come but there are not so many of them. Britain's fraternal Party is Sid French's breakaway from the now defunct Communist Party of Great Britain, the New Communist Party, which sends groups to talk *Juche*. Ordinary North Koreans tend to avoid speaking to foreigners. Few have the language skills, and fewer still the foolhardiness.

The only two ways to visit Pyongyang are either as a member of an officially invited delegation or on one of a limited number of organised tours that the North Koreans allow in. The biggest and best of these is Koryo Tours (website: http://www.koryogroup.com; email: koryo-tours@mac.com). If you wish to join such a tour, your answer to the question 'Profession?' should not be 'Journalist' (although occasionally and fleetingly journalists become *persona grata* for the *Arirang* Festival, the colourful and spectacular Mass Games or other major celebrations). Tourists in the DPRK will have an interpreter and driver. The interpreter is with you all the time and you negotiate a programme. This can be arbitrary to a degree. During one visit I asked to travel to the northern city of Huichon. The response was that it was out of bounds to foreigners. I then explained that I had travelled there on an earlier trip, and suddenly it was back on the itinerary. Free movement or access to many parts of the country is impossible, though with prior notice you can indulge European eccentricities and visit Korea's last working steam trains, visit the funfair for what must be one of the world's top ten roller coaster rides, or go to the Pyongyang golf course where Kim Jong Il with his first ball hit a 'hole in one'.

Double-loop roller coaster at Mangyongdae Funfair

Fuel shortages and a sporadic electricity supply make public transport desperately unreliable. Pyongyang can be explored relatively freely, but until recently foreigners were limited to shops and restaurants that accept hard currency. This is beginning to change in Pyongyang, with money being changed discretely on the street and with kiosk capitalists on the streets bargaining and even accepting payment in Chinese RMB. Visits to public buildings and museums require a guide, but you can travel fairly freely to parks, restaurants, shops and the Tong-il Market. Here you can see an embryonic consumer society at work. Buying and selling was traditionally dependent on serendipity – to buy a television, a person needed money, a coupon giving permission to buy a television and a vendor with televisions for sale. Two out of three wouldn't do. But in 2005 to celebrate the 60th anniversary of the Korean Workers' Party a handwritten sign in one store read: 'To celebrate the important holiday, we are selling many goods at a 10 per cent discount from October 10 until October 31.'[4] Visitors see a partial view of the North then that bears little resemblance to the North Korea depicted in the Western media.

The North is still isolated in a way few in the West can imagine. International air traffic is often limited to a twice-weekly Air Koryo flight to Beijing. Rail traffic is two carriages four times a week tacked on to the Beijing–Dandong train which are shuttled across the border at Sinuiju. Road traffic is not much better. In a couple of hours at two of the road borders, barely half a dozen lorries crossed the line. The planes are relics from the Soviet era that do not meet current standards for Beijing's International Airport, but the Chinese have given them a temporary waiver. Under French urging, Air Koryo is banned from EU skies, although it is intriguing to wonder where French knowledge of its safety record comes from when there are no flights to Europe. Currently there is a third flight from Beijing on Thursday, and weekly flights to Shenyang and Vladivostok. The Vladivostok route to Russia was launched when bird flu in China threatened to leave the North totally isolated with the Chinese border totally closed for weeks.

From Beijing to Pyongyang, the flight takes just over an hour. Flight attendants wheel the usual drinks trolley loaded with local beer and spirits, plus non-alcoholic cider and mineral water but the merits of the water are sold over the loudspeaker system:

> The water you are drinking here is special for your health and longevity. Even if he's very busy, the Dear Leader, the benevolent father of our people, has studied in detail the problems of distribution in our country in order to give water to everybody. If you drink it, you will sense the endless love of our people for the great leader Kim Jong Il.

One hopes the water was Pugang's Hwangchiryong. The journey's progress is marked by history:

> Eighty-one years ago, our President Kim Il Sung went across the Amnok River with great ambition to liberate our country from the colonial rule of the Japanese imperialists. Amnok River quietly flows telling the history of the bloody struggle of Korean revolutionaries who sacrificed their lives for the liberation of our country.

The train from Pyongyang to Beijing, in contrast, takes 27 hours, allowing foreign travellers to see scenery that is otherwise out of their reach although there are no announcements. There are fewer than 10,000 passengers per annum each way. The great majority are North Korean or Chinese and under 10 per cent of the travellers are foreigners. There is a line from Pyongyang to Vladivostok and on to Moscow, but currently no timetable.

The only way until recently for South Koreans to visit the North was to travel by the Hyundai Corporation's Sokcho ferry that provides tours of Mt Kumgang in the southeast. Recently, this was augmented by buses crossing the DMZ. There was also a ferry link from Niigata in Japan, primarily for Korean residents of Japan, which was suspended by the Japanese government after the missile test in July 2006. US citizens not of Korean origin find it particularly difficult to travel as tourists, although 150 were allowed in 2007. When US tourists do visit, it is not unusual for at least one couple to request hotels to provide twin beds; after all CIA operatives have to keep it clean.

# 2 Drawing the Iron Curtain

## Introduction

To understand the DPRK is to understand how it had to fight to survive amidst powerful neighbours. Korea, partly due to its size (equivalent to the UK) and geography (positioned between Japan, China and Russia), has been subject to intervention and invasion throughout its history. When Japan took over the administration of Korea in 1905, it was a feudal country with no history of democracy or civic society, save amongst the aristocracy. It then remained a Japanese colony until the end of the Pacific War when it was carved up between the Soviet Union and the United States at the 38th Parallel. One occupier was exchanged for two. This legacy of the Potsdam Conference agreement between Stalin and Truman (July 1945) left a 250-kilometre dividing line separating the northern Soviet sector (55 per cent of the country) from the southern US one (45 per cent). It was an arbitrary division, with the US conceding the minimum they thought the Soviet Union would accept.

The subsequent Korean War drew an iron curtain between North and South along the demilitarised zone (DMZ), a line roughly following the 38th Parallel, a little to the south in the west and to the north in the east. North Korea is an isolated country – learning the lessons of time it rejected outside influences. Now completely separated, with the passage of time, two sharply different countries emerged on the peninsula, one being the DPRK.

## Geography

The Korean Peninsula stretches from the plains of eastern Manchuria and Siberia to within 110 kilometres of Japan's western island of Kyushu. The 1425-kilometre border with China follows the River Yalu/Amnok between Sinuiju and Taedong to Korea's west coast, and the Tumen River to Korea's east coast (on the Sea of Japan). The source of these rivers, Lake Chon on Mt Paektu, completes the natural border. Mt Paektu (2750 metres) is the peninsula's highest mountain and regarded as a national monument. Although it was for a time the subject of a border dispute with China the issue was settled in 1956, with the majority of the mountain now lying firmly within North Korea. The border with Russia has only existed since 1860 when Tsar Nicholas II acquired the Maritime Territories from China. This isolated border along 19 kilometres of the Tumen River estuary has only a single crossing point, a railway bridge. Large sections of the rivers forming the Sino–Korean border can be swum or waded for most of the year, and when the ice forms in winter can be strolled across.

Almost 80 per cent of the North is mountainous; this leaves little room for agricultural land, which is concentrated along with North Korea's 22.3 million people along narrow coastal plains in the east and wider ones in the west. It is this geography that has moulded the country, with flooding, deforestation and famine as its tools. But North Korea's wealth of natural resources such as coal, zinc and magnesium contributed much to the success of heavy industry in the 1960s and 1970s. The South in comparison is mineral resource poor but farming rich.

Korea first emerged out of the mists of pre-history 2500 years ago. As usual it was a kaleidoscopic arrival and departure of kingdoms that waxed and waned, born of division and dying from fusion. Some, like the Koguryo kingdom, spilt across today's borders deep into contemporary China. These kingdoms were often semi-vassal states of China and more recently Japan, neither of which hesitated to intervene to protect their interests. The Koguryo kingdom's footprint across today's national demarcation line excites contemporary historiography. Right-wing revanchists in South Korea look towards a

The only crossing – by rail – into Russia

Greater Korea that incorporates Manchuria's Korean-speaking majorities and minorities, while China sees the mirror image with a Chinese Koguryo, which stretches deep inside North Korea. This cocktail of kingdoms lives on in the names of airlines, hotels and restaurants.

## The Yanks arrive

Throughout the nineteenth century, the Western powers attempted to convert Koreans to Christianity to create an easier climate for trade. In 1836, French Catholic priests entered Korea from China and began a process of conversion, gaining an estimated 20,000 followers by the 1860s (including the mother of King Kojong). However the king's father, the *Taewongun* (Lord of the Great Court), persecuted these converts, who were undermining the principles of Confucianism. The *Taewongun* distrusted foreigners. Korea's and China's experience served him well – far too often letting Europeans in proved a prelude to foreign occupation. China's position had been catastrophically transformed with the arrival of Western gunboats and Western traders. The Opium War (1839–42) between Britain and China led to Korea shutting its doors even more firmly. This retreat into isolation only disguised how far behind was the country's economic development and military capacity.

Foreign ships arrived and then swiftly departed as the Koreans fired upon them. By the middle of the nineteenth century European nations and the United States were impatient for new trading routes in Asia. In 1853 Commodore Perry and his 'black ships' forcibly prised open Japan, but the gunboat *USS South America* which anchored off Pusan for ten days, received a friendly welcome. Americans shipwrecked off Korea in 1855 and 1865, were also treated well and repatriated via China. Such common courtesy and humanity, however, were confused with a willingness to open their doors.

US businessman W. B. Preston arranged for the gunboat *USS General Sherman* to sail to Korea in 1866. The ship steamed up the Taedong River and became beached at Turu islet near Pyongyang. The governor of Pyongyang sent his deputy, Lee Hyon Ik, to inform the captain the ship must leave immediately or the crew would be killed. The captain and crew kidnapped Lee and four days of fighting ensued. Eventually the ship was set ablaze, the crew jumped overboard and they were promptly butchered. The *General Sherman* incident, proved to be the beginning of the end of Korean isolation. The United States returned in 1871 with the Korean Expedition, a force of five ships and 650 men, to establish the fate of the *General Sherman*. Fighting ensued and 350 Koreans were killed. The US force was neither strong enough nor had the authority to open up Korea for trade. Nevertheless Korea's ruler read the writing on the wall. When a Japanese military expedition arrived off Seoul in 1876, Korea reluctantly signed the Treaty of Kanghwa and opened its ports. Further Treaties with European countries and the United States followed. In 1882 Korea signed the Treaty of Chemulpo with the United States, establishing mutual friendship and non-interference in missionary activity. However, few Confucian clerics travelled to the United States. The traffic the other way was heavy.

Propaganda poster depicting the *USS General Sherman's* surrender

## Revolts, riots and invasion

Korea suffered from massive revolts and food riots throughout the nineteenth century, culminating in the *Tonghak* Uprising of 1894–95. All were driven by hatred of the Choson dynasty's corruption and oppression. *Tonghak* was an indigenous religious movement founded in the early 1860s in opposition to Christian evangelism. The rebellion spread from the southwest to the centre, menacing the capital, Seoul. Desperate, the court pleaded with China to send troops to quell the rebellion. China sent an expedition. When the Chinese appeared to be there to stay, Japan invaded with a force three times larger. The first Sino-Japanese War (1894–95) had begun. The Japanese promised Koreans their freedom when they were victorious but reneged on the promise, keeping Korea under Japanese control. With China out of the picture it was the Russians who were the next to be defeated, while the United States was bought off, leaving Japan free to act. The Chinese had granted Russia, in the late 1890s, the right to extend their Trans-Siberian railway across Manchuria and had leased Port Arthur (now Lüshun) to the Russians to give them a strategic base for their naval forces in the Pacific. The line's completion would have enabled the Russians to transport troops swiftly to Manchuria and Korea. Japan, as an early rehearsal for Pearl Harbor, launched a surprise attack on Port Arthur starting the Russo-Japanese War (1904–05). Japan came out the winner. For the first time East had defeated West.

## Annexation and resistance

The Japanese sent troops into Seoul the day after the Russo–Japanese war broke out. The Koreans were forced to sign a Japanese Protectorate Treaty in 1904, effectively depriving Korea of its sovereignty and placing it within Japan's 'sphere of influence'. Within twelve months Japan had assumed administration of Korea and installed a Resident General (later replaced by a Governor General) in Seoul to direct affairs of state. Despite the Treaty of Chemulpo, the United States acknowledged Japan's control of Korea in the Taft–Katsura Agreement signed in 1905 by US Secretary of War William Howard Taft and Japanese Prime Minister Taro Katsura. This agreement balanced US approval for Japan's subjection of Korea with the recognition of US control of the Philippines – an agreement clearly violating the 1882 treaty. Treachery had its own reward with Theodore Roosevelt picking up the 1906 Nobel Peace Prize for his role in the settlement.

King Kojong declared the Protectorate Treaty invalid in the absence of his signature. He was forced to abdicate in 1907 in favour of his pro-Japanese son – and the last Choson monarch – King Sunjong. Popular resistance to Japanese occupation was widespread, but poorly led. There were acts of individual terror such as the assassination in Harbin of the former Resident General (1906–09) Ito Hirobumi in 1909. This resort to individual terror not only demonstrated the weakness of the opposition but its counterproductive nature. The killing provided an excuse for the Japan–Korea Annexation Treaty (1910) that turned Korea from protectorate to colony.

## Rising nationalism

Korea was quickly subdued. Initial opposition was brutally repressed. Resistance was led by the irregular Korean troops known as *Uibyong* or Righteous Army. 20,000 died before the remainder were driven into exile. External events promoted the emergence of a new nationalism that superseded monarchism and demands for a restoration of the monarchy. In January 1918, Woodrow Wilson submitted to Congress principles for the settlement of the First World War that included the right to 'national self-determination'. Wilson made no reference to Korean independence; after all the Taft–Katsura Agreement had served the United States well and 'national self-determination' was certainly not intended to include the Philippines. Nevertheless, it was these principles that provided the impetus for Korean students in Japan to issue a Declaration of Independence in February 1919. This was launched in Seoul by 33 Korean leaders on 1 March 1919 when hundreds of thousands rallied in support. Thousands were killed when Japanese troops fired on the demonstrators, and tens of thousands were arrested. This became known as the March First Movement.

Japanese repression was initially effective but served to strengthen nationalist sentiment, and for the first time Communists appeared both inside Korea and amongst the exile community. A Korean Communist Party with strong nationalist overtones had been formed as a section of the Soviet Communist Party in January 1918. One result of the March First Movement was that Koreans in exile in Shanghai announced the formation of a Korean provisional government with the conservative Syngman Rhee as its President. Another was that Communists – and socialists – began to infiltrate into Korea, organising youth and labour groups. In 1925, towards the end of Japan's brief liberalisation of its rule during the *Taisho* democracy, the Korean Communist Party (KCP) was formed in Seoul. One of the founders, Pak Hon Young, became Communist leader in the South after the division of the peninsula in 1945.

The Communists concentrated their activities amongst the peasants and on the small group of industrial workers. Lenin's theory of working-class emancipation combined with Krestintern's 'Red Peasant International' gave an organising framework and appealed to Korean peasants since it was the Japanese that owned the farms and the factories. Red Peasant Unions became influential, particularly in the northeast. To the suppressed Koreans, the pairing of national independence and material improvement by the Communists proved attractive. Yet by 1928 the Soviets had grown tired of the sectarianism and squabbling of Korea's Communists. The Party was dissolved and its members told to join the party in the country in which they were operating, either Japan or China. It was too late. Japan was now repressing its domestic Communists along with their colonial cousins. The year before, the remnants of moderate and radical opposition had formed a united front organisation, the *Singanhoe*. It moved leftwards as it shrank under the weight of Japanese repression, before dying as Communism went into its 'social fascist' period. By 1931 Japan was in its final and most brutal phase of colonisation with the military in control. Japan and its colonies were on a war footing. Japan drove an assimilation policy for Korea with forced worship at imperial shrines, the use of Japanese in schools, restrictions on Korean script and language, and the forced adoption of Japanese names. Despite savage repression and sectarian division, peasant uprisings and labour disputes continued to increase.

### Kim enters stage left

In 1931 Japan invaded Manchuria. In China's defence, strong anti-Japanese guerrilla groups were formed with over 200,000 Chinese and a sprinkling of Koreans, some left over from the *Uibyong* (righteous armies). Kim Il Sung, the North's future leader, was one of them. Kim's family was one of many that had left Korea after its annexation, establishing themselves in Manchuria in 1919. Kim Il Sung had been born on 15th April 1912, the day that the *Titanic* sank. His original name was Kim Sung Ju. He was educated in China but left school at 14 to found the 'Down with Imperialism League'. By the time he was 17, Kim had been arrested for helping to establish the Korean Youth League in Manchuria and imprisoned for eight months. When he was released, he focused more and more on agitation work which gradually shifted over into armed struggles. He joined the Anti-Japanese People's Guerrilla Army, adopting as his pseudonym Kim Il Sung, the name of an earlier well-known resistance fighter.

By 1933 he was fighting with the Chinese Communist Party as a part of the North East Anti-Japanese Allied Army under the banner of the renamed Korean People's Revolutionary Army. Japanese attempts to suppress the guerrilla movement drove the 15,000 strong army deep into the countryside, forcing them to abandon fixed positions and to break up into smaller mobile units. Between 1935 and 1941, Kim Il Sung was under the command of Chinese Communists and he rose through the ranks. His largest and most famous operation was the June 1937 attack on the Japanese garrison based in the Chinese–Korean border village of Pochonbo with a company of 200 men – barely a skirmish in some wars. Nevertheless, despite what was said by his many detractors, Kim was a determined resilient patriot favoured with good luck.

Eventually the weight of the Japanese offensive forced Kim and his guerrilla band to seek safe haven in the USSR, which was technically at peace with Japan under the Soviet–Japanese Neutrality Pact of April 1941. In the cold, harsh terrain of Siberia they were armed, trained and put to study Communist ideology. Kim was assigned to the Khabarovsk Infantry Services School's 88th Brigade located close to the USSR's border with China. This is where he married a fellow guerrilla fighter, Kim Jong Suk, and where his first son Kim Jong Il was born (although Korean history locates Kim Jong Il's birth in a small guerrilla camp – now a visitor attraction – on the slopes of Mount Paektu).

Kim Il Sung had been effectively in exile from his homeland since the age of seven. Since his teenage years, apart from his time in the USSR, he had never lived in a town or city and had been cut off from books, newspapers and radio. Consequently, he was largely ignorant of the international situation and world events. Moreover, there was little evidence of any detailed study of Marxism-Leninism apart from a youthful reading of the *Communist Manifesto* and his courses in Stalin's Soviet Communism. But Kim had learnt by experience. His days as a guerrilla shaped his leadership style and management skills and moulded the future shape of the DPRK. The Chinese Communists were paranoid about spies and betrayal. They had much to be para-noid about. Suspected spies and infiltrators were executed, and these victims included a disproportionate number of Koreans. Kim's experi-ence taught him tenacity and self-reliance plus a deep mistrust of outsiders. His experience of Soviet military training and mass mobili-sation and his studies of Stalin and Stalinism were all applied to the modernisation of post-war Korea. Its big construction projects and the development of heavy industry were shaped in the Soviet image.

Partisan resistance to Japanese imperialism became the founding myth of the nation, legitimising its leader, his policies and his actions. It was from this resistance milieu that the 'Great Leader' Kim Il Sung emerged as philosopher-king, and for decades from the early 1960s the wider North Korean leadership was dominated by the legacy and personalities of this period.

## Colonial consequences

Japan's colonisation of Korea was atypical. Japan did not create a country out of native tribes or educate in self-government to promote state building, as colonialism is usually pictured. Rather, the Japanese seized a country that since 1876 and the Treaty of Kanghwa had been on its way to modernisation – that was already nearly there – and tried to deconstruct it and rebuild it anew in their own image. It was a colonialism of occupation in which they attempted total remodelling, incorporation and assimilation. Japanese objectives went further than just economic exploitation. Japan in the end attempted to destroy Korean culture and society and turn Koreans into 'second class' subjects of the Japanese Emperor. Koreans were supposedly such enthusiastic pupils that, as reported by George Orwell, a Japanese Radio broadcast announced that: 'in order to do justice to the patriotic spirit of the Koreans, the Japanese government have decided to introduce compulsory military service in Korea.'[1] By 1945, 2.4 million Koreans were by choice or by coercion in Japan. Those that fought died. Hundreds of thousands of Koreans died for a 'homeland' that was not theirs, in a war where their sympathies were with the enemy.

Japan destroyed Korea's decaying feudalism with an army of government officials, bureaucrats and entrepreneurs who took over and remodelled institutions. As early as 1907 the Japanese owned 14 per cent of the land, and by 1910 there were 170,000 Japanese in Korea. Japan brought infrastructure, industrialisation and rising agricultural productivity to their colony. Investment from Japan's ministries poured in, with the use of new planting techniques and chemical fertilisers to increase rice output. Agricultural development was concentrated in the south, with industry and mining in the north. Japan built houses and factories, road and rail networks. The system worked well. The rate of economic growth in Korea was higher than in Japan. The benefits however flowed not to Koreans, but to Japan and the Japanese.

The peninsula became a cog in Japan's Greater East Asia Co-Prosperity Sphere, a supplier of food, manual and sexual workers, war materials and industrial production to Japan and its empire. War work was offshored to Korea's cheap labour but it was two-way traffic. When necessary, labour was shipped to Japan – the men to the mines and factories and the 'comfort women' to Japanese army brothels. South Korea, citing Japanese documents and statistics, claims that by 1945 over 800,000 men and 50,000–70,000 women had been forcibly shipped to Japan; North Korea goes further, claiming two million working as slave labour. They were invisible workers. The Hiroshima Peace Park commemorating the victims of the world's first nuclear bomb had no memorial to the 30,000 Koreans who died until years later one was erected on the obscure periphery of the park.

Japan sowed the wind and is reaping the whirlwind 60 years on. Japan's violent and unrelenting repression, at least for the last 15 years of its occupation, drove into exile large sections of the traditional nationalist leadership. Away from their homeland, these would-be leaders lost touch. The transformation of Korea eluded them. They experienced neither the modernisation nor the dramatic changes wrought. For all the Koreans hatred of Japan and the Japanese, the changes leapfrogged Korea's economy and industry from late feudalism to twentieth century. The changes were irreversible. The Koreans did not want to go back, they just wanted the Japanese to go. Thus when the traditionalist leaders finally returned, they found the population unenthusiastic about their attempts to turn back the clock.

Those who stayed possessed first-hand experience of the system, but were targets of the Japanese security forces. The life expectancy of nationalist leaders in Korea was brutally short. The Japanese produced a political vacuum in Korea – leaders in exile without followers, and followers without leaders at home. Japan beheaded the possibility of developing a national capitalism run and managed by a modernising indigenous elite. The vacuum was soon filled by Communists and Communism, whose democratic centralism had a historic memory and collective will that survived the loss of individual leaders, and whose programme resonated with the post-feudal aspirations of peasants and workers.

The Pacific War brought the Japanese occupation to an end. When Japan surrendered unconditionally to the Allied Forces on 15 August 1945, Korean hopes for independence soared. After all the Cairo Conference in December 1943 had stated: 'The US and its allies, mindful of the enslavement of the people of Korea, are determined that in due course Korea shall become free and independent.' Hopes were soon dashed; betrayed again, the people of Korea learned that the victorious allies had decided that 'in due course' was definitely not now. Roosevelt and Stalin agreed that Koreans did not have the required institutions or experience to govern themselves, being both politically immature and divided; instead someone had to do it for them. The United States' initial proposal was to expel the Japanese and to place Korea under Trusteeship, administered initially for five years by the United States, the Soviet Union, China and the UK. (The UK was thus rewarded for its role in fighting to subdue Japan in Operation Iceberg off the South Okinawan Islands.) In the end, Korea did not achieve independence, self-government or even Trusteeship. It was occupied.

The fate of the Korean Peninsula was left to the US military in the absence of any clear decision at Potsdam in July 1945. A few days before the Japanese surrender, US War Department officials proposed a US–Soviet joint occupation, with the 38th Parallel acting as the dividing line between the two zones. The decision had no logic save cutting the peninsula into two roughly equal parts – with Seoul, the capital, conveniently on the US side – and giving the Soviets enough of the cake to stop them wanting more. The US knew it had no way of stopping the Soviet occupation of the whole peninsula as US troops were fully occupied elsewhere and the Soviet Union had already marched into northern Korea the day after its Declaration of War against Japan on 8 August, seven days before Japan's unconditional surrender. Stalin's lack of ambition on the peninsula was demonstrated by his acceptance of what was a pretty poor deal in the circumstances.

## The Soviets come and go

Under pressure from the United States and Britain, the USSR made a secret agreement at Potsdam to declare war on Japan three months after the ending of the war in Europe. It has been argued that it wanted to regain the regions lost by Tsarist Russia after its defeat in the Russo-Japanese war in 1905.[2] While the Soviets were clearly aware of the advantages of regaining this strategic foothold, it was not a priority for Stalin. If so why wait three months? An early intervention would have almost certainly allowed him to occupy the whole of the Korean Peninsula, and much of Northern Japan including Hokkaido, both initially sideshows for the United States. Why agree to the US proposed division of Korea with nothing to stop it occupying the whole peninsula? Why withdraw in 1948 if Korea was so vital for Soviet regional control, especially as the cold war had already been 'declared' twelve months earlier?

Stalin had no clear plans for post-war government in the Soviet zone in Korea – a fact that reinforces the view that the invasion was no complex Soviet plot. There was no evidence Kim or his Korean partisans were seen as major players during the endgame of the Pacific War. The Soviets had regrouped the Korean fighters along with other remnants of the Manchurian guerrillas in the first of four battalions forming the Red Army's 88th Brigade, responsible for reconnaissance and infiltration, and made Kim Il Sung its commander. Yet the brigade was not included amongst the Soviet forces that initially entered and occupied Korea. Kim and his fellow officers only returned six weeks later on 19 September when the Soviet warship *Pukachev* landed them at Wonsan. Initially, Kim was presented by the Soviets as a guerrilla hero rather than political leader. If at this stage Kim was being groomed for the top, one might have expected him to be portrayed as one of Korea's liberators.

Kim Il Sung had been away for a quarter of a century. He was completely unknown outside his narrow circle of warrior Communists. Japanese censorship had ensured that few details of the heroic, if limited, successes of the guerrillas were circulated. As an obscure potential puppet of yet another foreign occupier, Kim's consolidation of power would not be easy. The Soviet approach to forming a people's democracy initially established an interim coalition government that included a number of non-communist parties. This was achieved by taking Cho Man Sik's Preparation Committee for Korean Independence (PCKI) in Pyongyang and liberally adding Communists. Kim and his followers within the government acted as an unofficial liaison between the Soviet high command and the local population. The interim government collapsed as a result of divisions over Roosevelt's proposal for Trusteeship. While the Communists, following the Soviet line, expressed their support, the other parties, who favoured immediate independence, expressed outrage. Kim's superiors in the CPSU, quickly impressed by his dedication, discipline and ruthlessness, abandoned Trusteeship and promoted Kim as a 'house-trained' Communist leader.

On 8 February 1946, Kim Il Sung was appointed Head of the Provisional People's Committee. He rapidly began to transform Korea. First he turned the Communist Party into a mass rather than a vanguard party, inducting tens of thousands of poor peasants into its ranks. In August 1946 the North Korean Workers Party was established from the Communist Party and another smaller left party. The party, later renamed the Korean Workers' Party, embarked on the road of popular reform. Laws on social security and labour protection were enforced as well as equal rights for men and women. A land reform law redistributed land previously owned by the Japanese or local landlords to the peasants. In August nationalisation gave the state control of 90 per cent of industry.[3] Economic reform, based on the Soviet model, gave priority to heavy industry over agriculture. The Soviets provided 212 million roubles (€6.1 million) worth of loans to smooth the process. The North's GNP doubled between 1946 and 1949. With a little help from his Soviet friends, Kim soon enjoyed strong popular support and a loyal following amongst militant nationalists and former guerrilla fighters.

While both the United States and the USSR had initially worked within the administrative framework put in place by the Japanese, Kim's nationalisation of industry swiftly changed the situation in the North. In the South however, almost all significant enterprises were the property of Japanese colonists who had fled to their devastated homeland, leaving Korean collaborators in charge. Retaining them did not endear the United States to nationalists in the South who had suffered under the occupation. The People's Committees, which had a breadth of support that belied the later claims they were no more than Communist front organisations, organised huge popular protests against the US Military Government in Korea (USMGIK).

In the North alongside social and economic change came political consolidation. Kim's key strength was his relations with the Soviet administration, which provided him with valuable political leverage.

Under the Soviet umbrella he welded together a coalition of domestic Communists – many of whom had fled to the North from the US-occupied South in a reverse flow to the North's fleeing factory owners – Chinese Koreans who had fought with Mao's Communist forces, Soviet Koreans, and his own small but cohesive group of partisan fighters.

Kim and his allies took control and began to systematically eliminate the opposition and arrest non-Communist leaders such as Cho Man Sik, who had led the PCKI and the initial coalition put in place by the Soviets between August 1945 and the formation of the Provisional People's Committee in 1946. In 1948 as the government in the South began outlawing Communist activities, more southern leaders fled north. When the North Korean Workers' Party merged with the South Korean Workers' Party to form the Korean Workers' Party (KWP), Kim Il Sung was named as chairman while the South's leader became vice-chairman; with the political situation consolidated and the economy growing Kim Il Sung could concentrate on unification.

## Gerrymandered elections

The division of the Korean Peninsula was intended as a temporary measure, like in Austria. The United States and the Soviet Union were to organise nationwide elections to enable a single Korean government to be established. But the United States–Soviet Joint Commission on Korea failed to find any agreed way forward. Elections in which both sides attempted to manipulate the vote for their favourite sons suited neither the United States nor the USSR, for while the South was much more populous than the North, the political climate gave an enormous bias in favour of left parties. The United States turned to the newly established UN. In September 1947, a General Assembly Resolution proposed the holding of a plebiscite under a UN guarantee of a free and fair election. The Soviets regarded the UN as a wholly US-owned subsidiary and rejected the UN proposal.

Had genuine elections taken place across the whole of the peninsula, Kim and his left coalition would have won. The Communists and their left allies by then were widely perceived as having led the struggle against Japanese occupation and more importantly were espousing a package of populist policies. The plebiscite went ahead in the US zone. The May 1948 elections, deeply flawed and corrupt, saw a National Assembly replace an Interim Legislative Assembly. Syngman Rhee was elected President of the Republic of Korea (ROK) and on 15 August formally took control from the USMGIK. The UN immediately recognised the National Assembly and its President as the official government of Korea.

The United States chose Syngman Rhee as its sponsored South Korean leader. Rhee, the late 1940s answer to Iraq's Ahmad Chalabi, was a graduate from Princeton University and the first Korean to have received a doctorate from a US university. He was flown in on 16 October 1945 on General MacArthur's personal plane. Rhee was one of a number of potential leadership candidates but his fierce anti-communism and his long exile in the States gave him the edge. Rhee had little credibility or support inside Korea. While few Koreans remembered his brief spell in 1920 as president of the Shanghai-based Korean provisional government in exile, he had the backing of powerful US patrons who saw him as a malleable tool. They misjudged him. Once in place Rhee was almost impossible to manage and even less grateful to the United States than Kim Il Sung proved to be to the Soviet Union.

The North's response was to hold its own elections for a Supreme People's Assembly. The DPRK was born on 9 September 1948. With full Soviet support, Kim Il Sung set up a parallel state north of the demarcation line. The North–South border was closed. Neither government recognised its counterpart, each claiming it alone represented the entire nation. The South left one-third of its seats in the National Assembly empty for future members from the North, while the North claimed that 360 out of their 572 new assembly members already represented the South. North Korea requested the withdrawal from the peninsula of US and Soviet troops. The Soviet troops departed in October 1948, leaving behind weapons and newly established arms factories as an aid to the North's defence. In response, driven by US public opinion that wanted the war over and the 'boys' home, US forces withdrew in June 1949 leaving behind just 500 military advisors. On the peninsula, with both governments completely at odds with each other and pledging to reunify the whole country by any means possible – the question was not war, but where and when?

## Pre-war war

USMGIK, under the command of General Hodge, had strict instructions to prevent a Communist takeover. Thus the United States stood back and allowed the South Korean regime to murderously put down popular protests as well as Communist insurgencies, with mass arrests of 'suspects' and the complete suppression of the People's Committees. By December 1946, the first round of insurrections had been contained with hundreds of Koreans killed and thousands jailed, but sporadic violence continued until the spring of 1948 when it turned to armed struggle and guerrilla warfare, involving Pak Hon Young's South Korean Workers' Party. Cornelius Osgood, a US anthropologist living on Kanghwa Island summed up the situation:

'Communist' has become a strange word in our time and it may refer to a political philosopher, a Russian spy, a member of any other political party, a labour organiser, a traitor to one's own country, or someone who happened to be regarded as an enemy. On Kangwha it seemed to mean just 'any young man of a village'.[4]

In the run up to the elections of 1948, the Korean National Police under Rhee's command fired upon a demonstration on Cheju Island. The result was an escalation into armed resistance and guerrilla fighting against the US/Rhee regime which culminated in a rebellion on the island in April. This was followed in October 1948 by a mutiny of the 14th Regiment of the South Korean army in Yosu-Sunchon. These insurrections were viewed as Communist inspired and were crushed. Cheju Island experienced a year of barbarism and brutality in which as many as 30,000 were killed (the official figure is 27,719) out of the total 300,000 inhabitants, and 40,000 people were forced to flee to Japan, with more than half the villages totally destroyed.[5] The brutal campaign on Cheju was intended as an example to deter other insurrections spreading to the mainland. Yosu's military rebellion led to the killing and the execution of 2000 alleged participants. Park Chung Hee, the ROK's future right-wing dictator, was sentenced to life imprisonment for his part in the rebellion. Before the Korean War started, the number of civilian deaths in the South had reached at least 200,000 – some claim as many as 800,000. The increasingly dictatorial Rhee was attempting to cleanse the South of Communists and Communism and to impose himself on a reluctant population that had a sneaking sympathy and admiration for Kim Il Sung and his patriots who had fought their war rather than watched from the comfort of US exile. By 1949, 100,000 political prisoners were crowded into in Rhee's jails.

Civil war was inevitable. North and South were driven by a mutual feeling that the arbitrary division in the aftermath of Japan's defeat was deeply unjust. North and South wanted one Korea. Rhee's 'March North' and Kim's 'Fatherland Liberation' were both calls to arms. Border clashes and conflicts provoked by the South started in May 1949 but died down by December, with the North coming off distinctly better in the exchanges. Kim was waiting to be let off the leash.

Kim's ambitions were encouraged by US Secretary of State Dean Acheson's speech to the National Press Club in Washington on 12 January 1950. He defined the United States 'perimeter of defence' in Asia to include Japan and the Philippines but not South Korea or Taiwan.[6] His failure to put the ROK inside the line was taken by Kim Il Sung as a clear signal that if the South was attacked the United States would not intervene. Acheson added a prescient addendum: 'should such an attack occur... the initial reliance must be on the people attacked to resist it and then upon the commitments of the entire civilised world under the Charter of the United Nations'. Kim saw a window of opportunity for the North. Stalin and Mao concurred.

Conspiracy theorists believe that Acheson laid a trap for the Soviets by omitting Korea in order to lure the Soviets into kick-starting the war. This view assumes that Stalin ran the North. The United States, keen to pick a fight with the Soviet Union before it could deploy atomic weapons, needed an excuse and the peninsula could provide it. There is no evidence to back this theory up. In contrast Rhee at the time was trying to persuade the United States of a Soviet threat. He was partly successful. In March 1950 Congress voted an extra $11 million of military aid to the ROK, enabling them, in line with Acheson's speech, to better defend themselves in the future. The vote pushed up the date of Kim's attack.

Kim had reasons and resources for war. North Korea had, as the backbone of its army, tens of thousand of battle-hardened troops who had fought with Mao's Communists in China plus a substantially smaller number of troops trained by the Soviets in the early 1940s. When the United States withdrew its troops in June 1949, not trusting Rhee and reluctant to be drawn into any major conflict by Rhee's military adventurism, the United States limited his ambition by leaving the ROK army without heavy weaponry. [7] The idea was to leave him strong enough to put down internal unrest but incapable of conducting an aggressive war, disadvantaging the South in the event of an attack from the North.

## Stalin says yes

In March 1949, Kim Il Sung went to Moscow to secure political backing for his plans from his mentor Stalin. He tried to convince Stalin that the North would quickly subdue the South. Stalin did not endorse Kim's plans. His focus at that time was on Europe, not Asia, and he wanted to avoid a direct confrontation with the United States. However, to compensate, Stalin did agree to provide some limited material assistance to the Korean People's Army (KPA). A second attempt to persuade Stalin in August 1949 also failed. Stalin was still not persuaded that the North was capable of a swift victory, unaware of the KPA's successes against the South in armed clashes along the 38th Parallel because of the failure of the Soviet ambassador in Pyongyang to report them to Moscow. This omission may have cost Kim dearly. Had Stalin known he might have given his backing then, and an earlier invasion would have favoured Kim.

On 14 February 1950, a Treaty of Friendship, Alliance and Mutual Assistance was signed between the Peoples' Republic of China and the Soviet Union. This treaty eased Stalin's mistrust of Mao and made Communist revolutions in Asia a Chinese franchise. Stalin had decided that there would be advantages to opening a surrogate second front in Asia to draw US resources away from the cold war stand-off in Europe. China was to be the subcontractor and proxy partner. In April 1950, after Acheson's apparent disavowal of Korea, Stalin finally approved Kim's invasion plan and gave the undeclared war his approval, with the USSR dispatching substantial quantities of weapons and equipment to the North.

## Mao concurs

Since their collaboration against the Japanese in the 1930s and 1940s, the Chinese and Korean Communists had a close relationship. There were particularly strong links in Manchuria where Kim Il Sung had fought with the North East Anti-Japanese Allied Army and become a member of the Chinese Communist Party. Tens of thousands of Koreans from both sides of the Yalu/Amnok and Tumen Rivers had fought against the Japanese. After August 1945 many had continued the fight as part of Mao's People's Liberation Army against Chiang Kai-Shek's Nationalist *Kuomintang* (KMT) in China's Civil War. Kim Il Sung supplied aid and assistance. When Lin Biao's forces fell back before a Nationalist offensive in South Manchuria at the end of 1946, it was North Korea that provided shelter for the families of Communist troops forced to flee the region.

The victory of the Communists over the Nationalists on the mainland and the subsequent founding of the People's Republic of China encouraged Kim's own ambitions to reunite Korea. In May 1949, Mao had returned to Kim two Korean divisions of 14,000 soldiers who had fought in the Chinese Civil War. With Stalin's agreement in his pocket, Kim Il Sung travelled to Beijing the next month to secure more military assistance. Mao, entering the end game of the Chinese Civil War with his planned final assaults on Taiwan and Tibet, was initially reluctant to become embroiled in another war, especially one where the United States might get involved. Yet Mao wanted Stalin's help with the invasion of Taiwan. After their Friendship Treaty in February and the promise of Soviet military supplies, Mao gave grudgingly his agreement to Kim's attack. The agreement was secured by personal assurances from Pak Hon Young, the Communist leader in the South, that the South Korean masses would rise up in support immediately the North marched South. This view was echoed by Ho Kai, the leading Soviet Korean at the time.

## Who kicked off?

There has been a continuing debate as to who started the Korean War. Kim Il Sung claimed the first attack came from the South on 25 June 1950. If it had been the South that launched a pre-emptive strike, their subsequent collapse and headlong retreat suggests their generals had all the tactical skill of General Custer at the battle of Little Big Horn. In reality there is little doubt it was Kim who launched the 25 June attack. But the more interesting question is: when did the Korean War start? It was inevitable long before June 1950. Was it back in December 1946 with the General Strike and riots, Pak Hon Young's guerrilla warfare in defence of parts of the population in 1948, Cheju or Yosu the same year, or the 1949 skirmishes between North and South? Here there is a real choice as to when escalation became inevitability.

The CIA had predicted North Korea's June attack. Major General Charles Willoughby, Chief of Intelligence G-2 in the Southwest Pacific Asia command, had alerted MacArthur over a twelve-month period to the build-up of troops on the border, as well as the despatch to the North of the large numbers of battle-hardened Chinese troops of Korean descent. The reports were ignored, repeating Roosevelt's mistake in disregarding warnings of the attack on Pearl Harbor by the Intelligence Services. Yet I. F. Stone's suggestion in *The Hidden History of the Korean War* that the United States deliberately kept quiet about the North Korean troops massed on the 38th Parallel and took no countermeasures in order to trick the North into invading is another conspiracy theory too far.

## Civil war to cold war conflict

At 04.00 on 25 June 1950, 90,000 North Koreans troops equipped with Soviet weapons and Soviet tanks crossed the 38th Parallel. Ongoing manoeuvres on the border turned into invasion. Korea invaded Korea. The North swept south. Within four days they seized Seoul, and within a month reached the foot of the peninsula. Only a small pocket in the southeast around the port of Pusan, known as the Pusan Perimeter, continued to resist. The ground invasion had been accompanied by a series of landings on the east coast. A North Korean ship carrying 600 men who could have easily occupied a defenceless Pusan was serendipitously intercepted by the South Korean Navy and sunk, a single event that may have determined the final outcome.[8]

Civil war turned into an international conflict with 25 countries involved. The Korean War was the first battle of the cold war and became the UN's first military engagement. The world divided along ideological lines, with the West fighting for or sympathising with the

UN and the South. The Soviet Bloc and China provided the North with material aid and assistance, and when the North startled to buckle under the weight of the US counter-attack China put in more than a million troops.

The Korean War shares features with the Spanish Civil War (1936–39). In Spain, Franco's attempted *coup d'etat* failed and turned instead into a grinding three-year war of attrition. Both sides sought outside help. Franco enlisted Italian fascism from the start (and even earlier), with Italy effectively at war with Republican Spain. Germany sent its Condor Legion to practise its techniques in live combat. In response, the Republic sought support from France and Britain, but on being rejected, turned for materials and manpower increasingly to the Soviet Union, along with Mexico. Volunteers flooded in from the Soviet Union's overseas armies – the European Communist Parties sent their men and some women – to fight the fascist menace in Spain. They were joined by a levy of independent socialists who either were absorbed into the Communist ranks or who, like George Orwell, joined the heterodox Marxist militia of the Partido Obrero de Unificación Marxista (Workers' Party of Marxist Unification) and ended up being hunted by their erstwhile Communist allies following the counter-revolution within the revolution.

The difference was that public opinion in Europe had been with the besieged Spanish Republic coping with a military *coup d'etat*. In Korea it was the Communists not the fascists who were seen to have launched the war. Communist parties around the world backed the North – with the exception of Yugoslavia's Tito who labelled the North 'aggressors' – but with the onset of the cold war the mainstream left was much more equivocal. Britain's Labour government sent troops to fight, as did the left governments of a number of other European countries. In Korea, Kim had secured Stalin's and Mao's authorisation that it was his show, save for some Soviet military advisors. When the United States read the events as Soviet expansionism rather than national liberation – it may not have mattered – they threw their forces into the fray just in time. Stalin played pass the parcel. The Chinese were given the job of saving the revolution and the Chinese People's Volunteers took the field. They turned the tide, resulting in the UN's long retreat, just as the International Brigades had done in the defence of Madrid. But 'Volunteer' was in the title only. They had as little choice in the matter as Mussolini's Italian Blue Legion had in fighting with Franco. The wars in Spain and Korea were transformed from civil wars to wider ideological conflicts, and Spaniards and Koreans suffered and died in their millions in someone else's fight.

But to step back, international reaction to the war was swift. The UN Security Council passed a resolution on the day of the invasion, calling for: 'immediate cessation of hostilities' and for 'North Korean authorities to withdraw forthwith their armed forces to the 38th parallel'. The Security Council also asked UN member states to 'refrain from giving assistance to the North Korean authorities'. A second resolution two days later recommended member states provide 'assistance to the ROK as may be necessary to repel the armed attack and to restore international peace and security in the area'. The Soviet Union was boycotting the UN over its refusal to recognise Mao's People's Republic of China instead of Taiwan and lost the opportunity to veto UN intervention. Not that that would have stopped the United States.

The United States used its control of the UN to internationalise the conflict. The US response was in line with domestic political concerns. The Communist victory in China had come as a profound shock to Washington, particularly in the wake of the 'Iron Curtain' descending across Eastern Europe. Obsessed by fear of Communism at home – the 'red scare' and McCarthyism – and abroad, the United States felt the need to stop a Communist takeover in Korea. After all Japan, with the world's largest Communist Party outside of the Soviet block could be next. Now was a good time for a fight. The United States was no longer the only country with the secrets of fission. The Soviet Union had tested its first atomic bomb in 1949. It was the last window of opportunity for the United States to take on the Soviets, or at least their proxy partner, before it became an order of magnitude more dangerous with Soviet deployment of the bomb. As today in North Korea the United States wildly over-estimated the threat from the Soviet Union. Following the USSR's first test in August 1949, the CIA estimated in mid-1950 that the Soviet nuclear stockpile was already 10–20 bombs, which would rise to 25–45 by 1951, 45–90 by 1952 and 70–135 by mid-1953. In fact it was not until December 1951 that the USSR's Avangard Electromechanical Plant, with 150,000 staff on the programme, produced its first bomb. To organise the United States' response, President Truman immediately assigned General MacArthur, the Second World War hero based in Tokyo, as Chief of US forces in the Far East. MacArthur as an added bonus got to command the South Korean army as well.

The first US troops landed in Korea on 1 July 1950, pre-empting formal approval to intervene by a third Security Council resolution on 7 July 1950 which established a United Nations Command (UNC) and a UN intervention force under MacArthur. The United States' 'coalition of the willing' was Australia, New Zealand, Britain, France, Canada, South Africa, Turkey, Thailand, Greece, the Netherlands, Ethiopia, Colombia, the Philippines, Belgium and Luxembourg, while Denmark, Sweden, Norway, India and Italy provided hospitals and medical personnel. 'UN' was more myth than reality. Like Iraq it was a very American or Anglo-American affair, with 300,000 out of a total of 342,000 UN troops from the United States. In all, 92 per cent of those that fought were Anglo-American, with token detachments from the other countries, down to Luxembourg's 44, of whom seven were killed in action.

The first non-US troops did not arrive until 29 August. The United States was on the defensive until 15 September when an amphibious landing behind enemy lines at Inchon, a port west of Seoul, proved a decisive success. It was the breakthrough which rescued the ROK army herded into the Pusan Perimeter. The next 15 days saw the recapture of Seoul and the retreat of the KPA forces back north of the 38th Parallel, their initial jumping off point. The United States saw and seized the opportunity. Containment of Communism became rollback. US government lawyers were soon advising that the previously inviolable border at the 38th Parallel had 'no legal basis'. By early October, concern was being expressed at the UN by the President of the Security Council, India's representative Benegal Rau, that the UNC should not try to reunify Korea by force. After all, UN troops had been despatched to stop exactly that. The United States had its way. The Resolution of 7 October 1950 gave the UNC the green light to move into the North. Both sides were fighting for one Korea. The tables were turned; dispatches now talked of 'liberated areas'. Pyongyang fell. Just like the KPA three months earlier, the UNC encountered little resistance, moving rapidly on to occupy almost the entire peninsula.

The United States wanted a decisive victory over Communism. Any failure to crush Kim would mean the North would merely reform and regroup at the 38th Parallel and try again in the future. The United States misread China's intentions as badly as Kim had misread Washington's. The US administration was convinced that China would not enter the conflict as it was only just beginning to recover from its – not quite concluded – civil war. Truman and MacArthur had discussed the prospects of Chinese intervention on 15 October. MacArthur reassured the President that the superiority of US air cover would deter China from entering the conflict, but that if it did get involved, he could counter the attack. MacArthur advanced to the Yalu/Amnok River, the border between Korea and China, secretly bombing Chinese and Russian targets, a blind eye being turned as it was two decades later in Laos and Cambodia.

The aggressive US approach proved counterproductive. After only a brief hesitation the Chinese became convinced that war with the United States was inevitable, and they preferred to fight their battles on Korean territory rather than on their own.[9] The Chinese People's Volunteer Army was ordered to cross the border, which it did undetected on 26 October 1950, within ten days of Beijing sending 30,000 troops into Tibet. MacArthur only became aware of the Chinese intervention when its forces began to sweep down in human waves on his front line. UN forces overwhelmed broke in disarray. It proved impossible for them to regroup, split as they were between the east and west coast by the inhospitable central mountains.

## The process

The heaviest fighting of the war took place during the extremely cold winter of 1950 – Kim Il Sung and his comrades were holed up in Kanggye. The United States attempted to decapitate the leadership with five-tonne 'bunker buster' Tarzan bombs. They failed; no major commander died. With the Chinese intervention criticism of Kim's handling of the war rose sharply. By December 1950 a Party plenum in Kanggye saw him blame his subordinates for the military defeats, relieving a number of high-ranking officers of their positions and expelling them from the party.

With the Chinese now involved, the UN forces suffered a series of devastating defeats and virtually collapsed, fleeing southwards. Communist forces captured Seoul for the second time on 4 January 1951. This advance proved less successful than the first. The Chinese and North Korean forces were overextended with weak supply lines. When the UNC launched a counter-attack, they took Seoul on 15 March and pushed the Communists back north of the 38th parallel once more. By late spring, the conflict was at a stalemate virtually along the initial line of division between the US and Soviet zones. Both sides were suffering heavy losses of men and materials. The Chinese troops suffered particularly badly from a lack of proper winter equipment.

MacArthur was determined on total victory. He asked for authorisation to send US planes across the border to attack Chinese bases in a public expansion of the war. The request was officially refused, with Truman believing that such an expansion of the conflict could lead to a Third World War. MacArthur protested too much and he was relieved of command on 11 April 1951, replaced by General Matthew Ridgway, who was prepared to obey his President and fight a limited war.

War was brutal on both sides. Besides the deaths in action and collateral damage there were executions. Neither South Korean government officials, nor Communist cadres were spared. With both sides, at one time or another, controlling the vast majority of the peninsula during the war, tens of thousands were executed. Credible reports have the North executing prisoners in Seoul's jails prior to their second withdrawal. UNC soldiers were killed to prevent them from being freed by advancing forces. There were also reports of Chinese troops looting and raping. Yet generally both North and South Korean forces treated their fellow countrymen as exactly that. Both were fighting to reunite a single country and a single people.

This was not always the case with the US troops. In recent years, reports of US atrocities have surfaced. *The Bridge at No Gun Ri* gives details of how, in the summer of 1950, US military forces opened fire on a large group of South Korean refugees at the No Gun Ri railway bridge.[10] Retreating US commanders had issued orders to shoot approaching civilians to guard against North Korean infiltrators among refugee columns. As many as four hundred refugees, mainly women and children, died. The book also records that a South Korean officer, who blew up the Naktong River bridge, trapping soldiers and civilians in front of advancing North Korean troops, was court martialled and executed after the war. But that, in contrast, was manslaughter not murder. No American was even tried for No Gun Ri.

Worse problems were the army, air force and navy attacks on refugees attempting to cross UN lines, carpet bombing and racism. The first, depicted as far back as 1952 in Tay Garnett's *One Minute to Zero* starring Robert Mitchum, showed retreating civilians and North Korean infiltrators being shelled by US artillery. The film was banned at the time from US military bases as the Pentagon cautioned that it would be used for anti-American propaganda.[11] As for carpet bombing, the United States just levelled the North. More bombs were dropped there than on Germany in the Second World War, with 600,000 tonnes of bombs razing cities, towns and villages. Many of these bombs contained napalm, used as a weapon of mass destruction for the first time. The liquid petroleum jelly stuck like glue and burned its victims alive. Oceans were poured over the civilian population, who died in their hundreds of thousands. When the United States arrived, it took control of the skies. The North had no planes and no bombs available to do the same, even if it wanted to.

During the Second World War, the United States projected the view that the Germans were 'misled' while the Japanese were 'monkeys'. The Japanese may have been fanatical, but not that fanatical. The US captured less than 1 per cent of the 22,000 Japanese engaged in the battle for Iwo Jima, but thousands more were killed trying to surrender or shot while wounded. Five years on there was little evidence that US military racism had disappeared. It viewed Koreans in 1950 no more favourably than Japanese in 1945. There were claims that the United States used chemical and biological weapons in North Korea and China. A supposedly independent commission of experts, including chemist and sinologist Dr Joseph Needham from Cambridge University, accused the United States of developing and deploying chemical and bacteriological weapons in

Women wounded by US napalm at an aid station in Suwon,
4 February 1951

Source: Reproduced from the National Archives and Records Administration
and printed in *Living Through the Forgotten War: Portrait of Korea*,
Patrick Dowdey, Mansfield Freeman Center, 2003.

collaboration with Shiro Ishii, a Japanese microbiologist who served
in the Second World War as head of the Japanese germ and chemical
warfare 'Unit 731' in Harbin. The full truth may never be known, but
Ishii certainly traded the result of his inhuman experiments on
Chinese prisoners to the United States in exchange for immunity
from prosecution as a war criminal.

## Going for a draw

Total defeat and total victory were both taken off the agenda. At a press
conference in November 1950, President Truman announced that he
would not rule out the use of nuclear weapons in this war. Labour MPs
in Britain were outraged and under pressure from Labour Prime
Minister Clement Atlee, Truman was forced to clarify his position.
Nuclear bombs would only be used to prevent a forced evacuation of
the peninsula or a military disaster. It was this threat that pushed Mao
into early development of nuclear weapons in 1955.

With a limited war, the United States and the UN needed a negotiated solution. The UN's first Secretary General, Trygve Lie, urged the Soviet Union to intervene in favour of armistice talks. On 23 June 1951, Jacob Malik, the Soviet ambassador said in a broadcast in New York: 'the Soviet people believe that, as the first step, discussions should begin between the belligerents for a cease-fire and an armistice providing for the mutual withdrawal of forces from the 38th parallel.'[12] The Chinese agreed and the truce talks opened on 10 July 1951. Between 1951 and 1953, the two sides talked while their soldiers died, first at Kaesong then at Panmunjom, the 'truce village' ten kilometres east of Kaesong, which now straddles the border between North and South in the middle of the DMZ.

The Chinese and the North Koreans, formally led by the North's Lieutenant General Nam Il, sat on one side of the table and the UNC, led by American Vice Admiral C. Turner Joy, on the other. Allowing Kaesong, formerly in the South but now held by the North, to be used as a venue was a tactical mistake by the United States in the middle of a struggle to secure strategic territory. Initially the United States had wanted the talks on a Danish hospital ship but the North refused. Instead, the North offered Kaesong, a city once renowned for its anti-communism and now in their hands. Washington just wanted to end the fighting and get the troops home. The public in the United States had lost any appetite for war, so they acquiesced. The result was that the immediate vicinity of Kaesong was out of bounds to military action. It gave the North the home advantage for the talks, a quiet ride in a potentially difficult military area and strategic advantage in any future conflicts.

The two main issues at stake were the demarcation line between the two sides and the fate of the prisoners of war (POWs). Negotiations dragged out over two years. The first round stalled after six weeks and only resumed on 25 October. Ground fighting continued on both sides, bombing on one. Lives were squandered in the ground war for little territorial gain. It was First World War-style trench warfare. The bloody nature of these battles was epitomised in names like Heartbreak Ridge, Punch Bowl and Pork Chop Hill.

In terms of the military demarcation line, the UNC wanted it at the current line of control while the North wanted it at the 38th Parallel. This was not altogether surprising as the UNC held slightly more North Korean territory than the North Koreans held of the South. The North claimed that the 38th Parallel was 'recognised by the whole world' and that it had also been the dividing line before the conflict had erupted. The UNC, abandoning any remaining pretence that the UN's intervention was meant to force a return to the *status quo ante*, turned the argument around, asserting that it was precisely the conflict that showed the vulnerability of the line. In the end the UNC got its way.

Unfortunately the line at sea, the Northern Limit Line (NLL), was left in dispute. The UNC unilaterally set it between the mainland portion of Kyonggi Province and the adjacent offshore island, the former under North Korean control and the latter South Korean. Pyongyang always refused to accept a straight extrapolation of the land border as the basis for the maritime demarcation line. Ever since, it has continued to cause problems, with clashes between North and South naval units protecting their own fishing boats, and giving an easy opportunity for provocation for either side when one is wanted. The South's interpretation of the NLL is so distinctly partisan that even the United States expresses reservations that it goes beyond what was intended.

## POWs

The Chinese and North Koreans demanded the repatriation of all POWs, in line with custom and practice and Article 118 of the 1949 Geneva Convention: 'prisoners of war shall be repatriated without delay after cessation of hostilities.' After the Second World War, the allies returned all Russian POWs to the Soviet Union, including tens of thousands who had fought with the Nazis, while the Soviets returned captured members of the British Free Corps, mainly members and sympathisers of Oswald Mosley's British Union of Fascists, who had fought on the Eastern Front with the Germans, where one even won the Iron Cross.

In Korea the United States refused to abide by the Geneva Convention, demanding instead 'Voluntary repatriation'. For many on the US side it became a matter of principle, almost an article of faith. This blocked negotiations while the killing continued. Some Americans were more sceptical. Admiral Joy, Head of the UNC at the truce talks, who eventually stood down over the POW issue, wrote after the war:

> voluntary repatriation put the welfare of ex-Communist soldiers above that of our own United Nations Command personnel in Communist prison camps, and above that of our United Nations Command personnel still on the battle line in Korea. I wanted our own men back as soon as we could get them. Since we were not allowed to achieve a victory, I wanted the war halted. Voluntary repatriation cost us over a year of war, and cost our United Nations Command prisoners in prison camps a year of captivity. The United Nations Command suffered at least 50,000 casualties in the continuing Korean War while we argued to protect a lesser number of ex-Communists who did not wish to return to Communism.[13]

Kim Il Sung agreed with Admiral Joy: 'the continuation of the war is not advantageous because the daily losses are greater than the number of

POW's whose return is being discussed.' Kim's problem was the Southern Communist faction were determined to fight on to the bitter end.

The pressure on POWs in the South was enormous. Chinese novelist Ha Jin in *War Trash*, a thinly disguised biography of his father, writes about the fate of Chinese soldiers who fought, were captured and spent years in South Korean POW camps.[14] For the Chinese the choice was to be China/Taiwan and for the Koreans North/South. Apparently a third option of neutrality existed, but few knew of it and even fewer chose it. Former Chinese nationalist KMT troops, who had been forced to fight with the Chinese 'volunteers', and the Taiwan regime worked together to ensure it was 'Hobson's choice' for many. Within the camps rival gangs of POWs fought for or against repatriation, with camp guards complicit with the anti-communist groups. Many who wanted to return were forcibly tattooed with 'death to Mao' or 'death to Kim Il Sung'.

The North's leadership became increasingly concerned about the turn of events, and their POWs had their leadership strengthened when a senior KPA general was ordered to let himself be captured so he could take command of the North's POWs. Manipulation and coercion were used by both sides, with hundreds dying in a series of riots. Britain's *Daily Mail* on 18 December 1952 demonstrated the absurdity of the position: 'the United Nations refuse to return captives who would almost certainly be shot when they got home ... but the effect of this humanitarian policy will be weakened by continual shooting of prisoners, even in self-defence.' The experience of the POWs in the South was even worse than the brutality endured by the UNC prisoners in the North. But that was not how it was viewed back home in the United States and Europe. Asians doing these things to each other was one thing; having Europeans and Americans suffering was very much another.

## The end

Dwight Eisenhower's promise to end the war in Korea helped get him elected in 1952. But final agreement did not come until there was a change in leadership in the USSR. After Stalin's death in March 1953 Vyacheslav Molotov returned as Foreign Minister. He and his Chinese counterpart Zhou Enlai decided to end the conflict. They conceded on 'voluntary repatriation' on 8 June 1953. Each side was given the opportunity to persuade POWs who refused repatriation to change their minds, but few did. Months and years of intimidation and indoctrination were not to be overturned in a five-minute interview. Besides Kim Il Sung would not have been forgiving of those initially doubtful of the merits of the North. Almost two-thirds of the 21,374 Chinese prisoners chose to go to Taiwan and a substantial number of North Koreans chose to stay in the South. Captured South Korean soldiers were given the option of joining the Korean People's Army (KPA) or going home. Some 50,000 former ROKA remained in North Korea, while 21 US POWs chose to stay in North Korea or go to China along with one British prisoner who opted for the North. He eventually returned to Britain in the 1960s.

It turned out that not all the returnees were who they seemed. By 1959, the United States claimed to have identified 75 former POWs as Soviet agents, including the most notorious, George Blake, who acted as a spy in the British Foreign Office. It was not entirely clear how they chose the Soviets over the Chinese, although from time to time there were reports of senior Soviet officers in POW camps. This did give rise to the notion of the agent as mindless automaton, as portrayed in Richard Condon's novel *The Manchurian Candidate* and its two film adaptations. The US administration, unable to believe that Americans could have voluntarily converted to Communism, blamed it all on hypnotism and brainwashing. How many North Koreans and Chinese went the other way as US spies will probably never be known, but it is scarcely conceivable that the CIA did not have its own programme.

Syngman Rhee had wanted to use the UNC to unify the peninsula by force; he rejected armistice negotiations that threatened to leave a divided Korea, and so did everything he could to wreck them. He tried to sabotage the last stage of negotiations by releasing 27,000 North Korean POWs on 18 June who he claimed had indicated they wanted to remain in the South. This infuriated both the United States and the North Koreans, but by then everybody had had enough. The armistice agreement was signed without Rhee on 27 July 1953 at Panmunjom, by the chief negotiators of the UNC, North Korea and China. The North's copies, in English and Korean, now a little frayed, with their bright red silk bindings are proudly displayed in a small museum near the DMZ.

The armistice never moved on to a peace treaty. The United States and North Korea are still at war. The agreement established a 2 km demilitarised zone either side of the agreed line of control, as well as a Military Armistice Commission (MAC) to oversee the compliance of both armed forces with the agreement. The five positions designated for the UNC were filled by two South Koreans, one American, one Briton, and one on a rotational basis among the other members of the UNC. However it was not a democracy. The United States made the decisions. The MAC served to keep a channel of communication open between the two Koreas in the darkest days of the cold war. The foot soldiers went further. Fraternisation between members of the opposing forces was dramatised by Park Chan Wook's film *Joint Security Area* (2002).

Arrival in England of the first group freed;
from left to right: George Blake, Bishop Cooper,
Commissioner Lord, Norman Owen, Monsignor Quinlan.

Source: *Pencilling Prisoner: The Story of an Australian Prisoner in North Korea*,
Philip Crosbie; Hawthorn Press, Melbourne, 1954.

## Hangover

Without US intervention, the war would have been over in six weeks. Korea would have been unified at a cost of 50,000 lives rather than divided at a cost of 5 million, but 'Better Dead than Red'. The human cost of the Korean War was enormous. There were 4 million Korean military and civilian casualties, a million Chinese troops dead or disabled, 144,000 Americans and 14,000 from the rest of the UN coalition. On top of the maimed and scarred, the lives of all the survivors were devastated, with half of industry and a third of all houses destroyed. Countless civilians on both sides of the DMZ, including war orphans and napalm victims, roamed the rubble of the cities in hunger and despair. Eleven million Korean families were separated and remain so half a century on.[15] Worst of all, the war created a mutual fear and hostility that poisoned North–South relations for decades and turned them for so long into mirror images of each other. As late as 1999 when I checked in for a flight from Seoul and the desk clerk saw a North Korean visa in my passport it was shown around the neighbouring staff and I was asked if North Koreans were normal people like us. What did the North and the South Korea gain from the three years of fierce fighting and bloodshed? As John Halliday and Bruce Cumings put it in *Korea: The Unknown War*, 'each side proclaims that it won, yet each actually seems to feel that it has lost.'[16]

Viewed from the North, the situation was dire. The whole country had been devastated and Kim's promise to Stalin and Mao of a swift and easy victory lay buried in the battlefields along with Mao's own son, Mao Anying, who had been killed in a US bombing-raid on Pyongyang while serving with the Chinese People's Volunteers. Kim Il Sung's decision to invade, it turned out, had been a serious misjudgement.

Kim's belief that he would enjoy the vigorous support of a South Korean population opposed to Rhee's government proved wrong. At best they were welcomed from the balconies rather than the barricades. The massive rebellions in the south before the war were not a sign of growing support for Kim and the KWP but a broader left nationalist opposition to Rhee's growing authoritarianism. When Kim invaded and people were forced to take sides, there was no automatic left turn. It was no longer 1945; a degree of separation had taken place as Communists and capitalists passed each other on the border between the zones, heading in opposite directions. The South had started to move on. Most importantly, the Communists remaining in the south had been savagely repressed and eliminated as a mass movement. When Pak assured Kim that tens of thousands of Southern Communists were prepared to give their lives in the battle for national liberation, he failed to take into account that most already had. Two years earlier the Southern Communists would have been a fifth column willing to fight and die. Kim invaded too late. By 1950 most were dead or had fled.

Kim factored in Southern support and factored out US intervention. Not alone amongst Communist leaders, he judged from Acheson's statement that the United States did not see Korea as vital to their interests and therefore would not intervene. After all, the United States had not reacted to China falling into the hands of the Communists in 1949. Neither miscalculation alone would necessarily have stopped Kim, but the two together proved fatal. Kim portrayed the end of the war as North Korea's victory but it just didn't feel like that. Although he had failed in his ambition to take over the South and reunite the Korean peninsula, he claimed political legitimacy from direct negotiations with the United States and forcing them to beg for peace. Not all his Communist colleagues were as impressed. Kim was in trouble and he knew it.

## Winners and losers

There were few winners. The North had lost and so had the South. In the South, the feeling was one of bitterness. As Chuck Downs simply put it in *Over the Line*: 'limited war led to limited objectives and produced limited results.'[17] South Korea gained little from the conflict apart from heavily reinforced anti-communist authoritarianism. Syngman Rhee was 're-elected' in 1952. When it became clear the National Assembly would not re-elect him, he sought a constitutional amendment to have the president elected by direct popular vote. When this was rejected, he had dissenting National Assembly members arrested, with the remnant at the second time of asking giving him the change he required. Democracy was sacrificed in the name of national security. Rhee manipulated the law and, in a manner befitting Kim Il Sung, arrested those who threatened him for alleged communist links. Anti-communism became the excuse rather than the cause for decades of political repression.

Of the interventionists China had best reason to be pleased. It had fought US-led UN troops to a standstill, proving its military was capable of holding its own with the West. Within the Communist camp, the USSR was the biggest loser in the long-term, even though it had no troops of its own in the conflict. Korea gave the US military-industrial complex the green light for rearmament. Moscow had no choice but to follow where Washington led, resulting in the Soviet economy living a 40-year long lie that ended with the Soviet Union on its knees as military necessity deprived the civil economy of scarce resources that were desperately needed.

Washington suffered its first defeat in a major war and failed to convince the American people of its purpose and mission. They equally had fought the Communists to a standstill, but had been unable to deliver final victory. The Korean War became the first 'unpopular war' among Americans and prefigured the next conflict in Vietnam, when the United States again intervened, this time with much less international support, to fight another proxy war against Soviet Communism. The Korean War fuelled the rising intolerance and paranoia of McCarthyism; American Communists were persecuted, but so too were thousands who had done little more than attend a meeting or donate a few dollars to some organisation Joe McCarthy decided to name as part of a 'communist front'.

The United States increased its national defence budget by a factor of five and set up a global network of military bases. In Western Europe, the effect was the same, with a new military build-up. Winston Churchill said: 'Korea does not really matter now. I'd never heard of the bloody place until I was seventy-four. Its importance lies in the fact that it has led to the re-arming of America.'[18] The United States went onto a war footing with an increased and increasing commitment to the North Atlantic Treaty Organisation (NATO), established in April 1949 as a counterweight to the perceived Soviet threat in Europe.

Japan, the one country that gained most from the conflict, never fought on either side. The United States, forced to take the lead role in northeast Asia, decided it needed Japan's help. Japan's economy took off with US aid and trade, plus financial assistance to rebuild its industry. Enormous orders for material to support the war effort, proved Japan's 'get out of jail free' card. By 1952 with the San Francisco Peace Treaty, the occupation of Japan was over – save in Okinawa, never really part of Japan – and it was independent again, even if it had a US-imposed constitution. The Korean War turned Japan from enemy to ally.

More than half a century since the 1953 armistice, the number of surviving Korean War veterans is rapidly shrinking. Overshadowed in Europe by the Second World War and in the United States by Vietnam, Americans call it 'the forgotten war'. It is this twisted perception which explains the United States failure on the peninsula, for it is certainly not forgotten in China or Korea. A million Chinese died. For Korea, it brought death, separation and division. How would the Korean War have turned out if things had happened differently? It is impossible to tell, but what is clear is that it reinforced and consolidated the cold war and superpower stand-off. Today, Korea and its division is the last dangerous remnant of a period rapidly passing into history, but which might still have a vicious sting in its tail.

# 3 Kim's Korea

## Introduction

After the Korean War Kim needed to consolidate power and consolidate it quickly. Those critical of his handling of the war had history on their side and he had only a narrow window of opportunity to deal with them. He did. By the late 1950s he was in total control of Party and country and was free to set about building a world in his own image where Kim was Korea and Korea was Kim.

Kim took the North from Stalinist orthodoxy to a Confucian cult communism that resonated more with the pre-war Japanese Emperor cult than with Marxism-Leninism. This *Juche* (self-reliance) ideology came to permeate every aspect of society and provided guidance for everything from film making to potato farming, manufacturing to martial arts. Although the pattern of economic and social development was initially modelled on the Soviet Union, self-sufficiency soon came to replace it. This was not economic nationalism, but the more extreme economic isolationism reminiscent of nineteenth-century Paraguay under José Rodriguez de Francia and Burma under Ne Win.

Economic recovery from the Korean War happened much more quickly in the North than the South. In the 1950s North Korea could boast one of the fastest growing economies in the world, and in the 1970s it was one of the top 30 industrialised economies. Yet as with the Soviets, the reliance on heavy industry proved not to be a viable long-term strategy. After peaking in the late 1960s the economy went into steady decline, not helped by the increasing diversion of resources into military spending, culminating in the economic meltdown and famine of the 1990s.

Ultimately, Kim left the country where he found it, destitute, starving and broke. Yet his legacy lives on through self-sufficiency and succession – the Kim Dynasty has now ruled for more than 60 years. Kim Il Sung was the last survivor of the post-war Communist conquerors. All the others are long gone and forgotten. Mao and Tito died of natural causes in 1976 and 1980, and Ceausescu – a late comer – was executed by firing squad in 1989. Mao's China was buried by the new dynamic of Market-Leninism, Tito's Yugoslavia shattered into fragments with very different trajectories, and Ceausescu's Romania is now part of the EU.

## Divide and rule

As early as the 1920s the Soviets despaired of faction fighting amongst Korean Communists, closing down the Party in 1928. Moscow was right. Korean sectarianism was alive and well in 1945. The Soviets may have belatedly selected Kim Il Sung to take on the leadership, but he was 'first amongst equals' as a complex set of parties and of factions vied for power and influence in the immediate aftermath of liberation. They were all Leftist organisations; indeed the Soviets would have tolerated no other. It was a two-way street with Communists driven north by Syngman Rhee's brutal persecution, passing on the road those going south to escape Soviet repression.

In Manchuria two main Communist guerrilla groups operated. Kim's, which fought directly under the leadership of the Chinese Communist Party (CCP), and those that remained outside until 1938 when they were forced by the Japanese deep into China and then fought alongside the CCP. This latter group was to form the basis of the Yanan faction. Immediately after liberation they formed Sinmindang (New People's Party) led by Kim Tu Bong. In August 1946 Sinmindang merged with Kim Il Sung's North Korean Communist Party to create the North Korean Workers' Party, which three years later merged with its southern counterpart the South Korean Workers' Party to become the Korean Workers' Party (KWP).

The KWP inherited four main factions. First was a domestic faction comprising those who had remained in Korea, generally in jail or in hiding during Japanese occupation; this was split internally to a degree between North and South. Second was the *Yanan* faction. A third group, made up of second or third-generation bilingual Korean immigrants from the USSR sent by Moscow, formed the Soviet faction. Finally, there was the *Kapsan* (Partisan) faction led by Kim Il Sung, comprising those who had first fought with him in China and then accompanied him to the Soviet Union, with an inner circle of those he commanded in the 88th Brigade. Apart from the Communists, competition came from an eclectic group of progressive nationalists organised around two main parties, the Korean Democratic Party, set up in November 1945 and led by Cho Man Sik, and the Party of Young Friends of the Celestial Way (*Chondoist Chungu Party*) established in February 1946 by followers of the Chondoist religion, an anti-Western movement originating in the late nineteenth century and central to the Tonghak uprising in 1894.

While Kim had the advantage of Soviet sponsorship, it was by no means inevitable that he would be the last man standing even amongst the Communists. The struggle for power started immediately, but the final rounds were played out long after the Soviets had withdrawn. At times Kim's position was far from secure, particularly after the disaster of the Korean War, and many would have laid odds against his survival. But he proved a master of factional infighting, playing off group against group and individual against individual. Divide and rule.

Within months of liberation Kim began his purge. The first to go were the other parties. The Nationalists were sidelined, with Cho Man Sik and other non-communist leaders arrested by the Soviets in January 1946 for opposing the Trusteeship plan. The Chondoist Party was forcefully incorporated into the Popular Front led by the KWP. Kim modelled his government on the Soviet empire's People's Democracies. The Communist Party was in control, but buttressed by house-trained partners in what was a very one-sided coalition. Even today there are two other parties represented in the North's Supreme People's Assembly, the Chondoists and the Social Democrats. They occasionally make a token appearance, the former as suggested hosts for the South Korean Democratic Labour Party's planned delegation in 2005 and the latter as candidates for membership of the Socialist International (SI). Not that either potential partner took kindly to the proposals.

## Kim under threat

At the end of the Korean War Kim Il Sung was in trouble. He had led the country into a disastrous war that had cost millions of lives and totally devastated the country, and it had been all for nothing. No territory had been gained, indeed some had been lost, Syngman Rhee's weak position had been consolidated and now the US were in the South to stay. During the war the KWP lost up to half its 700,000 members through desertion, expulsion and death. Although Kim enrolled almost half a million new members – predominantly peasants or workers – who took control of the party organisation from the Soviet Koreans, he still needed a scapegoat in a hurry. Fortunately one was available. It was Pak Hon Young, leader of the domestic faction, who had personally assured Mao and Kim that the South would rise with his initial onslaught. Pak paid the penalty for his optimism. He was arrested in August 1953 and executed in December 1955 after a Soviet-style show trial in which he confessed all that was necessary. Kim branded Pak:

> a spy on the payroll of the American scoundrels (who) bragged that South Korea had 200,000 Party members and that in Seoul alone there were as many as 60,000. But, in actual fact, this rascal, in league with the Yankees, totally destroyed our Party in South Korea.'[1]

There is no evidence that Pak was anything other than a loyal Communist for whom the wish was father to the thought. His faction went before him. The Yanan faction's military leader Choi Chang was dismissed from office and the most prominent member of the Soviet faction, Ho Kai, who had shared Pak's optimism, apparently committed suicide in suspicious circumstances within days of the armistice being signed. Within a month he was branded a 'traitor to the party, the government and the people'.

Even with a scapegoat, Kim's responsibility for the war had not been forgotten or forgiven and Kim's opposition harboured a growing resentment of his burgeoning personality cult. But the next battle was over economics. There was no consensus, with polemics back and forth in the pages of *Rodong Sinmun* and the Party's theoretical journal *Kulloja*.[2] The question was how to apply the principles of Marxism-Leninism to the realities of Korea. Kim Il Sung and his supporters advocated a forced march towards post-war reconstruction via an almost exclusive emphasis on heavy industry, while others argued for a more balanced development. It was an echo of the Stalin–Bukharin struggle in the Soviet Union of the late 1920s and a rehearsal of Mao–Liu Shaoqi in the 1960s. As with the USSR and China, it was Korea's 'reds' that triumphed over the 'experts'.

In late 1955 Kim began to criticise senior members of the Soviet faction. After Khrushchev's denunciation of Stalin and Stalinism at the Party's 20th Congress in February 1956, Politburo members affiliated to the Soviet group and the Yanan group attacked Kim. May's KWP Congress was quiet, but at the August meeting of the KWP's Central Committee matters came to a head. Kim was derided as Korea's Stalin with a second-hand personality cult and industrial policy. Choi Chang Ik, the new leader of the Soviet faction and Deputy Prime Minister, and Yun Kong Hum, Minister for Commerce from the Yanan faction, attacked Kim for concentrating power in his own hands and for pursuing a policy on heavy industry that contributed to the widespread starvation in the countryside which had forced Kim to ask for food aid from the Soviet Union and China. Attempts were made by senior members of the Soviet faction in consultation with the Russian ambassador in Pyongyang to orchestrate a coup. This was betrayed when the conspirators mistakenly included a Kim loyalist in the planning.[3] Kim Il Sung got his retaliation in first, making minor concessions on agriculture and pre-empting the coup and purging Choi Chang Ik, while senior figures in the Yanan faction, including Yun, were exiled to minor posts in the provinces or stripped of their power entirely. Some fled to China, even though China and the Soviet Union had acquiesced in the purges. Kim Tu Bong, leader of the Yanan faction and the North's largely ceremonial President, who had not been directly involved in the coup attempt, survived until 1958 when he was purged and accused of being the plot's 'mastermind'.

Khrushchev's denunciation of Stalin's terror, cult and economy led to the opening of the Sino-Soviet rift, which left Kim Il Sung between a rock and a hard place. Korea could become an adjunct of China or the Soviet Union or risk going it alone. He chose the last option, reinventing himself and his politics in a new framework of independence, nationalism and autarky. By 1958 only Kim's faction was left, dominated by the veterans of the 88th Brigade. Politics was dead and *Rodong Sinmun*'s (newspaper of KWP) days of debate were over. Politics had withdrawn from the public arena and was now seen second-hand in a 'shadow' world of hint, nuance and nepotism.

## Then there was one

Now Kim and his fellow guerrillas were in undisputed control. The 1960s was to be the era of the partisan generals. But this autocracy had its price as North Korea was left isolated. Kim turned necessity into virtue and promulgated self-reliance through *Juche* and then began to intensify his personality cult. He was in good company with the personality cults of Stalin and Mao, Tito and Hoxha, but Kim created a personality cult exceptional in its scope, intensity and longevity.

Kim was the father of the nation, and as he left orthodox Communism behind his sanctification began. Korean history became a family affair. Kim Il Sung's parents were rediscovered as exemplary revolutionaries. His father Kim Hyong Jik, who ran a small store selling traditional medicines until he was killed in a raid by Communists, was made into an indefatigable revolutionary fighter in the vanguard of the movement. Kim's mother, Kang Ban Sok, became both a revolutionary fighter and the leader of the Korean women's liberation movement. His late wife and Kim Jong Il's mother, Kim Jong Suk, became venerated as mother of the nation. Even Kim's great grandfather, Kim Ung U, turned out to have led the destruction of *USS General Sherman*.

Kim – and subsequently Kim Jong Il – were omnipotent and omniscient. Like all religious prophets they became synonymous with miracles. Kim Il Sung became the man who had participated in more than 100,000 victorious battles, could turn sand into rice and cross rivers on a piece of paper. Kim Jong Il's birth on Mt Paekdu, was accompanied by thunder and lightning that shattered the ice on the lake causing bright double rainbows across the sky. When four-year-old Kim smeared ink across a map of Japan he created violent storms across that country. KCNA even reported a rainbow over Kim Jong Il's car which apparently followed him for miles.

The cult penetrated every aspect of society and manifested itself not just in history but in daily life. The North Korean calendar counts up from the year of Kim Il Sung's birth. Pictures and plaques, busts and badges of the 'Great Leader' Kim Il Sung, and to a markedly lesser extent the 'Dear Leader' Kim Jong Il, are everywhere. Excerpts from the Kims' writings are read daily and their speeches are replayed constantly. Their *Collected Works* plus Kim Il Sung's autobiography *With the Century* – new volumes of which continue to appear a dozen years after his death – are prominently displayed in every bookshop and library, workplace and school. From the nursery to university, all classrooms are decked out with pictures of the two Kims, as are all homes. Inside the two portraits hang side by side; outside, propaganda posters and murals adorn the walls while statues, plaques and shrines are prominent street furniture.

The ubiquitous Kim badge pinned to every lapel exists in a variety of styles and sizes. The claim that they are sophisticated indications of status doesn't seem to ring true, apart from the fact that senior party members sport the more elegant and smaller badges from the cocktail of designs available. In 40 years at the helm Kim managed to visit almost every farm and factory in the country providing 'on the spot guidance' and leaving in his wake a trail of holy relics. Chairs he sat on are roped off, papers he signed framed, photos of the visit mounted and his words memorised. Kim Jong Il carries on the good work.

In Laos there is a mini-cult of Kaysone Phomvihane, the leader of the Lao Communist Party from its foundation in 1955 until his death in 1992. As recently as March 2007 a number of comrades were still wearing his Kim Il Sung-style badge in Luang Prabang, Laos' second city. In 1995 memorial busts were distributed throughout the country. It's perhaps not surprising that 150 were produced and presented by Pyongyang. The style is classic Kim Il Sung, save for the stylised lotus petals at the base. But as an export industry it was very much a shrinking niche market. Whereas other personality cults died with their subject – with the noted exception of Che Guevara – the Kim cult survived and thrived on his demise. Interestingly Che is probably the only Communist cult figure to appear in contemporary North Korean propaganda posters. One on sale at an exhibition of propaganda art in London in July 2007, had in English and Korean, 'An Internationlist Fighter, Che Guevara will be remember [sic] by our posterity'.

Following Kim's death in 1994 his presidential office was turned into a mausoleum at the cost of $750 million (€564 million), and his body was embalmed and put on display in a glass coffin. The Kumsusan Memorial Palace is now a place of pilgrimage where tens of thousands file slowly by every week as they circle the coffin, bowing three times. As you enter the Memorial Palace the words 'Great Leader, Comrade Kim Il Sung Will Always Be With Us' are emblazoned above the door. Groups from the outer provinces can wait years to be allocated a visiting time. To the tune of 'When the Carnival is Over'

Ubiquitous lapel badge

women cry and men look stern, before select groups are taken off to view Kim's train, his V12 600 SEL Mercedes and the display of his hundreds of doctorates and honours from around the world.

## Leaving Marx

According to *With the Century* Kim considered himself a Communist from his teenage years. However, he rejected the sectarianism and opportunism of the various Communist Parties and groups he observed in China. Many believe he fell into the self-same trap after 1956 when he adopted a new driving ideology *Juche* (self-reliance).

Marxism-Leninism from its inception had its schisms and its heretics. Trotsky and Bukharin were two early examples, along with English Communist J. T. Murphy, who ironically moved Trotsky's expulsion from the Comintern in 1927 only to be expelled himself from the Central Committee of the Communist Party of Great Britain (CPGB) on charges of Trotskyism five years later. More successfully after the Second World War Albania's Enver Hoxha, Yugoslavia's Tito and later Romania's Ceausescu never entirely followed Moscow's dictates to Stalin's fury with their own variant national Communisms. Kim was to go further.

*Juche* was launched in the speech 'On eliminating dogmatism and formalism and establishing *Juche* in carrying out ideological projects' to the Propaganda and Agitation Unit in the KWP on 28 December 1955. Kim was getting ready to purge some of the Soviet Koreans. The launch was possibly triggered by Kim's visit to Moscow in May where Khrushchev had hinted at the 'Wind of Change' that was to blow through World Communism with the 20th Congress of the CPSU. While *Juche* as a fully blown concept followed rather than preceded Khrushchev's iconoclasm, the speech emphasised: 'Marxism-Leninism is not a dogma, but a creative theory and guide to action.' A clear sign of heresy on the horizon.

The word *Ju-che* is a combination of two Korean letters (*Ju* – master and *Che* – oneself), thus literally meaning 'master of one's self'. The term was a flexible one that over time indicated a varying amalgam of national identity, self-reliance, patriotism and national assertiveness. In the 1960s four guiding principles were laid down to encompass *Juche*: identity in ideology, independence in politics, self-sufficiency in economy, and reliance on Korea's own forces in national defence. These principles legitimised the state and its policies. Interviewed by Japan's *Mainichi Shimbun* in 1972, Kim defined *Juche* as:

> the idea ... that the masters of the revolution and construction are the masses of the people and that they are also a motive force of the revolution and construction. In other words, it is an idea that one is responsible for one's own destiny and that one has also the capacity for hewing out one's own destiny.[4]

*Juche* was a direct challenge to Marxist economic determinism which argues that society is a reflection of technology – the water mill feudalism, the steam mill capitalism, with socialism inevitably flowing from capitalism's subsequent development. For Koreans will and leadership overrode economics and technology: 'Man is master of all things and decides everything and man is capable of anything, unrestrained by the narrow realities of the world.' Explicable in North Korea's situation – after all, how else would one explain that socialism chose to visit itself on a small backward country on the periphery of global economic activity? North Korea was the product of the will of one man, a conclusion carrying within it the logic that transformed that man into god.

*Juche* legitimised building Communism in one small country. If Stalin's socialism in one country was seen as an absurd betrayal of Marx, then how much more so in a country a dozen times smaller? *Juche* legitimised arrogance and untied the Gordian knot of choosing between the Soviet Union and China. It provided a paradigm within which Korea's industrial policy choices played themselves out. *Juche* evolved. When it first appeared it was a national flavouring to Marxism-Leninism. The link between the two continued to be emphasised throughout the 1960s and 1970s. In 1967 Kim wrote: '*Juche* ideology referred to the most correct Marxism-Leninism oriented philosophy designed to carry out our revolution and construction.'[5] The North's new 1972 constitution specified in Article 4 that *Juche* was a creative application of Marxism-Leninism to Korean reality. This began to shift in the late 1970s, as references to Marx in official party publications began to disappear. The amended Constitution of 1992 excised the final references. The Constitution's commitment to socialism remained, but was no longer described in traditional Communist terminology. *Juche* and the revolutionary thinking of Kim Il Sung were the sole guides. A religious heresy had become a new religion and broken with its past.

North Korea is the only Communist state that transformed itself into a theocracy. It has a messiah figure who performs miracles. It has a church of the elect who have a totally internally coherent set of ideas that explain the world and how it works. They are imbued with a missionary zeal to spread the gospel *Juche*, combined with an internal self-discipline that requires no sanctions to work. They have a belief in Holy Scripture that needs to be studied continuously and an unconditional faith in the system. They have millions of worshippers. Albeit with Christian overtones, these are features not so much of any particular fundamentalism, but all. The mass grief at the funeral of Kim Il Sung in July 1994 was genuine. The whole phenomenon goes some way to explain the deep and sincere condolences I was offered by North Korean officials over the death of Princess Diana when I visited Pyongyang for the first time in autumn 1997. It came naturally to them to empathise with those overwhelmed by the death of a beloved national idol.

## Economy takes off

Kim Il Sung's formal training in Marxism-Leninism would have started with Stalin's *The History of the Communist Party of the Soviet Union (Bolshevik) – Short Course* (only 392 pages) and the trilogy of centralisation, collectivisation and the plan. The North replicated Stalin's economic model of state ownership and control. It re-ran the tape of Soviet history on fast forward. The first stage to be implemented after liberation was the state or collective ownership of industry in 1946. Korea prior to 1910 had been a feudal economy and during Japan's occupation the mines and factories were under Japanese ownership – after all, the Japanese had built them. The North's nationalisation of industry proceeded smoothly with little resistance. In 1945 those Japanese that could flee did so, and those that remained had other things on their mind than pursuing claims for ownership or compensation. Disgruntled Korean capitalists (and there were a few) whose factories, workshops and shops had been seized could flee south. Indeed, the line was porous even up to the start of the Korean War. By 1947 private companies that had initially been transformed into cooperatives were converted into centrally or locally owned enterprises. The public sector, which had accounted for 72.4 per cent of industrial production in 1946, expanded to 99.9 per cent by 1958.

The North had inherited the heavy industry and power-generating facilities that the Japanese had developed during the occupation, topped up by substantial economic and technical assistance from the Soviet Union. This aid however paled in comparison with that provided by the United States to the South. Figures vary, but it is estimated that grants and loans equivalent to $3.5 billion (€2.6 billion) were provided by Soviet Bloc countries between 1946 and 1984. As Table 3.1 shows, about 45 per cent of assistance came from the Soviet Union, 18 per cent from China, and the rest from Eastern Europe.

Kim in 1946 concentrated on land reform, breaking up large farms and redistributing the land. This was massively popular with the peasants who were able to farm their own land for the first time, providing a massive underpinning of support for Kim and the KWP that made it possible for him at this time to sideline his left nationalist opposition. The aftermath of the Korean War saw a changed political landscape, and phase two began. Individual plots gave way to collective farms, which successively grew in size and number as demands for increased productivity drove attempts to find greater and greater economies of scale after the 1955 collectivisation. This worked for a time, allowing a rapidly shrinking number of agricultural workers to maintain and improve production with the millions moving from farms to factories with rising living standards. Not everything went smoothly in Korea. The machine tractor stations from the Soviet Union were tried and deemed to have failed; they came in the 1950s and went in the 1960s.

After the Korean War, progress came with the 'plan'. The first was the Three-Year Plan (1954–56) that rebuilt the country's shattered infrastructure, followed by a shortened Five-Year Plan (1957–60) that laid the foundations of industrialisation, completed the rebuilding of the housing stock and brought the North near self-sufficiency in food production. By 1958, with Kim in complete control, the state came to own and manage everything.

Table 3.1 Economic assistance from the Communist countries
(US$ millions)

| | 1945–49 | 1950–60 | 1961–69 | 1970–76 | 1978–84 |
|---|---|---|---|---|---|
| Soviet Union | 53 (ln) | 515 (gt) 199 (ln) | 197 (ln) | 906 (ln) | 0 |
| China | 0 | 336 (gt) 173 (ln) | 105 (ln) | 2 (ln) | 259 (gt) |
| East Germany | 0 | 101 (gt) | 35 (ln) | 0 | 0 |
| Other Eastern Europe | 0 | 326 (gt) 4 (ln) | 0 | 0 | 0 |
| Total | 53 (ln) | 1,278 (gt) 376 (ln) | 337 (ln) | 908 (ln) | 259 (gt) |

Note: ln = loans; gt = grants

Source: adapted from the Republic of Korea National Unification Board, *Statistics of North Korean Economy*, Seoul: 1986.

## Heroes of labour

Stunning growth rates were achieved, with the leadership mobilising the masses through rabble-rousing propaganda and appeals to good practice and patriotism. During a visit to the Kangsong Steel works in 1956, Kim stated that rising productivity was a precondition for socialist advancement. He subsequently used this speech and visit in 1957 as the launch pad for his Chollima Campaign. Named after Korea's legendary flying horse, this campaign was a nationwide exhortation for harder work and improved productivity. It worked but at a cost. The lack of skilled workers hindered progress and the failure to achieve targets was blamed on sabotage, with hundreds arrested. It was the skills shortage that led to the 1959 drive to bring Koreans in Japan back home. The Chollima Statue on Mansu Hill overlooking Pyongyang sums it all up, embodying the continuous advance of the workers under socialism, with a worker spurring Chollima forward holding the symbol of the Central Committee of the KWP and a young woman behind carrying a sheaf of rice.

In 1960 Chollima was augmented by the Chongsanri campaign, named after a cooperative farm where Kim Il Sung's 'on the spot guidance' had married the usual exhortations to work harder with the idea that productivity gains could come from drawing on craft practice and local knowledge through direct dialogue between workers and farm managers. It worked, driven by the incentive that agricultural labourers, unlike workers in heavy industry, got to share the profits from increased production.

The success led to the notion of untapped knowledge being applied to industry. Modelled on the Chongsanri campaign, the *Taean* work system applied bottom-up management techniques to industry by encouraging top management to learn both from middle management and shop-floor workers, replacing one-man management with a love for the party. It also introduced material incentives for the workers.

These campaigns shared aspects of both the mass mobilisation of China's 'Great Leap Forward' (1958–60) and the Soviets' Stakhanovite movement of the mid 1930s when heroic individual workers set new productivity records, by example driving up output and allowing the early fulfilment of the plan.[6] The 'heroic' workers themselves were awarded certificates, medals and more (Stakhanov, when presented with a banana, didn't know how to eat it).

The results were remarkable. Economic growth rates of over 20 per cent per annum throughout the 1950s and early 1960s made the North one of the fastest-growing economies in the world, far outstripping the South. Corruption was kept down, with savings maximised. However, serious imbalances amongst the different industrial sectors contained the germ of what was ultimately to undermine the economy. But those who had earlier debated and warned of the consequences of an over-emphasis on heavy industry in *Kulloja* magazine in the early and mid 1950s had been silenced by the purges. There was no one left to protest.

The Seven-Year Plan (1961–1970) shifted the focus of industrialisation.[7] Heavy industry, especially the machine tool sector, was given continued priority. Kim Il Sung argued in 1965:

> the keystone of socialist industrialisation lies in the priority development of heavy industry. Only with the establishment of a powerful industry it is possible to ensure the development of all industries, transport and agriculture, and the victory of the socialist system.[8]

In the 1950s the DPRK had fewer troops than the South but this was to change: there was now a new over-reaching emphasis on the defence industries, prompted by the military regime in the South, the widening Sino-Soviet split, and slightly later the US invasion of Vietnam.

The machine-building and metal working industries' share of gross industrial output rose from 1.6 per cent in 1944 to 17.3 per cent in 1950, 21.3 per cent in 1960 and 31.4 per cent in 1967.[9] The economy had been transformed from rural to urban, agricultural to industrial, underdeveloped to developed. In 1946, industrial and agricultural outputs had been 16.8 per cent and 63.5 per cent respectively of GNP. By 1970 this had been reversed, 57.3 per cent for industry and 21.5 per cent for agriculture.[10]

## Economic turbulence

Nevertheless in sharp contrast to the rapid and uninterrupted growth during previous plans that had resulted in the early completion of the plans, 1961's Seven-Year Plan took nine years. Economic growth for the first time began to stutter and slow. Economic growth based on the continued construction of heavy industry, rather than rising productivity led by technical innovation, had reached its limit. In addition to decreasing external assistance from the Soviet Union and China (see Table 3.1) the workforce was increasingly exhausted as 'speed battle' followed 'speed battle'. Agriculture and light industry were both suffering from a serious lack of investment, which led to a slow-down in the production of consumer goods. The heavy industry sector shrank by 1965, to 51 per cent of output from the 55 per cent of two years earlier, but this was more a reflection of a temporary lack of material inputs rather than any change of direction. The problem was that the North's engineers and technicians had been so well schooled in how to manage and run heavy industry that they just could not think any other way. They over-performed, and in doing so diverted vital resources away from light industry and agriculture against the plan's targets making the asymmetry of the economy worse. By 1970 heavy industry accounted for 62 per cent of the total industrial output.

Reflecting the over-ambitious targets of the previous plan, the growth targets of the Six-Year Plan (1971–76) were substantially scaled down. In an attempt to compensate, the plan placed more emphasis on technical change, greater self-sufficiency particularly in raw materials, better product quality, and the development of the power and extractive industries. An attempt was also made to shift some resources into light industry.[11] A new mass mobilisation was launched with the Three Revolutions Campaign (technical, cultural and ideological). The ideological and cultural revolutions aimed to raise the political consciousness of the workforce driving workers to yet higher levels of effort, while the technological revolution aimed to modernise process and product.

## Economic autarky

Kim believed economic independence was a key to national independence. As he said in 1971:

> only when a nation builds an independent national economy can it secure political independence. ... A country which is economically dependent on outside forces becomes a political

satellite of other countries. ... Without building an independent national economy it is impossible to establish material and technological foundations for socialism, or build socialism and Communism successfully.[12]

Kim resented the growing pressure from the Soviet Union to join COMECON (The Council for Mutual Economic Assistance), with its policy of industrial integration inevitably creating a dependence on the Soviet Union for the products of advanced technology. He rightly regarded it as an attempt to lock North Korea into the Soviet sphere of influence, undermining and restricting his autonomy.

Initially established in 1949 by the USSR, COMECON was a Communist Common Market where an integrated economic area would allow each country to specialise in producing the raw materials and products it did best – or was allocated in the great plan – and rely on others for the rest of its needs. It was an economic trap. Once in, dependency increased year by year. Kim rejected all advances claiming, rather disingenuously, that economic self-reliance aided rather than impaired socialist solidarity:

only by building an independent national economy can we meet each other's economic need with fraternal countries, ensure more effective mutual cooperation and division of labour with them on principles of proletarian internationalism and of complete equality and mutual benefit, and contribute to the strengthening of the entire socialist camp.[13]

Kim recognised that the North needed to import raw materials not available domestically and to purchase some advanced technology. Nevertheless, this was to be kept to a minimum. Necessity was turned into ideology, with self-reliance becoming a catechism, not a choice. The plan called for a self-sufficiency rate of 60 to 70 per cent in all industrial sectors by import substitution, replacing imported raw materials with domestic ones wherever possible, and by re-organising and modifying technical processes to reduce the demand for imported materials. The new innovative technology would enable skill levels in the workforce to be enhanced. To meet the manpower and technological requirements of this new Three Revolution economy, the education sector needed to produce more and better technicians, and to expand the training of specialists, particularly in the fields of fuel, mechanical, electronic and automation engineering.[14]

The subsequent plan followed the same logic. Aiming at mechanisation and automation of all industrial sectors utilising modern production and management techniques, the second Seven-Year Plan

(1978–84) had the goals of greater self-reliance, modernisation, and 'scientification' of the economy. It was an echo of the previous plan. The emphasis on utilisation of indigenous materials became even more shrilly imperative, reflecting the fact that outside capital and resources were becoming increasingly difficult to obtain. This was due to the disaster of North Korea's venture into borrowing from the West, and its defaulting on repayments in 1976. The debt originated with massive purchases of capital goods such as machinery and equipment from Western countries in the early 1970s at the start of the Six-Year Plan. The loans were to be repaid by increased export earnings and new short-term credits, neither of which happened. After initially suspending payments, North Korea rescheduled, but debts as well as unpaid interest continued to mount. North Korea's inability to pay its debts destroyed any possibility of future loans. The second Seven-Year Plan failed rather than just under-achieving like its predecessor. North Korea only reached its production target in a single sector of the consumer goods market – textiles. An economy that had once been an object of envy was showing signs of systemic failure.

### Economy in reverse

From the mid-1960s, economic growth in the North slowed year on year before finally grinding to a halt at the beginning of the 1990s. Previous targets were rolled over yet again in the third Seven-Year Plan (1987–93), which sounded empty echoes of the previous two. Targets were once again adjusted downwards while more emphasis was put on light industry and the production of consumer goods. The plan died at birth as the economy slammed into reverse gear. North Korea de-industrialised almost as rapidly as it had industrialised. By the end of 1998, the economy had recorded a negative growth rate for nine straight years, with some years in double digit decline.[15] The failure to invest, or to find investment, the refusal initially and inability later to switch from heavy to light industry cost North Korea's economy all its forward momentum. To make matters worse the Soviet empire collapsed in 1989 and North Korea lost one of its last remaining benefactors.

The natural disasters of the mid-1990s were the final blows. It was all over bar the shouting. North Korea's economy and its society were paralysed by indecision and indifference, famine and isolation. It was not until a new leader and a new millennium, prompted by the successes of China and Vietnam, that the North attempted to redress its difficulties with economic reform that laid out a path to Market-Leninism. Only with the new century did the North's economy start to reverse its decline and slowly grow again from a dramatically reduced and narrower base.

## Welfare state

Initially, industrialisation and economic growth led to improved standards of living, modernisation and urbanisation in the North. After 35 years of colonial rule and centuries of feudalism, Communism at least delivered material well-being. It was through mechanisms such as the Public Distribution System (PDS) that the state delivered basic needs such as food, housing, health care, education and employment, while social insurance programmes provided for the sick, gave maternity benefits and paid pensions. As with the economy, Kim's model for social development was the Soviet Union. The state-funded and managed health service was one to be proud of and schooling was radically reformed, with seven years compulsory education introduced in 1950. The state provided everything from schoolbooks to board and lodging. The previous, woefully inadequate, education system had been destroyed by the years of Japanese occupation. Most adults were illiterate and only a third of children had attended primary school.[16] The literacy rate was close to 100 per cent within a decade. Education did not stop with the classroom. Kim established an adult learning programme, and by 1983 over 70 per cent of the population was undergoing on-the-job training.

The result of education and industrialisation was massive upward social mobility and a changing social architecture. The proportion of farmers in the population declined from three-quarters to a quarter between 1946 and 1987. In contrast, industrial manual workers jumped from a 12.5 to 57 per cent of the population in the same period.[17] Industrialisation drove urbanisation. From 1953 to 1960, the urban population grew by between 12 and 20 per cent per annum, with one in nine of the population living in Pyongyang.[18] By 1987, 60 per cent of the total population lived in cities, marking one of the world's highest levels of urbanisation.[19]

Despite dramatic social changes, families and individuals could not escape their past. Aspirations were constrained by class and commitment. The classification of citizens began in 1958. In-depth investigations were conducted to identify criminal elements and those hostile to the regime. The political history of three generations, including in-laws and relatives as distant as sixth cousins, was taken into account. Families were placed into one of three broad categories: 'friendly', 'neutral' and 'hostile'. Direct translation from the North Korean terminology would be into 'main class' (*haeksim kyech'ng*), 'wavering class' (*tongyo kyech'ng*) and 'hostile class' (*chuktae kyech'ng*).

The 'friendly' class was trusted to support the regime unconditionally and included former revolutionaries and the families of victims of the Korean War. The 'hostile' were families who owned land during the Japanese occupation and therefore comprised the bourgeoisie,

Table 3.2 Political classification system in North Korea by social origin

| Categories | Sub-categories | Treatment |
|---|---|---|
| 'Friendly' (28%) | 1) workers who originated from working families; 2) former farm hands; 3) former poor peasants; 4) the staff members of state organisations; 5) KWP members; 6) the family members of deceased revolutionaries; 7) the family members of participants in the revolutionary and national liberation movements; 8) revolutionary intelligentsia (that is, those who received their education after Liberation); 9) the families of civilians who were killed during the Korean war; 10) the families of soldiers who perished during the Korean war; 11) the families of servicemen; 12) war heroes; 13) families of the socialist patriotic victims. | Qualification for becoming cadres in the Party, government and the military. Privileged treatment in receiving rations of food and necessities, promotion, housing, place of residence, medical care, etc. |
| 'Neutral' (45%) | 1) former small vendors; 2) former medium traders; 3) former independent craftsmen; 4) former owners of small enterprises; 5) former owners of small service businesses; 6) former owners of medium-sized service businesses; 7) the families of people of good social origin who went to the South but did not actively oppose the North Korean political and state regime; 8) former middle-level peasants; 9) returnees from China and Japan; 10) old intelligentsia who received their education before Liberation; 11) those who studied abroad; 12) people prone to hooliganism; 13) 'suspicious women' – former mudang (shamans), kisaeng (courtesans) and the like; 14) people from the South who did not participate in the so-called 'factional activities' (that is, those who were not related to the Communist movement in South Korea); 15) the wealthy in small villages. | Qualification for becoming low-ranking officials or engineers. A chance to be reclassified as friendly, though limited in number. |

*Table 3.2 continued*

| 'Hostile' (27%) | 1) workers who had become workers after Liberation, but had formerly been entrepreneurs and officials; 2) former rich peasants; 3) former traders who represented small and medium capital; 4) former land-lords; 5) people who participated in pro-Japanese or pro-American activities; 6) former officials in the Japanese colonial administration; 7) families of people of bad origin who fled to the South during the war; 8) Protestants and people observing Protestant rituals; 9) Buddhists and people observing Buddhist rituals; 10) Catholics and people observing Catholic rituals; 11) Confucian scholars; 12) people expelled from the KWP; 13) former party cadres fired from their posts; 14) people who during the occupation of North Korea by the American and South Korean forces served in the police and state apparatus of the South; 15) the families of prisoners; 16) people involved in spying activities and their families; 17) anti-party and counter-revolutionary elements, as well as members of various factions; 18) the families of people punished for political crimes; 19) people released after serving prison terms for political crimes; 20) people released after serving prison terms for stealing, embezzlement and other non-political crimes; 21) former members of the Party of Young Friends of the Celestial Way; 22) former members of the Democratic party; 23) former capitalists. | Forced labour in remote places. No qualification for becoming Party members or entering colleges. Forced move to remote areas or segregation. Being placed under constant surveillance. Limited chance to be reclassified into the 'wavering' stratum. |
|---|---|---|

Sources: adapted from the '3 class 51 group' classification system in H.J. Chon (2004), p51–2, Tables 7 and 8. Detailed discussion of social classification structure can be found in Oh and Hassig (2000), pp.133–5.

families of defectors, Japanese and US collaborators, and families of those who had opposed Kim. The rest were 'neutral'. It was possible to escape one's lot in life by meritorious actions or through political re-education but relegation was always easier than promotion as it only took a single slip. In 1967 the composition of the three classes was summarised as a series of 51 sub-groups.

Social status was the key determinant of education, occupation and residence, plus the ability to travel at home and abroad. Kim Il Sung stood capitalism on its head. Superior living standards and opportunities were the preserve of the children of the working class and the Party.

## Alone abroad

*Juche* shaped not only domestic politics but also foreign affairs. Independence began to define North Korea's international relations from the time of Khrushchev's denunciation of Stalin in 1956. Initially Kim was close to the Soviet Union – the country that had given him military training and a route to power – but it was Mao not Stalin that came to his rescue in 1950. Although he proved harder to convince than Stalin of the inevitable victory of the Fatherland Liberation War, Mao did his Communist duty, intervening to stave off the North's defeat and 'save the revolution'. In contrast, Stalin was cowardly and extended meagre material assistance that was well short of the promised military support, and even asked for payment. The few Soviet fighter pilots seconded to the North's air force were only allowed to undertake missions over North Korean-occupied territory to avoid the possibility of being captured by US troops if shot down and triggering an escalation of the war.

Soviet support did flow after the armistice with $700 million (€526 million) of grants and loans to reconstruct the devastated North Korean economy. Despite China having its own reconstruction in hand, less than four years after the end of the civil war on the mainland it nearly matched the Soviet Union with $500 million (€376 million). North Korea owed its survival to its two Communist neighbours, who became its major trading partners – almost its only trading partners – and source of oil and military equipment at 'friendship' prices. Pyongyang after the Sino-Soviet rift was forced into a delicate balancing act. Kim opted for independence over alignment, and thus after the rift maintained his distance from both.

In July 1961, North Korea signed Treaties of Friendship, Cooperation and Mutual Assistance with the Soviet Union and then with China. These Mutual Assistance Treaties guaranteed support should one of the parties be attacked as a check to US ambitions, while acting to deter imperial ambitions by either neighbour. By 1963 Kim was emboldened to complain that:

certain persons propagandise as though a certain country's armed forces alone were defending the entire socialist camp, as though the latest military technique of a certain country alone were maintaining the security of the socialist camp and world peace. They make light of the role of the other fraternal countries in the defence of the socialist camp and neglect their due cooperation in strengthening the defence power of these countries. All who are truly concerned about the security of the socialist camp and world peace cannot agree to such a stand.[20]

This was part of a sharp criticism of Moscow's refusal to transfer nuclear weapons technology to North Korea.

The Sino-Soviet split and Kim's refusal to choose sides, coupled with the Soviets' (and after 1955 China's) refusal to transfer advanced weapons technology, meant the North had no choice but to develop a powerful independent military capability. This necessity was only reinforced by – in Kim's view – Khrushchev's craven surrender to the United States with his policy of peaceful coexistence and Park Chung Hee's coup in Seoul. Initially Park was welcomed as 'leftist' by Pyongyang, but he soon showed his true colours. Military government in South Korea meant rising military budgets on both sides of the DMZ and a view that outstanding problems warranted military solutions. In December 1962 Kim launched the 'Equal emphasis' policy, balancing a commitment to continued economic growth with indigenous weapons production. The inexorable logic of going it alone meant an increase in the defence budget and expansion of the North's military-industrial complex.[21]

The Sino-Soviet rift intensified with Khrushchev's policy of 'peaceful coexistence'. When the Soviet Union backed down during the Cuban Missile Crisis of October 1962, China denounced Moscow; Kim agreed in private and so did the Cubans. In response to China's denunciation of 'socialist imperialists', Khrushchev cancelled China's aid package and backed India's aggression that led to 1962's Sino-Indian border war. Kim felt similarly betrayed and temporarily leant towards China and away from the Soviet Union. Yet his failure to endorse Chinese criticism of the Soviets for their unilateral claim to the leadership of world Communism annoyed Beijing. During the Cultural Revolution Red Guards labelled him 'Korea's Khrushchev'. Growing tensions between the Soviet Union and China as the 1960s progressed continued to make Pyongyang's position increasingly uncomfortable. Kim's condemnation of both Soviet imperialism and Chinese dogmatism did little to endear him to either.

By 1966, Kim was proclaiming the KWP as entirely independent. Empathising with the Communist Parties of other contested parts of the Soviet empire, Kim reflected: 'our Party, too, has had the bitter experience of interference by great-power chauvinists in its internal affairs. Needless to say those great power chauvinists met with rejection they deserved.' In October 1966 Kim also proclaimed self-reliance in national defence, stating that the Military Four Lines policy must: 'make our army a cadre army, modernise it, arm all the people and turn the whole country into a fortress'.[22] Military expenditure tripled, from 10 per cent of GNP in 1966 to 30.4 per cent in 1967.[23] In 1967–68 relations with China worsened, with Kim resisting Beijing as strongly as he had earlier resisted Moscow.

## Switching partners

Relations with the Soviet Union remained cool, China and the North enjoyed renewed warm relations for most of the 1970s. Zhou Enlai went to Pyongyang in 1970 and Kim Il Sung went to Beijing in 1974, despite his shock at Nixon's 1972 visit. China even replaced for a time the Soviet Union as the DPRK's leading supplier of military hardware. However, this trend was to be reversed at the end of the 1970s after China signed the Sino-Japanese Treaty of September 1978 and normalised relations with the United States four months later.

When Deng Xiao Ping came to power in 1978, his pragmatic approach to the economy and his implicit advocacy of market socialist reforms was summed up in his infamous aphorism: 'White cat, black cat; who cares as long as it catches mice.' The Chinese Communist Party's new direction emphasised modernisation and economic reform at the expense of revolution and ideology and there was a continued and accelerating move towards the market throughout the 1980s. Despite this there was an exchange of high-level visits in the early 1980s. For North Korea it was Hobson's choice. Friendly relations were necessary for economic and military reasons.

The Soviet Union, like the DPRK, did not welcome the US–China rapprochement.[24] Its own relations with the United States had been severely compromised with its Afghan 'invasion' of 1979. Ties with the North began to strengthen, especially when Andropov replaced Brezhnev as Soviet leader in November 1982. Kim visited Moscow in 1984, and in 1986 Soviet Foreign Minister Eduard Shevardnadze visited Pyongyang. Moscow consolidated and strengthened its military cooperation with the North with annual joint naval and air force exercises between 1986 and 1990. But the end of the decade brought a fundamental change in Soviet-DPRK relations. Mikhail Gorbachev, elected General Secretary of the Soviet Communist Party in March 1985, began to pursue domestic economic and political reforms, *perestroika* (transformation) and *glasnost* (openness), and at the same time altered the emphasis of Soviet foreign policy to favour economic development over great power rivalry. Gorbachev continued to engage with Pyongyang, but the consequences of reform swept all before it.

The waxing and waning of the respective influences of Moscow and Beijing is colourfully demonstrated in the North's philatelic history. Russian themes alternated with Chinese across the decades, as the DPRK's partner of choice switched.[25] The North's last remaining confidence in its erstwhile allies was undermined in the early 1990s. Moscow's establishment of diplomatic relations with Seoul in 1990 was a first, followed two years later by Beijing. But the collapse and disintegration of the Soviet Union in 1991 ended the ability of Pyongyang to play one off against the other.

**Alternative to the Soviet bloc**

Kim had tried to find a third way in the mid-1970s with the Non-Aligned Movement (NAM). *Juche* acted for North Korea as a cross to ward off the vampires of its two Communist neighbours. The NAM, with its rhetoric of 'neither Moscow nor Washington', appealed to Kim as his own relations with the Soviet Union and to a lesser extent with China deteriorated.

The NAM had its origins in the 1955 Bandung Conference in Indonesia. It was a meeting of Asian and African states, most newly independent, that condemned colonialism, including that of its Soviet variant. While China and Vietnam attended Bandung at the time the DPRK could not because it was too close to Moscow. The NAM was formally established in Yugoslavia in 1961 with the objective of grouping together third-world states experiencing 'similar problems of resisting the pressures of the major powers, maintaining their independence and opposing colonialism and neo-colonialism, especially Western domination'.[26] The NAM refused to take sides in the East–West ideological conflict, believing the opponents were two sides of the same coin.

Kim's delicate balancing act during the Sino-Soviet split threatened to topple him into one or other camp. He was looking for support to underpin his struggle against the United States and help win the diplomatic battle with the South. The NAM seemed an ideal forum to promote his own particular vision of the Third Way and to promote himself as a third-world leader. Initially his strategy was highly successful.

North Korea began to expand its diplomatic relations with third-world countries from the 1960s but did not join the NAM until August 1975, along with the Palestine Liberation Organisation. The number of nations having diplomatic relations jumped decade by decade from two at the end of the 1940s to 113 by the turn of the millennium. Kim's first success was to have South Korea's bid for membership of NAM rejected in the same meeting as the North was accepted. South Korea was told 'no' because the massive and continued US military presence was proof of alignment. But success was short lived. Pyongyang's lobbying led to a series of pro-North resolutions, but turned counter-productive as member states reacted to excessive pressure. The North's support for international terrorism and Kim's growing personality cult did not help. Resolutions on the Korean Peninsula began to favour the South. Kim's hopes were dashed, while the NAM virtually disappeared, destroyed by its own internal conflicts. One vestige from this period is the special relationship between Pyongyang and Jakarta. Former President Sukarnoputri Megawati was a regular visitor, both in and out of office, to the North, and her successor President Susilio Bambang Yudhoyono plans a visit in 2007, seeking the role an 'honest broker' on the peninsula. Indonesia was also responsible for saddling North Korea with the world's most inappropriate national flower, with the adoption of an Indonesian orchid, named the *Kimilsungia*, at the suggestion of President Suharto.

## Friends and foes

The experience of Japanese colonisation and the United States' role in the Korean War left the North with an intense antipathy towards the two that continues today. Animosity toward Japan is twofold. Japan has not only chosen to ally itself with the United States, but it is still unapologetic about its colonial past. Around 600,000 Koreans live in Japan. As many as 2.5 million were in Japan at the end of the Pacific War. A few had come in the early years of Japanese occupation to study or work, and later some went as volunteers, but most were coerced or forced to Japan after 1937. Many were able to return to Korea after the end of the war, but a large group was left behind; however tens of thousands returned to the North in the 1960s after the North Korean Red Cross and its Japanese counterpart concluded an agreement in August 1959. These overseas Koreans chose sides according to their political beliefs. Chosen Soren, formed in 1955, supported the North and grouped together a majority of Koreans in Japan. While its foundation was not organised by Pyongyang, the DPRK extended generous financial aid – substantially greater than that from Seoul to its counterpart organisation, Mindan. Initially a receiver, Chosen Soren turned into a giver of funds and a recruiting ground for the North. For many years its leadership acted as the voice of Pyongyang. Now as the third generation has begun to take over, the organisation has begun to distance itself a little. Some former members have broken off to attack human rights abuses in the North, particularly in relation to those who returned from Japan in the 1960s.

With its intervention in Korea's civil war, the United States replaced Japan as 'number one enemy', making itself the prime target of Pyongyang's anti-imperialist rhetoric and more. A particularly sore point was the continued presence of nearly 70,000 US soldiers in the South. While both sides were serial violators of the armistice along the DMZ, US intervention in Vietnam and Cambodia gave the opportunity to fight a proxy war. Following Lon Nol's coup against Prince Norodom Sihanouk in March 1970, Kim Il Sung offered the prince North Korean troops for his war of resistance. Sihanouk politely declined the offer. Earlier in 1964 the ROK sent tens of thousands of troops to support the United States in Vietnam. Pyongyang in response provided a range of military assistance and KPA advisors to Hanoi. Hundreds of North Korean pilots flew missions against the South and US troops. The casualty rate was high and recently a number of graves of North Koreans who died have been discovered near Hanoi. North Korea also sent about 100 tunnel warfare experts to Vietnam to help dig the 250 kilometres of tunnels that the North Vietnamese and Viet Cong troops used to infiltrate into South Vietnam. After the United States withdrew and South Vietnam fell, relations between Hanoi and Pyongyang deteriorated as North Korea became close to the Khmer Rouge regime of Pol Pot and its titular head of state Sihanouk. At one time the only flight into Phnom Penh was a monthly Air Koryo flight from Pyongyang. Thus when Vietnam invaded Cambodia, Pyongyang, like Washington, sided with Pol Pot and denounced Hanoi.

Nearer to home the North captured the National Security Agency (NSA) spy ship *USS Pueblo*. In January 1968, North Korean naval ratings boarded and seized the vessel, with Pyongyang claiming the ship had violated their territorial waters. The initial seizure was a huge embarrassment for the United States, which made frantic attempts to put together a rescue mission. The United States suffered further humiliation when it was forced to apologise to the North in exchange for the return of its 83 officers and men. All the fuss about the *Pueblo* was another example of US double standards. The *Pueblo* crew were considerably luckier than that of the *USS Liberty*, which a year earlier had been attacked by the Israelis to stop the NSA monitoring the massacre of captured Egyptian soldiers. That assault had left 34 dead and 171 wounded. The *Pueblo* story with a single death lives on in the United States, while the 34 dead to Israel action against the *Liberty* is all but forgotten in the interest of US foreign policy. In 1969 it was the turn of US Navy reconnaissance plane EC-121, shot down because of its incursion into North Korean airspace. This time there was no apology from the United States. Instead, nuclear-capable B-52s flew up and down the DMZ.

Until 1998 the *Pueblo* was moored in Wonsan harbour on the east coast, adjacent to where it was captured. Kim Jong Il decided that a

The first North Korean soldier to board the *Pueblo*

new generation in the capital should learn from the lessons of the past. As a result, the *Pueblo* was disguised and sailed from Wonsan to Nampo in great secrecy through international waters around the southern tip of the Korean peninsula and up the Taedong river to Pyongyang. Concerns that the United States would attempt to seize the vessel proved groundless. The United States did not see it despite all the tens of billions of dollars spent on the NSA and its spy satellite partner, the National Reconnaissance Office. In Pyongyang, the ship was restored to its original condition before being opened for business in October 1999. The ship is now proudly on view to tourists and visitor groups, with original NSA documents still intact, as a floating relic of cold war history. More recently Pyongyang has offered to consider its return as part of the negotiations with the US.

The next clash was the 'axe murder' in 1976. Two US servicemen were pruning a poplar tree that blocked the view from a UN observation post in Panmunjom. The tree was in the neutral zone and the US authorities should have informed, if not sought the approval of, their counterparts on the other side of the DMZ. As it was North Korean soldiers were ordered to stop the pruning and so one of them seized an axe and killed two US soldiers with it. As with the EC-121, the United States dispatched B-52s to flirt close to North Korean airspace while President Ford instructed that the tree be removed once and for all. Three days later it was chopped down with US fighters flying overhead. The axe is on display in the North Korean exhibition hall close to the DMZ.

## Reunification of the fatherland

Reunification was until recently a given for both North and South, though not a sentiment shared by the superpowers who had cut the cake in the first place. Kim Il Sung's attempt to unify the country by force was not only destructive but counterproductive. It consolidated Rhee's regime and kept US troops in the South for more than half a century. But that didn't stop attempted destabilisation by both sides. Throughout the 1960s Kim raised tensions through border incidents, the infiltration of agents and commando raids. These reached an all-time high at the end of the 1960s. Six hundred infiltrations were reported in 1968, the year of the unsuccessful assassination attempt on President Park Chung Hee[27] and a planned assault on the US Embassy in Seoul. A second assassination attempt two years later also failed, but a third in 1974 killed the President's wife. More recently it has been revealed, in a reprise of the film *The Dirty Dozen*, that in retaliation South Korea released violent criminals and murderers from death or life sentences to train for an operation to blow up the North Korean presidential palace and behead Kim Il Sung. The film *Silmido* (2003)

The axe on display

shows the secret training on the remote island of Silmi and their mutiny when a rapprochement between North and South in the early 1970s led to the mission's cancellation. The mutiny was put down with the death of the whole commando squad.

In 1960, even while guerrilla incursions were taking place, Kim laid out his formula for reunification. It borrowed the idea of confederation from Khrushchev (in 1957 the East German leadership had suggested it to West Germany). First, Kim stressed that the removal of US troops was imperative:

> At present the root cause of our country's division and of all misfortunes and sufferings of the people in South Korea lies in the occupation of South Korea by the US army and the aggressive policy of the Americans. As long as the US army is stationed in South Korea, it is impossible to accomplish the peaceful unification of the country, and the South Korean people cannot extricate themselves from the present miserable plight.[28]

Second, Kim proposed a confederation of North and South,[29] as Pyongyang's prime focus was on ending the inter-Korean armed confrontation, with the withdrawal of US troops from the South and an ending of the military build up on both sides. Confederation was to be 'Unity in Diversity' a 'one country, two systems' solution to ending the division.

The South Korean approach, in contrast, was peaceful coexistence based on 'peace first, unification later', with cross-recognition of the two political systems and mutual economic cooperation. The two sides were miles apart. The situation changed when, at the turn of the 1970s, Nixon went for détente in Asia. Learning the lesson from Vietnam, Nixon declared in 1969 that Asian nations had to be responsible for their own security, with the United States staying aloof. The 'Nixon doctrine' paved the way for a partial wind-down of US engagement in Korea and led to the rapprochement with China. In 1970, Nixon announced that the United States would be withdrawing troops from South Korea.

Neither North nor South was happy. In 1971 it was the two Red Cross societies that initiated inter-Korean talks, ostensibly around the issue of family reunion. Behind-the-scenes contacts brought a joint communiqué on 4 July 1972 declaring both sides accepted three principles: unification should be achieved independently without external interference; it should be achieved by peaceful means; and 'great national unity' should be achieved by 'transcending differences in ideas, ideologies and systems'. Both sides agreed to refrain from slandering and defaming each other and a South–North Coordinating

Committee (SNCC) was to be established. The SNCC held its first and third meetings in Seoul in November–December 1972 and June 1973, with a second held in Pyongyang in March 1973.

It was the first attempt to ease tension and foster mutual trust after 20 years of hostility. Negotiations floundered. North Korea declined to convene the fourth SNCC meeting scheduled for 28 August 1973 in Pyongyang. The North refused to negotiate with the head of the Korean Central Intelligence Agency (KCIA), Lee Hu Rak, because the agency had orchestrated the abduction and attempted murder of the former South Korean presidential candidate, Kim Dae Jung, from his Tokyo hotel. A second reason given was that the Seoul regime had 'mercilessly repressed Christians'.

In the late 1970s, there were attempts to revive a dialogue, but preliminary talks in 1979 failed. In 1980 the Sixth Congress of the KWP adopted a less confrontational concept of unification. But in October 1983, there was an assassination attempt on President Chun Doo Hwan. North Korean agents planted a bomb at the Martyr's Memorial in Rangoon which left 21 dead, including four ROK cabinet ministers. President Chun survived: behind schedule, he arrived after the bomb had exploded. This terrorist attack led to a worldwide condemnation and triggered mass demonstrations in the South. Pyongyang had again misread the situation. Although Chun had seized power in the South in a military *coup d'état* and killed hundreds, if not thousands, of civilians in the Kwangju massacre with the collusion of the US military, the population of South Korea didn't want him removed by Pyongyang.

In the aftermath it seemed that talks would be off the agenda, but reconciliation came sooner than expected. In September 1984 South Korea suffered serious flooding and the North offered aid. After some hesitation Seoul accepted, unfreezing North–South relations. The dialogue resumed but ended in January 1986 when South Korea's annual *Team Spirit* exercise with the United States forced Pyongyang once again to mobilise its forces in response, at an enormous cost estimated as up to 6–7 per cent of the North's GNP.

In 1987 two agents blew up a Korean Airline jet returning from the Middle East killing all 135 passengers and crew. The North Korean agents were captured and turned over to South Korean authorities. The male agent committed suicide by swallowing cyanide but his female partner was prevented from doing the same. Under interrogation she confessed her involvement and declared that the operation had been personally directed by Kim Jong Il. She ended up becoming a cult figure in the South.

The next round of negotiations awaited the Roh Tae Woo administration and its 'Nordpolitik' aimed at improving diplomatic and economic ties with the Soviet bloc in Eastern Europe and Asia. Lim

Dong-Won, Roh's advisor and later the architect of Kim Dae Jung's 'Sunshine Policy', persuaded the North to return to the negotiating table after he persuaded the United States to cancel the 1992 *Team Spirit* exercises. The talks produced two agreements: the 'Agreement on Reconciliation, Non-Aggression, Exchanges and Cooperation', which entered into force on 19 February 1992, and a 'Joint Declaration on the Denuclearisation of the Korean Peninsula'. The agreements were never fully implemented. Lim's efforts were compromised by both the United States, whose commander in South Korea announced that *Team Spirit* would resume, and by hard-liners within the KCIA who intercepted and blocked a message Lim sent to President Roh from Pyongyang seeking approval for the deal he had negotiated. By the time the KCIA had been brought under control the presidential elections were looming and Roh was out of time.

Kim Young Sam became President in December 1992. His initial stance was hardline despite, or perhaps because of, his perceived liberal leanings. It became even more uncompromising as tensions grew over the North's nuclear weapons programme. Nevertheless when Jimmy Carter went to Pyongyang to try to secure a freeze on the North's programme, Kim Young Sam asked Carter to convey to Kim Il Sung the offer of a summit meeting. Kim accepted and the summit was scheduled for 25 July 1994. The two Kims never met. Kim Il Sung died of a heart attack on 8 July. After more than 20 years of stop–start negotiations with four different administrations in the South, Kim never got close to an agreement to reunify the peninsula.

## Kim's legacy

The hereditary succession, a challenge more to Marx than *Juche*, protected Kim's legacy. Kim had seen in the Soviet Union and China how both Stalin and Mao had been betrayed, and wanted to guarantee the continuation of his work and his world. A successor had to be chosen and Kim Jong Il fitted the bill.

In the process of grooming his son as a successor, Kim arranged with his friend Dom Mintoff (Prime Minister of Malta 1971–74) to host and guard Kim Jong Il at a secluded specially built country house on the island. Kim spent over a year learning English and familiarising himself with Western music and European ways.

Quite when Kim Jong Il got the final nod is not known, but hereditary succession resonated with Confucian tradition. There was a long lead-in time. North Korean official sources began rather enigmatically to use the term 'Party Centre' to refer to Kim Jong Il from 1975. In these early days, Kim Il Sung's younger brother Kim Young Ju, was seen by some as heir apparent and supporters started to assemble. They

Kim's house, Ix~Xabbatur, near Mdina in Malta

jumped too early. Between 1975 and 1977, Kim Jong Il's opponents and those thought to be sceptical of the succession plan were purged from Party, state and military.[30] Kim Young Ju vanished from public life in 1976, reappearing in 1993 when he was elected to the Party Central Committee. The purges consolidated Kim Jong Il's position. Those who survived learnt to read better the writing on the wall.

The Sixth Congress of the Korean Workers' Party met in October 1980. The new members of the Central Committee were all Kim Jong Il loyalists. Apart from the softening of the line on unification (mentioned above) the Party platform was revised to give Kim Jong Il control of the Party, the administration and the military. He was elected a full member of the Politburo, the Military Commission, and all the Party's key committees. Throughout the 1980s Kim Jong Il played an increasing and ever more prominent role in the KWP as the North Korean people were introduced to their future leader. A decade later one of Kim Jong Il's half-brothers, Kim Pyong Il (born in 1954), was seen as another possible successor. His mother Kim Song Ae promoted his cause. A graduate of the military academy, he had support within the army. At one time Kim Il Sung was thought to have had a plan to make Kim Jong Il the Party Centre, with Kim Pyong Il the Military Centre. It never happened, with no love lost between Kim Jong Il and his stepmother or her children. Kim made it clear that you were for him or against him and there was no middle way. Despite his wife's entreaties Kim Il Sung decided – if he had ever thought any differently – that the leadership as job share was not on. Kim Pyong Il was dispatched to Hungary as ambassador in 1988. Further postings followed in Bulgaria, Finland, and most recently, Poland. With the decision taken Kim Il Sung wanted no confusion about his intentions and placed his other sons out of harm's way. The transfer of power from Kim to Kim continued and accelerated in the 1990s unchallenged.

Compared with China and the Soviet Union, where there was a significant turnover and diversification in the highest ranks of the Party during the 1980s, North Korea showed, at the expense of almost all else, stability and continuity. The North Korean ruling elite in the 1990s, shrank in size, became more exclusive and more homogenous, with its members closely linked by personal and educational ties.[31] They emerged as loyal supporters of Kim Jong Il, with the old guard, the second revolutionary generation and the military elite speaking with one voice. The inner dynamics of politics and decision making within the leadership mitigated against division and dissention. There had been no factions since the late 1950s, a credit to party management and the view that you hang together or hang separately.

By the early 1990s, Kim Jong Il was in complete control of the state and Party, subject only to his father's restraining authority. In 1992, despite his lack of military experience Kim Jong Il assumed the top two military posts of Supreme Commander of the Korean People's Army and the Chairman of the National Defence Committee (NDC). Kim Il Sung 'Liberator of the Fatherland' and 'Great Leader' died on 8 July 1994.

# 4 A life in Wonderland

## Introduction

For North Koreans, there is no 'outside' frame of reference. The Party promised they would live where 'all the people eat rice and meat soup, wear silk clothes and live in tile-roofed houses,' and although the state never delivered on this promise it did deliver basic necessities.[1] The standard of living rose throughout the 1950s, 1960s and 1970s. Until the close of the late 1980s living standards were higher than they had ever been. But by Kim's death in 1994 the decline was clear.

The economy stagnated in the 1980s and collapsed in the 1990s. As a result up to one in eight of the population died of starvation. Economic reforms in 2002 proved only partially successful, but did put more goods on the shelves and restaurants on the street as hard cash replaced the Public Distribution System (PDS). Despite the promise of a prosperous and egalitarian world, the North is now characterised by wide and growing social inequality. The elite lives well, while the rest are entirely dependent on position and place.

North Korea is a country whose people live isolated from the rest of the peninsula, and in millions of cases from families in the South – an arduous march indeed. It remains one of the most closed and controlled societies in the world. Yet sights of people shopping in the market, flirting during street festivals, or laughing over a beer reflect an everyday normality. Daily life in the North contains elements of the normal, abnormal and absurd.

## Building the nation

The first impression of North Korea is of a colony of the Soviet empire frozen in the 1950s or 1960s. US Bomber Command worked long and hard during the Korean War to ensure that the North Koreans had a *tabula rasa* on which to build anew. While it was the Chinese who saved the revolution with their 'volunteers', it was the Russians who provided the model and architects for the rebuilding of Pyongyang and the rest of the country.

Accordingly, life is now lived within Russian-style concrete boxes, with the furniture inside bearing the same stamp. Until recently, on street corners empty shops harked back to the designs and hues of post-war Britain, with pictures of what they should sell on the walls instead of goods on the shelves. After dark these naked emporia were palely lit with

The world's biggest bronze statue – Kim Il Sung

bare bulbs of a wattage more suited to romantic dining than shopping. Yet glued across adjacent walls are propaganda posters showing the people of North Korea triumphing over their US enemy who, in their eyes, continues to occupy the South. At the post office the most popular stamp shows a Korean soldier bayoneting a cowering US soldier. Meanwhile, in

남북이 힘을 합쳐 미제침략자들을 쫓 어버리고
자주통일을
이룩하자!

◎평양

1969

10전   조선우표

Philatelic propaganda

the 'hard currency' shop in the Koryo Hotel, home to most visiting Westerners, any Koreans can spend months or years of their salary respectively on tins of strawberries or bottles of Möet vintage champagne.

Pyongyang was rebuilt on a grand scale. Modern monuments, buildings and high-rise apartment blocks, interspersed with parks and open spaces, dominate the sky-line with the 170 metre Tower of the *Juche* Idea flickering above them all. A stone-clad tower with a metal torch and burning flame at the top, the tower was built for Kim Il Sung's 70th birthday, with each tier representing a decade and each stone a day of his life. No matter how many sectors of Pyongyang are blacked out by power cuts, the torch continues to burn. The tower has its own power supply. At its base, more than 500 tablets donated by groups around the world pay homage to Kim and to *Juche*. These include a *Juche* study group from Liverpool. 1982 was a great year for presents. Kim also received a remodelled stadium bearing his name, and next to it a replica of the Arc de Triomphe in Paris which is only a little larger than the original.

North Korea is built with concrete and is broad-brushed grey. The colour on the streets emanates from massive murals, propaganda posters and shrines celebrating the Great Leader Kim Il Sung. But there is beauty in its vast homogenous buildings, squares and open spaces. Squares free from pollution (there are few cars and factories only work sporadically) and crowds provide the ideal setting to admire monuments built to the glory of Kim. At the heart of Pyongyang is the Kim Il Sung Square, a 75,000 m² granite plaza dominated by the Grand People's Study House, built in traditional style but contemporary scale, for the education of 12,000 workers who each day file past an enormous statue of Kim Il Sung with muzak ringing out to the tune of the 'Song of General Kim Il Sung' to access its three million books. The square is the venue for all those rallies and parades, mass meetings and festivals pictured in the Western press.

Apart from around these stage-managed events, for a capital city there is little bustle. There are no lively neighbourhoods and, apart from the new state-controlled markets and the Pyongyang Department

Birthday celebrations

Store No 1, no lively shopping centres. Two million people are permitted to live in Pyongyang and checkpoints control movement in and out of the city. Inside the city there are closed suburbs where the Party and the army work and live, off limits to ordinary people. The inhabitants are responsible for keeping their city clean. Families clean the area around their homes and teams of older women are employed to tend public spaces. The cleanliness of North Korea is one of its most striking features, with no throw-away culture of capitalism.

There are multi-lane motorways stretching out from Pyongyang and few cars. The newest, built in 1998, spans ten lanes, and takes a handful of cars 46 kilometres to Nampo, Pyongyang's seaport. Within Pyongyang tree-lined boulevards are free of anything remotely resembling a traffic jam with or without the pretty white-gloved girls directing traffic (in the suburbs it is men with a very different selection criterion). Pyongyang has men on their bicycles riding to and from work and, although far removed from China of a decade or so ago where the streets would run black with hundreds and thousands of bicycles swarming about their daily business, the bicycle is an important part of daily life. It is only men though. For many years, women did not cycle in Pyongyang as the Dear Leader gave guidance, following a spate of accidents that women cyclists were a traffic hazard, although they could drive buses. But as of summer 2007 a few women are back on their bikes.

Trams and trolleys run when electricity permits, with long queues on the surface that is alternately frozen in winter and cooked in the summer. For the upmarket commuter, the transport of choice is the metro, with the *Hyokshin* and *Chollima* lines traversing the capital. The metro is sedate with un-crowded, former East German rolling stock shuttling backwards and forwards. Cathedrals to Communism, the metro stations are extraordinary Moscow-like constructs, built deep in the ground, where the trains run to a regularity which puts the London tube to shame and where the people of Pyongyang will rush with their gas masks to shelter behind enormous blast doors in the event of an air raid or nuclear attack. The platforms are clad in marble and stunning mosaics depicting the Great Leader leading the workers onward, smoking factories, abundant crops and doting women and children. The omnipresent radio broadcasts stirring tunes and the travellers take trains to uplifting destinations such as *Pulgunbyol* (Red Star), *Chonu* (Comrade-in-arms), *Kwangbok* (Liberation) and *Kaeson* (Triumphant Return).

In contrast to Pyongyang, the nationwide transport network is limited. Travel between towns and provinces requires a hard-to-obtain permit and consequently there is little demand. Outside the urban centres there are stunning coastal areas and mountainous regions, but these are difficult to access for individual travellers. An extensive electrified rail network does exist, but apart from the international route to

Beijing the services are unreliable, with mass cancellations and trains arriving days late because of power shortages and flooding. There are a small number of lines where steam trains still operate, attracting trips from Europe's more intrepid train buffs. Recently, the number of railway accidents has started to rise, with reports of one accident in spring 2006 killing hundreds when a train ran away out of control after the brakes failed. It was not always like this. In Britain, British Standard Time was a product of the coming of the railways and their need for a common measure of time. The same is true in North Korea. Pyongyang Station's imposing four-face clock tower was used to inform all local stations of the standard time by which to set their clocks for the accurate operation and control of trains.

North Koreans will walk or cycle for tens of miles or hitchhike to their destination on army trucks – the only real traffic on the roads in the countryside. A small, but increasing number of private cars can be seen in Pyongyang, owned in the main either by the new rich or by Koreans with family amongst Chosen Soren in Japan, who for a premium can either transfer money to Pyongyang to purchase a vehicle or ship the vehicle itself.

As in most other capital cities, living space in Pyongyang is limited, but here who occupies is not determined so much by price but political pedigree. The urban elite live in spacious apartments in gated communities, while lower-ranking bureaucrats and workers live in high-rise apartments with one or two rooms. Nevertheless standards are much higher than for those unfortunate enough to live in the provinces and countryside. In Pyongyang at least water comes out of the taps, even if only on the lower floors, and electricity is generally available rather than just for the three to four hours a day in the provinces. People used to pay a purely nominal rent for their apartments, but rents now consume a significant percentage of income following the 2002 wage and salary reforms. From the outside the tall, grey apartment blocks hide the circumstances of the families within them, but as a general rule the taller – even if the lifts don't work or don't exist – the newer and the closer to the centre, so much the better. Everything from education to health, employment to living space is based on your class and position, and while standards for the 'friendly' class do not match the West's, they were for many the difference between life and death during the famine of the 1990s.

## Shaping the nation

Politics shapes society and education reflects Kim Il Sung's precept:

> political and ideological education is the most important part of socialist education. Only through a proper political and ideological

education is it possible to rear students as revolutionaries, equipped with a revolutionary world outlook and the ideological and moral qualities of a Communist. And only on the basis of sound political and ideological education will the people's scientific and technological education and physical culture be successful. ... The continued education of all members of society is indispensable for building socialism and Communism.[2]

Education plays a central role in society and culture. Although literacy rates are on a par with the highest in the world and can be counted amongst the regime's proudest achievements, education standards in Western terms are poor, with massive redundancy from large amounts of school time spent on rote learning – as in Japan – and studies of Kim and *Juche*. Education is used by the regime to foster and promote collective ways of thinking.

Universal compulsory education is provided by the state (including educational facilities, textbooks, uniforms, and where necessary room and board) for eleven years from ages 4 to 15 including one year's compulsory pre-school education. But 'education' begins at a much earlier age with children as young as 3 months entering the Central Committee-controlled education conveyor belt. Most children are placed in a nursery (*t'agaso*) from three months to the age of 4 years, allowing their mothers to work. Many board six days a week even when their parents live nearby, only going home on Sundays. Orphans, and more recently abandoned children, are raised entirely in state run Children Centres. Standards are low, but it can prove a lucky escape as the children are considered untainted by family history.

The elite have their own school. The Mangyongdae Revolutionary School, North Korea's Eton and attended by Kim Jong Il, was founded in 1947 for the orphaned sons and daughters of revolutionary martyrs, but is now the exclusive preserve of children of senior Party and army officials. This residential school fast tracks its graduates into the Kim Il Sung Higher Party School, whence the 'best' go on to run the country after attending university, preferably the Kim Il Sung University in Pyongyang. After graduating from primary school, ordinary students enter either a normal secondary school or a specialist school that concentrates on music, art or foreign languages. More recently a fourth specialty has been added, computer skills.

School uniform is a standard 'blue bottoms', white shirts and red neckerchiefs, with armbands denoting positions of responsibility. The national curriculum is an amalgam of the academic and the political, with language, mathematics, physical education, drawing and music, plus the life and thoughts of the Kim family constituting the bulk of education the in early years. From the beginning the Kim dynasty is centre stage. In Kindergarten papier maché models of both Mt Paektu and Mongyongdae-Kiu, Il Sung's birthplace, dominate the classroom with the children sat around them learning about Il Sung's upbringing and the partisan war against the Japanese. Education begins with children memorising 'Mother of Korea' (Kim Il Sung's mother), 'Revolutionary Patriot of Iron Will' (father), 'Mother of the Revolution' (wife and mother of Kim Jong Il), and 'Dear Leader' (Kim Jong Il).

All classrooms, like all houses, have twin portraits of the Great Leader and the Dear Leader hanging side by side on the wall. On adjacent walls there are revolutionary posters and murals. For younger children pictures are cartoon animals, which graduate with age to full red-blooded battle scenes. Everything is taught collectively with the individual lost in identical school uniforms and expression channelled through group performances of folk songs, traditional music and team displays of gymnastics or dance.

What this translates to is shown in Sonia Ryang's *North Koreans in Japan*.[3] Ryang, born in Japan to a Korean family that considered themselves 'Overseas Nationals of North Korea', attended a school run by Chosen Soren. According to Ryang, memorising titles plays an important role, with student essays often little more than a 'meaningless list of epithets for Kim Il Sung and Kim Jong Il'. Chosen Soren's schools are totally separate educationally and financially from Japan's own system. Back in the late 1950s, Chosen Soren received funds from North Korea, which set the curriculum and provided teaching materials. More recently the schools were financed through fees and donations, and since 1993 with generational change in Chosen Soren's leadership, they have taken a more independent line. Ryang's account of her own schooling prior to 1993 was augmented by later interviews with teachers and students.

History is taught through the life of Kim Il Sung and his family. Moral and social study comes under the 'childhood of Father Marshal Kim Il Sung' or 'revolutionary activities of the Great Leader Kim Il Sung'. There is no escape even in maths. A textbook question is: 'Three soldiers from the Korean People's Army killed 30 American soldiers, how many American soldiers were killed by each of them, if they all killed an equal number of enemy soldiers?'

Essays refer to the teachings of Kim Il Sung. In the rare areas of knowledge where Kim never commented, vaguely relevant quotes suffice. Language is controlled and its use disciplined. Although there are some distinct dialectical differences between the North Korean and South Korean languages, this would not hamper communication. What makes the communication uncomfortable is the North's common and often subconscious use of a strong political vocabulary forbidden or out of favour/fashion in the South. Examples are 'revolutionary – *Hyokmyong*', 'ideology – *Sasang*', 'comrades – *Tongji*', 'self-criticism – *Ja-A bipan*', 'great/dear leader – *Wuidaehan/Kyongaehanun ryondoja*', 'anti-reactionary – *Bandong*' and so on. In Japan student vocabulary is monitored and controlled through self and collective criticism sessions where students are encouraged to report their friends for not using North rather than South Korean vocabulary and speaking Japanese rather than Korean.

Yet 'Overseas Nationals of North Korea' in Japan are in a different reality from that of students in the North. They live in two parallel worlds, the Japan of their daily lives and their school, and Chosen Soren's influence is waning as the third and fourth generation reject a distant homeland for the 'here and now' of Japan's affluent society. Ryang herself went further. She did her postgraduate degree at Cambridge University and is now teaching at the Johns Hopkins University in Baltimore. These days, school trips 'home' to the North merely reinforce the tendency to go 'native'. In contrast students in North Korea have no access to any alternative world. They are on a production line that turns them into loyal believers.

In the North to go on to higher education requires approval by the local, county and provincial college recommendation committees. Only 30 per cent make it. Students are from the 'friendly' class, salted with bright orphans and abandoned children. From the 'neutral' class it is only the exceptional that make it. Higher education institutions include universities, teachers' training colleges, colleges of advanced technology, medical schools and special colleges for science and engineering, art, music and foreign languages as well as military colleges and academies. In total there are about 280 universities and colleges and over 570 advanced technical and specialist institutions, ranging from the Universities of Light Industry, Construction and Building Materials Production, Mechanical Engineering and Technology through the University of National Economics and the prosaic Railway University of Communism to the Universities of Dramatic and Cinematic Arts, Music and Dance, Education, Medicine and Physical Education.

The 'Oxbridge' of North Korea is Kim Il Sung University with 12,000 students including a small foreign contingent. Competition for admission is intense. Only one student out of five is admitted even after passing the political tests. One senior official I know was particularly relieved when he discovered his son had, albeit narrowly, made the grade. As recently as 2004, two Vietnamese ministers, the Minister of Irrigation and Minister of Construction, had been educated in North Korea along with thousands of their compatriots during the Vietnam War. North Korea has extended this facility to other countries in the past, but today foreign student numbers are well down.

Outside formal school hours, 'social education' takes place. This includes not only extracurricular activities but also classes on family life and social relationships. The idea is to provide an environment in which children are protected from adverse outside influences. In Pyongyang, but also elsewhere, 'children's palaces' with gymnasiums and theatres have been built for extracurricular activities ranging from computer courses to calligraphy and circus, from science to sports. The Mangyongdae Schoolchildren's Palace and the Pyongyang Students and Children's Palace are two impressive examples. Children can also be seen at the weekend in the squares of Pyongyang or on the banks of the Taedong River practising for their next performance to commemorate or celebrate one Kim or the other. It's not all song and dance. The Pioneer Corps and the Socialist Working Youth League provide work experience to teenagers, drafting them in to help with the harvest and construction projects such as the above mentioned Pyongyang–Nampo motorway.

The British government and trade unions would see much to admire in North Korea's extensive lifelong learning programme at least in terms of process, if not product. There is a well-ordered study-while-working system based around colleges of technology. Universities and other specialist schools provide on-the-job training through evening and correspondence courses. Almost everybody participates in 'study groups' set up to reflect workplace needs. Office and factory workers also have two-hour political 'study sessions' every day. On top there are workplace branches of the KWP where secretaries organise weekly meetings to study social and political issues, using articles from the Party's internal theoretical journal, *Kulloja*, the latest speeches of the Leader, and editorials and special articles from *Rodong Sinmun*.[4] There are also schools for 'reorientating' officials in active service. In rural areas adults are organised into 'five-family teams', which not only serve a surveillance function but are also used for further education with designated teachers to coordinate learning.

Like generations of small-town businessmen in England who joined the Conservative Party and Freemasons to build up a network for mutual support and nepotism, Koreans see joining the KWP as one of the best ways to advance their careers. There are currently over 3 million members and a million who want to join. Those who make a good impression are selected to become Party cadres with all the advantages that follow. There are other clubs to join, but this undoubtedly is still the best one in town.

## Controlling the nation

In Western terms North Korea is possibly the most closed, isolated and tightly controlled society in the world. Only Burma, Turkmenistan and Saudi Arabia might run it close. Even in Enver Hoxha's Albania people could pick up Italian TV, although what they made of it at the time is unfathomable.

Apart from at the highest levels of the Party and the military, there is no access to information other than that propagated by the regime. The state controls the media and the Internet. Only authorised books are available. Travel at home – and abroad – requires a permit. All of this creates a situation where, unlike in the former Soviet Union, Eastern Europe and all the four remaining Communist states – China, Cuba, Laos and Vietnam – there is no overt sign of a domestic dissident movement. Mobile phones and services were introduced in November 2002, but were withdrawn from all but the invisible elite and the diplomatic community 18 months later in May 2004. The rumour was that mobile phones had been used in the attempted assassination of Kim Jong Il on his journey home from Beijing. That may have been a convenient excuse for those determined to slow the pace of economic reform. The existence of mobile phones certainly hampered the authorities' control of the distribution of information.

The most influential newspaper is *Rodong Sinmun*, the organ of the Central Committee of the KWP. It is Pyongyang's equivalent of the USSR's *Pravda* or China's *Renmin ReBao*, while *Minju Choson* is the mouthpiece of the government. *Rodong Sinmun*'s editorials reflect thinking at the highest levels of the Party and reinforce the messages in Kim Jong Il's key speeches. Particularly important editorials are published jointly with *Kulloja*, such as the New Year editorial outlining Party policy for the coming year. It had not engaged in policy debates since the late 1950s when Kim Il Sung purged the remaining factions. Since Kim Jong Il's accession *Rodong Sinmun* has seen, for North Korea, a vigorous exchange of views on the merits of economic reform and the role of the military within the economy. The reformists are winning the argument. The conservative case is to counter Deng's aphorism by saying 'A cat cannot catch mice after knowing the taste of meat' and that the danger is 'politics dominated by money'. Some conservatives defend military expenditure with the argument that military research and development produce process innovations that spin-off into the civil economy – Michael Kidron's argument for Britain's International Socialists in the 1960s. Others use shades of *Juche* to claim revolutionary spirit trumps science and technology – an argument that is dangerously close to a direct attack on Kim Jong Il's enthusiasm for computers and IT. The reformists both in *Rodong Sinmun* and the quarterly economic journal *Kyongje Yongu* do not challenge 'military first' policies head on, but rather argue that military power must be 'supported without fail, by strong economic power' and that military spending is not accumulative or productive, but resources lost to the system. In essence, they are demanding an increased emphasis on light industry and the civilian economy.

Newspapers are dominated by the Leader's visits and 'on-the-spot' guidance, the North's economic achievements, and successes in sport and elsewhere. There are human interest stories informing and warming with tales of individual heroics for the cause. International news denounces US and Japanese foreign policy alongside stories of the horrors of capitalism. Since the turn of the century, the media have highlighted China's economic success alongside Europe's anti-American stance. International news is normally relegated to the centre pages of six – some claim the six-page version is only available in Pyongyang and to the Party cadres. The centre pages are certainly often printed on different quality paper.

There are plenty of news stories and photographs of foreign visitors arriving, staying and departing (I have looked at back copies!). *Rodong Sinmun* is not generally for sale. Instead copies are on display in every park, metro station, public square and workplace in glass-fronted cabinets which passers-by and commuters group around to read. The only alternative source of news is gossip and rumour.

The DPRK's only newswire is the Korean Central News Agency (KCNA), which publishes daily *Korean Central News* and *Photographic News*. KCNA issues daily releases in English, Russian, French and Spanish, while the monthly magazines *Korea Today* and *Korea* and the weekly newspaper *Pyongyang Times* are published in English, Spanish, French, Russian and Chinese. These are complemented by a glossy pictorial magazine called *Democratic People's Republic of Korea*. The only foreign press agency to have a bureau in Pyongyang is the Associated Press Television News (APTN), but as it is staffed by North Korean 'journalists' there is little danger of any cutting-edge reporting. Al Jazeera English has applied, so far unsuccessfully, for accreditation.

Press pools of foreign correspondents are formed for official visits, the largest to date being for the visit by US Secretary of State Madeleine Albright in October 2000. Visiting journalists are accompanied by guides to ensure they do not find any unwanted stories. Not that it stops them from making news up. One journalist I accompanied into North Korea wrote up the visit making a point of how the North Koreans had confiscated her mobile phone – which wasn't in fact true, but why let the truth stand in the way of a good story?

There are three TV stations. Korean Central Television broadcasts daily while Kaesong and Mansudae only broadcast at the weekend. There are eleven radio stations on AM and FM, with Radio Pyongyang (alias Voice of Korea) and Korea Central Radio being the two main ones. Overseas broadcasting is in Chinese, Russian, Japanese, English, French, German, Spanish and Arabic. The content follows predictable storylines: the greatness of North Korea as compared with the evil United States and unrepentant Japan, and the wisdom and prescience of the two Kims. One suspects the number of listeners (apart from the broadcasts in

Reading the papers

Japanese) can be counted on the figures of two, if not one hand, with the remnants of Liverpool's *Juche* study group included.

In urban areas, most households have small black and white televisions, impossible to tune to anything other than domestic broadcasts. Now a few colour ones are beginning to be seen. The day's programming consists of news, films, soaps, dramas and 'pop' music performed by the Korean People's Army Choir with hit tunes such as 'Soldiers hear the rice-ears rustle' or by 'rock groups' like Pochonbo – named after the site of Kim Il Sung's only skirmish on Korean soil during the guerrilla struggle against the Japanese – and the Wangjaesan Light Music Band which produced the memorable 'No Motherland without you'. North Korean pop is sexless and sentimental with no passion or pin-ups.

For Western 'pop' you have to go to the Grand People's Study House where in the music library you can listen to Western music as modern as the Beatles. Listening to jazz is forbidden. In 1964, Kim ordered musicians to compose only certain types of music and did not approve of jazz: 'We should never allow the penetration of jazz in the future as in the past' – a sentiment German National Socialists would have approved of – 'it depraves and emasculates the youth and dulls their revolutionary consciousness. Jazz is an ideological weapon of the imperialists to degenerate revolutionary people.'[5] The regime's restrictions on the musical repertoire caused a North Korean pianist to defect to the South after discovering jazz music was exactly how Kim had described it. An identical storyline featured in *West Wing*, where President Bartlett rebuffed the whispered approach and left the musician to return home to the North.

Radios are to be found in every household, factory and workplace as well as in public places, with a steady diet of speeches and news interspersed with military music, propaganda songs or traditional melodies. Tuning is fixed and any attempt to tune into South Korean stations is strictly forbidden. Each radio has a registration number and radios are randomly checked by the head of the local party to deter tampering. A nationwide campaign to check radio sets was launched by the KWP at the end of 2003. Yet many refugees claim to have listened to foreign broadcasts, and the depth of knowledge of South Korean pop music amongst the younger members of the Party suggests they do too, albeit for very different reasons.

Any remaining control is fast eroding, with more and more radios being brought in from China and rumours of organised smuggling by the United States, which might tie in with US enthusiasm in the North Korean Human Rights Act of 2004 to establish US propaganda stations broadcasting into the North. A mixture of pop and propaganda, heavy on the first and light on the second, would make such stations compulsory listening for the children of the elite. That is almost certainly beyond the imagination of the US neo-cons who themselves censor groups like the Dixie Chicks who would find favour with the North's younger generation.

Very cheap DVD players produced in China are now 'illegally' flooding in, whether or not accompanied by Korean dubbed versions of the film *Team America* is not known. Bureaucrats in the relevant ministries have limited access to the Internet. Access is controlled by the Ministry of Posts and Telecommunications and restricted to approved users. A domestic intranet has been up and running since 2001. All the approved users are 'friendly', but they are exactly the class from which the winds of change will eventually blow.

From 2001 *Rodong Sinmun* began to feature articles about new computers in factories, offices and schools, and reported the establishment of a number of specialised IT training centres. The Korean Computer Centre, the largest state-owned IT company in the country, supervises and controls the examination, registration and dissemination of software. Outside Pyongyang and a small number of other major cities the population is lucky to have electricity for more than two or three hours a day, let alone a computer and modem.

North Korea's email service is confined to government and business customers and the small expatriate community. When Kim Jong Il waved off Madeleine Albright after her visit in 2001, he suggested that they should keep in touch by email. Whether the Bush administration has taken up the offer is unknown. Email addresses have yet to make their appearance on the business cards of even senior government officials. When they have business cards, which more often than not they don't, these are kept simple with name, position, telephone and fax numbers, and more rarely, office address.

## *Juche* culture

Foreign books are available in libraries and in a very limited way in the Foreign Languages Bookshop, but in the libraries the ones on open shelves are almost entirely technical and desperately outdated. Access to other books requires a permit. There are stories of visitors lending or giving foreign books to Koreans. The French animator Guy Delisle, who was working in Pyongyang, once gave George Orwell's *1984* to his interpreter. The book was soon returned with the mumbled excuse that he didn't like science fiction.[6] Kenneth Quinones, Foreign Service Officer under Clinton and the first diplomat to live at North Korea's Yongbyon nuclear research centre, passed on Tom Clancy's novel *The Hunt for Red October*, a cold war thriller about the efforts of the captain of a Soviet nuclear submarine to defect with his ship to the United States.[7] Back in the States, Quinones was cautioned by a member of the North Korean UN delegation not to give books in the future. He was later told that his interpreter had been sent to re-education camp for accepting the book without the permission of the KWP.[8]

My own experiences contradict those accounts. Interpreters have been eager to receive any written material available – newspapers, magazines and books. Novels have proved a disappointment, with a distinct lack of enthusiasm for Patrick O'Brian, while for rest the more political and the more anti-North Korean the better.[9] It is difficult to blame people for avoiding fiction. One of the few North Korean novels available in English is April 15th Writing Staff Central Committee of Korean Writers' Union's novel *Dawn of a New Age* (1978), which I can confirm once put down is very difficult to pick up again. After 1970 authorship was collective or anonymous.

The Party exercises its control over cultural expression through its Propaganda and Agitation and Culture and Arts Departments. Production and consumption flows from here. Koreans live in an isolated society and have an unparalleled homogenous ethnic culture, all sharing a common language and history. Mixed marriages are considered by some a crime against the Korean race. North Korean literature, music and art therefore look to traditional Korean genres and motifs, seasoned with revolution and with a filtering out of what is considered reactionary. Artists are state supported and censored, while Kim Jong Il believes 'we need a humanistic literature … which creates the image of the truly typical man of the new era, thereby contributing to the transformation of the whole of society in accordance with the concept of *Juche.*'

Art is a vehicle for politics. Its themes are the revolutionary struggle, heroes of Korea, the struggle against US imperialists and Japanese colonialism, the greatness of the two Kims and pride in being Korean. Novels, apart from *Dawn of a New Age,* include *Life Giving Water, New Spring* and *Men With a Passionate Heart.* Fine art ranges from the *Juche* artists with their oil paintings, through collectively produced propaganda posters of flag-flying workers and charging soldiers in the heat of battle to stylised Korean landscapes and saccharine tigers, kittens and flowers. More recently, a less overtly political school of painters has emerged from Pyongyang with portraits of house painters and air hostesses, construction workers and nurses going about their daily lives. From fairy tales to revolutionary operas, their themes have been cut and pasted from traditional Korean folk stories and songs into modern North Korea formats. Art is also seen as a vehicle for raising morale. When productivity is poor then 'Art Propaganda Squads' are sent to farms and factories to perform plays, poetry readings and sing songs to the tune of the latest speed campaign.

For Kim Jong Il, 'like the leading article of the party paper, the cinema should have great appeal and inform the audience of reality.'[10] Films include *An Jung Gun Shoots Ito Hirobumi,* the story of the assassination in Harbin of Japan's former Governor-General of Korea, traditional tales with a twist such as *The Sea of Blood* portraying Kim Il Sung as the father of the nation, Chinese-style Red cinema *Girl Chairman of the Co-operative Farm* and *The 100 Days Battle* showing how grit and self-reliance can ensure the plan's targets are met. Some films with anti-US themes feature appalling acting from US defectors, who play the 'bad guys'.[11] Defectors Larry Abshier, James Dresnok and Robert Charles Jenkins, appeared as Americans in the 21 episode 'soap' *Unsung Heroes,* and Jenkins also featured as a US army commander in *The People and Its Destiny.* Children are entertained by *The Boy General.*

The Korean Film Studio in Pyongyang is the site of this theatre of dreams with its reconstructed feudal villages and its parallel universe: Seoul overrun with US army brothels and Japanese casinos. The North produces around 200 films a year. Pyongyang hosts a film festival open to the public every two years in the Pyongyang International Cinema, which boasts a 2000 seat auditorium. The films shown are uncensored and are full of sex and violence, which surprises many Western visitors. They shouldn't be. The film festival serves the purpose of showing the inhabitants of Pyongyang the world as it isn't.

## *Manga* mania

North Korean comics are no joke. They maintain the same anti-American, anti-Japanese and anti-capitalist themes as all other reading material. Comic reading in North Korea, like everything else, is a collective experience with much swapping and borrowing. Comics or *Gruimchaek* (picture books) are pale imitations of Japanese *Manga* that target adolescents and adults rather than Western-style comics aimed at children. They are printed on poor-quality paper, normally in black and white, but occasionally monochromatic blue, brown or green, and are marooned in time with yesterday's clothes, furniture, houses and cars. The dialogue echoes strong nationalist and ideological themes. Plots are good versus evil, with roles determined by nationality, loyalty to the leadership and social origin. North Korean heroes and patriots sacrifice their lives fighting US imperialism, Japanese collaborators and South Korean infiltrators. The messages are clear and simple. In the comics North Korean soldiers, students and even heroic children are prepared to die for Leader, class and nation.

A look at ten random North Korean comics published between 2001 and 2004 shows three major themes.[12] First, and most common, is the 'James Bond' spy story where North Korean special agents penetrate US-run military bases in the South. The North Korean agents discover, subvert and stop US attacks on the North, saving the Korean people and the nation. Plots have the US military ready to use biological and chemical weapons and new deadly missiles against the North. Courageous KPA Special Forces infiltrate these WMD bases by fooling stupid US commanders and expose the US/Japanese plans, fulfilling their duty to the 'Great Comrade General' and of course dying in the process.

In the world of North Korean comics Americans are violent and cunning warmongers, Japanese contemptible opportunists and South Koreans sneaky and greedy US puppets. While the North's hero dies by blowing himself up along with his enemies, US scientists test bacteriological weapons on children and the elderly, US marines attempt to rape young Korean women, and tank commanders destroy entire Korean villages. In one case, a US officer threatens a seven-year-old child with 'execution by poking his eyeballs out and tearing his body into pieces'.

The second most popular theme is the resistance to Japanese occupation and the struggle against the exploitation of workers and farmers by the occupiers and their Korean collaborators. The ruthless Japanese kidnap and violate innocent Korean girls, kill and rob Korean peasants and pressgang them into forced labour to aid Japan's imperial ambitions in the Pacific War.

A third theme is the fight against internal subversion by counter-revolutionaries. These plots have former landowners, capitalists and

Japanese collaborators attempting to provoke chaos and collapse in the North in order to have their confiscated land and wealth restored under a post-Communist regime. Acting as CIA agents and saboteurs they set fire to cooperative farms, derail trains, sabotage the testing of new weapons and try to undermine the economy. All are defeated at the last moment by smart brave soldiers or students who report their suspicions to the authorities and help to arrest the perpetrators.

One comic unique to this sample had a 'missionary' story. A commercial aeroplane crashes in the African jungle where the leadership and bravery of two North Koreans save the group, in the process converting the survivors – including a priest – into followers of Kim-Il-Sungism. It all ends happily with the group chanting in unison: 'Long live the Great Leader Kim Il Sung and the Dear Leader Kim Jong Il'.

North Korean comics are earthy, littered with swearwords, brutality and violence – in reality little different from the average Japanese *Manga*. They are tools for ideological training outside formal education. They are very popular, with supply failing to meet demand. The batch I bought was read by interpreters, drivers and advisors before I got them back. Ariel Dorfman and Armand Mattelart, whose pioneering book *How to Read Donald Duck* (1984) analysed the role of US comics in promoting American imperialism, would find themselves entirely at home with North Korean comics.

**Bread and circuses**

Kim Jong Il may not be able to always give the North Koreans bread, but in a millennium-old tradition they get circuses. There are ten public holidays, including Kim Jong Il's birthday on 16 February, Army Day on 25 April, Independence from Japan day on 15 August and Korean Workers' Party Foundation day on 10 October. These and other feast days are celebrated by performance and pork – meat only obtainable from the PDS at holiday time. The largest celebration of all is the Arirang Festival held every year from the end of April to the end of June, although it can run on until August (in 2006 it was cancelled because of the floods that hit the North) in the May Day Stadium in Pyongyang. This impressive modernist building has a seating capacity of 150,000 – more than twice the size of Manchester United's Old Trafford.

The zenith of the festival is the Mass Games, a four-act show with gymnastics and acrobatics, ethnic dances and folk songs all telling the story of the DPRK performed by 100,000 'actors'. In the background a crowd hold flash cards which they flip on command every couple of seconds to create a gigantic slide show. In the foreground there are co-ordinated performances by teams of gymnasts and dancers. Children

금성청년출판사
주체93(2004)

Comic book superhero

selected for the mass games against enormous competition are removed from their schools for hours of daily rehearsals. Schools compete to be selected for the final stage, all documented in *A State of Mind*, produced in 2004 by Nick Bonner.[13] This documentary follows the daily lives and exhausting rehearsals of two schoolgirls preparing for the Mass Games and their desperate desire to perform in front of Kim Jong Il. The Mass Games is simply unique. For North Koreans, people working together with such precision and passion reflects the strength of collective thought and national unity. For Westerners it is brainwashing. The Mass Games featured in 2004 as the backdrop to the UK band Faithless's video clip 'I want more'.

And when the carnival is over? Days out include the circus, complete with acrobats and clowns mimicking idiot South Korean and US soldiers. There is the rather depressing Pyongyang Zoo where animals, including the virtually extinct Korean tiger, are in joyless captivity. A special Orchid House alongside the Taedong River proudly exhibit thousands of *Kimilsungia* (a purple orchid) and *Kimjongilia* (a perennial red begonia), the two national flowers of North Korea, an example of North Korea at its most absurd. Enormous energy is put into making them bloom for Kim Jong Il's birthday on 16 February. Every institution and factory, including foreign embassies, sponsors the cultivation of a plant requiring a minimum temperature of 18 °C over the winter period when outside temperatures reach –20 °C and when there is no power for factories, offices or homes for most of the day.[14]

There is the Mangyongdae Funfair, reputedly visited by 100,000 Koreans a day, although on the three occasions I have been it looked an order of magnitude less than that. It has several rides including two roller coasters as scary in age as size. The larger one features a double upside-down loop, which for roller coaster aficionados is a bit of a rarity as almost half the population of Europe just say no to being turned upside down. There is a gondola, as well as an amusement arcade complete with fruit machine, pool table and best of all a shooting range where Koreans practise shooting cardboard US soldiers. The one time I tried it KWP officials performed worse than visiting Westerners. Locals also head for the Taedong River where they hire pedal boats in the summer or skate on the frozen water in the winter under the watchful eye of the *Juche* Tower. For the highbrow the Mansudae Art Troupe, the Phibada Opera Troupe, the State Theatrical Company or the State Symphony Orchestra give performances of revolutionary operas such as *Sea of Blood*.

There are a dozen or so restaurants on Changgwang Street, Pyongyang's Ginza, where North Koreans with hard currency can pay directly but most queue with a voucher as part of a work unit's reward for outstanding hard work. Opening hours depend on food supply, but you can order such Pyongyang delicacies as *raengunyan* (noodles), *onban* (rice) and *tangogi* (dog) soup. *Tangogi* soup was Kim Il Sung's favourite and strongly recommended as nutritious health food. Once visiting a bare Korean home in the province with two colleagues we discovered a live puppy in a basin under a bed. My colleagues saw a family pet; I saw a family feast.

*Kimjongilia* donated by the British embassy

How to prepare *Tangogi* features in a recipe book available in English:

> First, the meat without offal and fat has to be in cold water to remove blood stained, then simmer it for three hours. Second, tear the simmered meat into strips, and season it with chopped leek and garlic, salt, ground red pepper and ground black pepper. Third, make a dressing by boiling some parts of the meat (offal and fat), minced skin, and some of the broth along with leek, garlic, chive, ground red pepper and salt. Fourth, put the broth over the seasoned meat along with some bean paste, pour in the dressing, and bring the whole thing with chopped garlic and ground black pepper to a boil. Serve Tangogi Soup hot after sprinkling with chopped coriander, perilla seed and dressing.

For most Westerners, the main ingredient would be the problem.

One culinary innovation has been the introduction of a beef patty in a bun. In October 2000, North Korea introduced 'Our-style Hamburger and Fries' produced in a food-processing plant specifically for university cafeterias. On 6 December 2000, *Rodong Sinmun* reported on this new nutritious meal praising Kim's 'benevolent affection for the future generations'. 'Kimburgers' are now available to a wide range of schools and other institutions, even making an appearance in Air Koryo's in-flight meals.

There are a range of bars where you can drink the most popular North Korean beers, Ryongsong, Pyongyang and Pohak, but the 'new kid on the block' is Taedonggang, produced in a plant Pyongyang moved, literally lock, stock and barrel, from Ushers in Trowbridge, Wiltshire.

There are a handful of nightclubs and karaoke bars with erratic hours that are kept open with hard currency. The Yanggakdo Hotel, perched on an island in the Taedong River, features a Chinese-run casino in the basement along with a sparsely populated disco. Expats from the European Community drink in the self-organised Random Access Club in the bowels of the cavernous former East Germany embassy, named after the long unfulfilled demand of European NGOs regarding food distribution. T-shirts are available.

## Games people play

Sport is big in the North. North Koreans participate in the Asian Games every four years and even hosted the 13th World Festival of Youth and Students in 1998, when the facilities built for the abortive joint Seoul–Pyongyang Olympic Games were finally put to use. North Koreans have participated in the Olympics since 1972. The only exceptions were when they joined the Soviet boycott of the Los Angeles Games in 1984 and their own boycott of the 1998 Games in Seoul. In 1988 socialist solidarity was a little thin, undermined by North Korean agents blowing up a Korean Airlines flight from Dubai to Seoul the previous year. Their only fellow abstainers were the Cubans. When they have been in the Olympics they have literally punched above their weight, with good showings in boxing, wrestling and weight-lifting.

North Korea – like the South – has a member on the International Olympic Committee (IOC), Chang Ung, a former basketball player, appointed in 1996. In Monte Carlo in 1993 during the IOC meeting to vote for the 2000 Summer Olympic Games venue, I was part of the Manchester Olympic Bid Team, and one of my target voters was the previous North Korean IOC Member. He was wined and dined, along with Chang Ung, then the head of the National Olympic Committee, by myself, Bobby Charlton, and Graham Stringer, then head of Manchester City Council and now Labour MP for Manchester Blackley. The only thing we had in common was football, so we replayed 1966. As it turned out, Beijing lost to Sydney by two votes. Chang Ung

Bottles of beer produced in a North Korea brewery
moved brick by brick from Wiltshire

confirmed, years later, that the instruction from Pyongyang was that if
Beijing were to be eliminated North Korea would switch its vote to
Manchester.

North Korea's first venture into the World Cup was in 1966 when they
qualified for the finals in England. They ended up in Group 4 and played
all their games at Ayresome Park in Middlesbrough. After losing 3–0 to
the Soviet Union, they managed a draw against Chile and then famously
beat Italy 1–0 with a goal by Pok Do Ik (in a prequel to South Korea's
victory by an identical score over the Italians in Seoul in 2002):

He scores. North Korea has taken the lead with five minutes of
the first half left. What a sensation, Italy a goal down to North
Korea. Whoever would have believed it? They are absolutely
overwhelmed.[15]

Not bad for a team that started the tournament as 1000–1 outsiders.

They held on, and in the quarter-finals were paired against
Portugal. Within 20 minutes of kick-off they were 3–0 up with goals by
Park Seung Jin, Lee Dong Woon and Yang Sung Kook. Their tactical
naivety proved their undoing. Instead of falling back and defending,

they continued to push forward. The result was that Portugal came out 5–3 winners with four goals from Eusebio. Since then it has been downhill all the way; they have withdrawn or not entered except in 1974 and 1982–94, when they failed to qualify. In their recent attempt in 2006, they failed to qualify from a group including Iran, Japan and Bahrain. The women's football team shows promise, winning the gold medal in the Asian Games twice in a row in 2002 and 2006, and made it to China for the FIFA Women's World Cup in September 2007.

Korea's normality might have been evidenced by an outbreak of the English disease – football hooliganism – in March 2005. Soldiers and

1966 World Cup squad

police were forced to intervene when bottles, stones and chairs were thrown onto the pitch after a North Korean player was sent off for diving in the world cup qualifier against Iran which they eventually lost 2–0. Violence spilled over outside the stadium with thousands of angry fans stopping the Iranian players from leaving until police stepped in. FIFA punished North Korea for the crowd violence by having their June home match against Japan played behind closed doors in Bangkok. Another unhappy night as they lost 2–0 and Japan qualified for the finals.

Sport is taken seriously. Chongchun Street in Pyongyang is a sports village with ten gymnasiums, an open-air stadium and a number of specialist schools. One sporting event growing in popularity is the Pyongyang Marathon, held every April, which starts and finishes at the Kim Il Sung Stadium after wending its way around Pyongyang. It was opened to foreign competitors in 2001, with the 2002 event sponsored by the Italian sports goods maker Fila.

## National health

North Korea boasted an extensive public health system before its economic woes left it in a state of near collapse. The infrastructure still formally exists with a network of hospitals, clinics and dispensaries, but they now lack basic necessities including medicine, functioning medical equipment, heating, clean water and sanitation. Most pharmaceutical drugs are no longer available except from hard currency shops or the foreign NGOs. The 'showcase' Pyongyang Maternity Hospital was built to impress with its 1500 beds. But now x-ray machines lack 'film' and anaesthetists gas. There are few, if any, working ambulances and no epidurals when you get there. Any remaining resources are devoted to the care of triplets, which are considered very special in the North. The rumour that they are treated badly because of a prophecy that Kim Jong Il will die at the hands of a triplet is belied by the special treatment they receive both in the hospital and children centres. Medical care is now rudimentary, and outside Pyongyang minimal.

As a result traditional medicines are making a comeback, alongside acupuncture. Traditional remedies are thought to cure almost anything, and include ginseng which is good for body metabolism, mental and physical well-being, detoxification and the immune system; bear bile for treatment of various liver and intestinal diseases; and bear bone powder for rheumatism. Pyongyang medicinal water is believed to cure everything from chronic gastritis to dermatitis.

Malaria and tuberculosis, once virtually eradicated, are returning. Climatic conditions in 1998 led to limited outbreaks of malaria in China and both Koreas. In China and South Korea they were rapidly brought under control. But North Korea had no insecticide, no drugs and no equipment – one Chinese expert reported that when he arrived, the only laboratory equipment available was a single Russian microscope from the 1940s. As a result, the outbreak spiralled out of control. By 2003, 300,000 people, mostly agricultural workers who got infected while sleeping out in the fields, were reported to have been infected with relapsing malaria which lays victims low for months on end, and returns repeatedly.

A typical medicine cupboard

At school recreational exercise is strongly encouraged. In school and the workplace hygiene, sanitation and healthy living are on the curriculum. Kim Jong Il is an ex-smoker, giving up in late 2003 on medical advice. Since then, he has become a 'born-again' anti-smoker. An effort to reduce smoking by 30 per cent before 2010 has been accompanied by an extensive anti-smoking campaign that includes exhortations in *Kulloja*. The government introduced a series of anti-smoking measures in May 2006. These included smoke-free areas, strengthening the law on selling cigarettes to those under 19, and promoting ways to quit through TV campaigns.

Even this was used as a stick to beat Pyongyang. The *Guardian* (1 June, 2006) carried the headline: 'University challenge: give up smoking or forfeit right to a degree.' Yet the original report in *Rodong Sinmun* revealed a typical anti-smoking campaign little different from those in Europe. In North Korea, university entrance is normally between 16 and 18 therefore under the legal age to smoke. According to the Deputy Public Health Minister, Choe Chang Sik, the smoking rate has fallen by 15 per cent since 2000.

## Equal opportunities

Despite claims that Pyongyang deliberately discriminates against the disabled (which led to Tony Blair questioning the then British ambassador following a particularly mendacious article in the *New Yorker* Blair had been given to read) and the belief that the Supreme People's Assembly (SPA) is a supine body, the SPA passed legislation promoting disability rights. Following a concerted campaign by foreign NGOs – in particular Handicap International – the SPA adopted new disability-rights legislation in 2003, providing the right to free medical care and rehabilitation services, the right to choose mainstream or specialist institutional education with all the costs covered by the state or institutions concerned, and equal rights in the workplace. The law also stipulates that all public and service buildings and public transport must provide disabled access. This was needed. While war veterans with physical disabilities are treated well, as are the long-term political prisoners returned from South Korea, there were no specific provisions for others with physical and mental disabilities. In Hamhung in July 2005, I visited a hospital where children and adults who had lost limbs were being fitted with artificial limbs manufactured on site. The most poignant case was a young boy of age five who had lost two lower legs from frostbite because of lack of heating in the house. There is a long way to go. Today's reality falls as short of the law in North Korea as it does in parts of Europe.

The Constitution states that 'women hold equal social status and

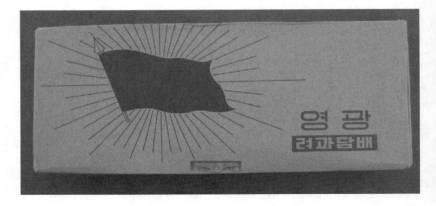

영 광
려과담배

North Korea's favourite cigarette

rights with men'. Fifty per cent of the workforce are women, as much a result of the Korean War as gender politics. With so many men killed, women, after centuries of discrimination, were needed in the workplace to get the economy back on track. Laws in themselves do not change hearts and minds, and a deep chauvinism prevails that is typical of much of East Asia. Men are on top, with the proportion of women falling sharply with each step up the ladder. There is only one woman, Ri Son Sil, in the Party Politburo, and the proportion of women in the Central Committee full membership has remained at less than 6 per cent for the past 30 years. Despite the Korean Democratic Women's Union having Kim Il Sung's wife, Kim Song Ae, as chairwoman, there is little evidence of any improvement in the status of women.

The 1948 Constitution guaranteed in Article 14 that 'citizens of the Democratic People's Republic of Korea shall have the freedom of religious belief and of conducting religious services.' Official attitudes toward organised religion have since hardened. Article 54 of the 1972 Constitution states: 'citizens have religious liberty and the freedom to oppose religion.' Article 68 in the 1992 Constitution grants freedom of religious belief and the right to construct buildings for religious use and religious ceremonies, but qualifies this by stating that 'no one may use religion as a means by which to drag in foreign powers or to destroy the state or social order.'

To demonstrate freedom of religion in the North, state-sponsored organisations (i.e. the Korean Buddhists' Federation, the Christian Federation, and the Chondogyo Youth Party) have been represented at international conferences. For the large majority of the population, their deity is Kim and their doctrine *Juche*. Religious freedom exists in theory, but not in practice. There are four official religions: Buddhism, Catholicism, Protestantism and Chondoism. The Buddhist temples resemble museums filled by men dressed as monks rather than active places of worship. There are one Catholic and two Protestant churches in Pyongyang, where Western ambassadors dutifully pay political homage accompanied by a congregation in their dotage. In 2006 a Russian orthodox church was added to the collection.

Chondoism developed out of the *Tonghak* (East Learning) movement of the late nineteenth century. The political party associated with Chondoism, the Chondoist Chungu Party, was founded in 1946 and still exists. There were once millions of Christians in North Korea – including Kim Il Sung's parents. Before 1948, Pyongyang was an important centre for Christian missionaries who established schools, hospitals and orphanages. But many Christians fled south between 1948 and 1953 to escape the socialist regime's atheism. Believers today are automatically classed as 'hostile'.

## Crime and punishment

North Korea has, in Western terms, one of the world's worst human rights records. Yet this is neither Chile under Pinochet, Argentina during the 'Dirty War' or Iraq – with or without Saddam Hussein. North Korea has the death penalty and uses it. No figures are published, but the indications are that executions run into hundreds per annum. Those held for political offences are kept indefinitely and arbitrarily – with their families – in camps. Yet the difficulty is not so much the camps but the cult nature of the regime itself with millions locked inside their own minds, in prisons of their own construction. They do not need to be controlled because they are true believers. North Korea's social conformity is not based on threats, but on indoctrination and belief.

North Korea, like any other country, has its common criminals whose crimes range from petty theft, through drunkenness and hooliganism, to assault and murder. Although there is a deep reluctance to admit criminality is on the rise, all indicators point in that direction. With the emergence of a market economy there are an increasing number of things worth stealing. The market has brought with it criminal gangs and prostitution. If their presence is a sign of progress, then North Korea is doing better than most external political commentators report. Tong-Il market in Pyongyang has an increasing number of shady characters lurking in its shadows, who are willing to exchange foreign currency on the black market at rates better than those on display in the market itself. While driving late at night from the embassy zone to the centre of Pyongyang, headlights pick out young women waiting for custom. The same phenomenon of rising crime is illustrated on the housing blocks of the towns and cities. Despite low levels of income every family on the first two or three floors has installed elaborate systems of security to protect windows and balconies.

The North's first fictional detective appeared in 2006. James Church, a pseudonym for a US intelligence operative, published *A Corpse in the Koryo* about Inspector O's fight against smuggling and military security. At least one more outing for O is in press.

The Ministry of Public Security (MPS – now called the Ministry of People's Security) and the State Security Department (SSD) are in charge of internal security, the former for general policing and social control and the latter for surveillance and intelligence.[16] The MPS with 144,000 personnel is one of the country's most powerful organisations, with 27 departments, twelve provincial offices and branches down to village level. The ministry maintains law and order; investigates common criminal cases; administers the prison system (i.e. detention camps and prisons); manages traffic control, transport and fire fighting; guards Party and government buildings, state facilities and senior officials' houses; keep census records and civil registration data; classifies citizens by social background; controls individual travel for business or family reasons; handles the government's classified documents; carries out construction of roads and major state facilities; and directs propaganda activities.

The SSD conducts intelligence work, investigates political suspects and manages the camps for political prisoners. Unlike the MPS, which is under Party control, the SSD reports directly to Kim Jong Il. It manages collective supervision and collective punishment, and has its agents everywhere in workplaces, organisations and neighbourhoods. Groups of 20–50 families are brought together and then subdivided into groups of five. The head of each subgroup monitors the activities and attitudes of everyone in his charge (the heads are almost always male) and passes the information up. A typical offence would be 'making anti-revolutionary remarks or listening to them'. This monitoring mechanism is similar to the Japanese *Koban* system of the 1930s, although Kim Il Sung claimed to have invented it in 1967. The SSD is also responsible for monitoring senior officials and staff seconded to government organisations, embassies, factories and co-operative farms.

During the interim between Kim Il Sung's death in 1994 and the formal succession three years later, there was a degree of turmoil caused by the political vacuum and the famine. In 1997 the Reinforcement Team (*Shimhwajo*) of the MPS launched a rectification campaign aimed at securing and consolidating the position of Kim's supporters. The result was that 20,000 people were demoted or purged, including a Chief Party Secretary, Mun Song Sul. Members of the Party and their families who fall seriously foul of *Shimhwajo* can end up in labour camps.

Those who engage in 'everyday, non-political' crime are tried and sent to prison. There are prisons for minor offenders and petty thieves and those for recidivists and those convicted of more serious offences. Until 1987 prisoners could be condemned to hard labour, but with the criminal law amendment this was officially abolished. Labour camps identified to date are Camp 11 (for women only, Jeung-san in South Pyongan Province); Camp 33 (for juvenile delinquents, Sook-chon in South Pyongan Province); Camp 55 (Hyongje mountain area in Pyongyang); Camp 66 (Dong-rim in North Pyongan Province); Camp 77 (Dan-chon in North Hamgyong Province); and camp 88 (Wonsan in Kangwon Province). These can be regarded as normal prisons by international standards.

The political camps are far worse. What constitutes a political offence is largely arbitrary and trials, when they occur, do not conform to Western norms of free and fair. In fact, it is who you are rather than your crime that determines your fate. Political re-education camps and prisons are not for ordinary Koreans, but reserved for former Party members and their families, relatives of defectors, and high-level officials accused of corruption. In many senses, it is similar to Cambodia where the notorious prison and torture centre in Phnom Penh, Toul Sleng, became the killing ground for those on the wrong side of the faction fight within Pol Pot's Khmer Rouge. North Korea makes it a degree worse with the Confucian notion of family responsibility. Those doing well out of the system who make a mistake take with them their whole family. Two examples are Kang Chol Hwan, the author of *The Aquariums of Pyongyang* (2000), who came from a wealthy Korean-Japanese family that returned voluntarily to the North and who enjoyed a privileged existence before being sent to the camps. Similarly, Lee Soon Ok, the author of the evangelical Christian memoir *Eyes of the Tailless Animals: Prison Memoirs of a North Korean Woman*, was the former general manager of the Chief Product Supply Office, an official of the Korean Workers' Party in charge of distributing consumer goods to high Party and government officials. (For more detail on Kang and Lee see Chapter 5.)

The first published account of the political camps came from Venezuelan poet and Communist Ali Lameda, recruited to the North in 1966 to translate Kim Il Sung's works into Spanish. Within twelve months he had been arrested, convicted of spying for the United States and sentenced to 20 years. International pressure from sources as diverse as Amnesty International and Romanian dictator Nicolai Ceausescu led to his release in 1974 after seven years imprisonment near Sariwon. In 1979 he published his experiences in an Amnesty International Report.[17]

Camps for political prisoners are normally in remote mountainous areas. They include Camp 14 (Kaechon, South Pyongan Province);

Camp 15 (Yodok family camp, South Hamgyong Province); Camp 16 (Hwasong, North Hamgyong Province); Camp 18 (Puk-chang Kun, South Pyongan Province); Camp 22 (Huiryong in North Hamgyong Province) and Camp 25 (Chongjin family camp, North Hamgyong Province). Normally there is no fixed sentence. Nevertheless political imprisonment and disgrace are not necessarily for life, nor fatal to one's career. Kang Chol Hwan was released from Yodok, went on to university, dropped out after a year in autumn 1991, worked on the black market, left as an economic refugee to China and eventually moved on to Seoul. More impressively, General Choe Kwang, who was threatened with execution during the Korean War for retreating in the face of the enemy, clashed with Kim Il Sung in 1968 and disappeared. He re-emerged in 1980 and went on to become one of the North's leading military figures until his death in 1997.

Kang's book also features the torture in Yodok camp of Park Seung Jin, a player in North Korea's famous 1966 World Cup squad.[18] According to Kang, on return from England, the whole team was accused of being bourgeois, reactionary and corrupted by imperialism for binge drinking at the hotel bar during the tournament, and was sent to the camps. It was claimed that Park had been at Yoduk for almost twelve years – although this does not fit with Kang's timescale – when Kang arrived at the camp, and was still there when Kang was released. Park made a miraculous recovery. When Nick Bonner took the whole team back to Middlesbrough in 2001 for his documentary *The Game of Their Lives* (2002), Park and the rest of the team seemed none the worse for their experiences.

North Korean defectors' accounts cannot be directly checked or confirmed, and 'bad news from the North' is good news for people's bank accounts. In a different context James Woolsey, former Director of the CIA said: 'if defectors are all you've got, that's a problem.' But even if not all claims are fully credible and a number have been disproved, the recurring elements and the sheer weight of evidence back the judgement of North Korea's inhumanity to its citizens, men, women and children.

## Coming out?

North Korea was forced to 'come out' as the famine of the 1990s led tens of thousands to flee across the border and seek refuge in China's Jilian Province. The famine also brought foreign NGOs and aid into the North, while the consequences of Kim Dae Jung's 'Sunshine Policy' was a rash of diplomatic activity with many new ambassadors and rather fewer new embassies. It has led, at least, to a superficial famil-iarity. Pyongyang now has probably close to a hundred 'Western' residents with 30–40 embassy staff, the same number of EU and attached NGO staff and a few representatives of organisations like the British Council, which at one time had two staff teaching English at the Kim Il Sung University. There are also a number of businessmen organised as the European Chamber of Commerce and the European Business Association involved in joint venture projects, including a new pharmaceutical plant making generic drugs for the local market and a very under-publicised and highly profitable British American Tobacco factory near Pyongyang churning out billions of cigarettes. Finally there are a few resident translators for the Foreign Language Publishing House, who seemingly are no longer expected to be politically sympathetic. Reports also put Ethiopia's former dictator Haile Mariam as a Pyongyang resident after Zimbabwe proved too hot to hold him, and of course, Prince Sihanouk has the Pyongyang palace that Kim Il Jung gave him.

# 5 Food, famine and fugitives

## Introduction

The international and domestic situation in the 1990s did not favour North Korea. The collapse of the Soviet Union and its empire, the US–DPRK nuclear crisis, the death of Kim Il Sung and the ensuing leadership vacuum, compounded by a series of natural disasters and consequent severe socio-economic problems culminating in a vicious famine, reform and an exodus of refugees left North Korea struggling for survival. Yet, despite all these challenges, the regime weathered the storm. North Korea's hidden strengths lay in its history and its culture, strengths the 'imposed regimes' of Eastern Europe never had. They continue to sustain the regime today.

The single most important cause of the economic meltdown and all that ensued was the collapse of the Soviet Union and its empire, which overnight ended decades of generous assistance and subsidies disguised as 'friendship prices' for oil and raw materials. It was all made worse by an obstinate attachment to a command economy obsessed with heavy industry, which had worked well in the initial phase of development, but for a decade and more distorted the economy and kept standards of living down with the failure to shift towards consumer-oriented light industry. The imminent causes were floods and drought, but the North was an economic train crash just waiting to happen. Failure to reform and failure to lead resulted in millions dying of starvation and an outpouring of refugees. Tens of thousands crossed the border into China's Jilin Province with its massive ethnic Korean community, some to seek relatives, others refuge.

In retrospect the famine and food crisis served as the tipping point for the North, providing the imperative for economic and social change. Kim Jong Il, when he finally took charge, started – not without opposition – to pave the way. The rhetoric of building a powerful and prosperous country followed. The famine and food crisis also exposed the country in an unprecedented way to the West. North Korea opened up to Westerners bringing humanitarian aid and at the same time questioning human rights. It was the testimony, real and rehearsed, of the many refugees that led to the current concerns regarding human rights in North Korea. Pyongyang established diplomatic relations for the first time with a score and more of countries, especially from the EU. Britain became the first Western Permanent Member of the Security Council to have an embassy in Pyongyang.

## Food and famine

Mountainous North Korea has limited fertile land and its climate, worsened by deforestation, means there is a propensity to flooding and drought. Food shortages have long been the order of the day (North Korea had failed to meet its agricultural or industrial targets since the 1970s). Under Kim Il Sung, *Juche* had worked the fields and in the drive for self-reliance farming had been mechanised, irrigation extended and fertilisers and pesticides deployed. The industrial stagnation of the 1980s inevitably affected agriculture. Spare parts could not be found and the machines stopped. Pesticides and fertilisers were no longer available. The poorer harvest could no longer be efficiently gathered in and floodwater could no longer be pumped from the fields. With the machinery old and the workforce exhausted, the regime's 'Let's eat two meals a day' campaign in the early 1990s left many wishing that they could only be so lucky. Raw materials were no longer available as importers wanted paying in hard currency. The collapse of the Soviet Union and market reform in China made a bad situation worse.

Pyongyang blamed the food crisis on a series of natural disasters – floods, hurricanes and drought – that struck the country in 1995 and 1996. The economic situation was already at crisis point, but these certainly propelled the DPRK from crisis to humanitarian disaster. Bridges were swept away, mines were flooded and tens of thousands of acres of good farming land were sterilised by saltwater. Millions of tonnes of cereals withered on the stalk, resulting in a catastrophic shortage of food. Two-thirds of the North's electricity comes from hydroelectric power. The floods damaged and destroyed many hydro units, and later the drought stopped the turbines that were left. Industrial production virtually halted in the absence of power and raw materials. Slogans from Kim Il Sung's Resistance-against-the-Japanese campaign were recycled. The 'Arduous March for Socialism' and 'March Under Trial' saw workers, joined by soldiers and children, leaving the factories for the fields.

Output plummeted well below minimum subsistence levels. By 1995, the grain ration distributed by the authorities to farming families was reduced from 167kg per person per year to 107kg, not enough to live on.[1] The harvest was barely 40 per cent of what was required, and basic food like rice, supposedly distributed by the Public Distribution System (PDS) ran out. In parts of North Korea, particularly Hamgyong Province in the northeast, the situation was even bleaker. People most at risk were not those in Pyongyang or even the countryside, but those in remote cities based around large heavy industry complexes that were no longer able to function. Although the sinews of society just about held together, many of the young, the old and the vulnerable starved to death. The World Food Programme's (WFP) nutritional survey in 1998 showed that one in six children had suffered brain damage from lack of food and that 50 per cent more would be permanently stunted. The UN Food and Agriculture Organisation (FAO) estimated that 13.2 million people in North Korea, or 57 per cent of the population, were malnourished in mid-2002.[2] Between 1995 and 1999 three million died.

## Korea's cry for help

People died amidst a conspiracy of silence. The North was not telling – after all it was hardly an advert for the system – while the US intelligence, which did not need to be told as it already knew, was happy to let them starve. After anguished internal debate lasting more than twelve months between ministry and military, the silence was broken. The Ministry of Foreign Affairs issued an international appeal for emergency food aid in 1995. The appeal initially had only a limited response, overshadowed as it was by the nuclear crisis. This was compounded by the North's lack of diplomatic relations with the West, its earlier reneging on its debt repayments and its history of providing military training and aid to the 'wrong side' of third-world conflicts and civil wars. When asked for money to feed the North and consequently sustain the regime, the West was understandably slow to respond.

However, after FAO and WFP visits and reports of 2.1 million children and 500,000 pregnant women near starvation,[3] the UN and NGOs sprang into action. The WFP along with UNDP and the United Nations Children's Fund (UNICEF) began delivering food aid. Between 1995 and 2005, the WFP alone provided North Korea with nearly 4 million tonnes of food worth $1.7 billion, helping to feed 6.5 million people a year, almost 30 per cent of the population. Direct emergency food aid from individual governments and their NGOs followed. For instance, in 1995 alone, South Korea provided 150,000 tonnes *gratis* while Japan provided 150,000 tonnes *gratis* and another 150,000 tonnes at subsidised prices. Between 1995 and 1998, the South Korean government provided $316 million, a third of the North's total aid. While China has its own bilateral assistance programme to the DPRK, which China claims constitutes 80 per cent of its total overseas aid, other assistance has largely been channelled through UN agencies with the next largest single contribution coming from the EU. The small US contribution was funnelled through the UN but clearly labelled with its point of origin.

The WHO provided medical aid. By 1997, the UN and NGOs had offices in Pyongyang with the WFP leading the charge with an office as early as November 1995.

US-labelled aid

## Calling on the EU

I had a visit from North Korean diplomats based in Paris in the spring of 1997. They described the terrible situation and the need for direct EU assistance, but had no idea of how to proceed. In the absence of formal relations with the EU, they had no access to or communication with the Commission and therefore no knowledge of the mechanisms to access European aid. At that time Commission officials were even forbidden to speak to North Korean diplomats. As an MEP with a long-time interest in North Korea, I offered to do what I could to help, but asked to see the situation on the ground for myself. I travelled with two fellow Labour MEPs, Clive Needle and David Thomas, to North Korea in October 1997. We met with Vice-Minister for Foreign Affairs responsible for North America and Europe, Choi Su Hon, international NGOs and the Flood Damage Rehabilitation Committee, and visited children's centres, hospitals and PDS distribution centres around the country. The diplomats were not wrong. The situation was dire.

Back in the European Parliament I tabled a resolution, which was passed, on the desperate need of the DPRK, including a paragraph demanding that an official delegation should be sent to the DPRK.[4] A further resolution on the food crisis in North Korea was passed the following March asking for the European Commission and member states to provide additional humanitarian aid, conditional on monitoring its distribution.[5] It also criticised the government for hampering a full assessment of the food crisis and the monitoring of aid distribution, and called for an independent evaluation of the food and energy situation.

The first official delegation from the European Parliament went to North Korea in December 1998. It was led by Leo Tindemans, former Belgian prime minister (Christian Democrat), along with Laurence Jan Brinkhorst (D66 – Dutch Liberal party), and myself.[6] This is a description of what we saw:

I visited the Huichon Children's Hospital, the only hospital in this city 200 kilometres north of Pyongyang in 1998. It was cold and damp. They have had no heating since the floods in 1995, which ruined the boiler. There was no medicine and no food. Huddled listlessly in the small communal rooms that serve as wards were groups of mothers with their thin, emaciated children in advanced stages of malnutrition, too weak to cry, too strong yet to die. Nearby, on the other side of the river that divides the town – and brought its destruction – was the local People's Distribution Centre. The cupboard was bare there was literally nothing there. Children received an allocation for 33 days, teachers, nurses and doctors 16 days and the rest of the population 11 days. But the daily allocation was only 250 grams, far short of the UN recommended minimum of 700 grams for long-term survival. All around the last of the harvest was being gathered in. An expected 3.8 million tonnes of cereals had slimmed down to 3.2 million tonnes. In Huichon, it was the Chinese cabbage that was being gathered in, the central component of *kimche*, the spicy vegetable dish that forms the basis of Korean cuisine. Men and women, young children and the army, all were systematically stripping fields and piling small trucks full with vegetables. Then they were dragged along by hand to the nearby river for washing, and onward transmission for pickling and storage. Traditionally kept in pots underground for two to three years to ferment, this latest batch probably did not last longer than two or three months.[7]

That month the EU opened, for the first time, an informal political dialogue with the DPRK. This led to a European Parliament resolution calling for the establishment of diplomatic relations, a dialogue on human rights, and the extension of assistance beyond food aid.[8] In April 1999, the European Parliament received a return visit from a North Korean delegation led by Vice-Minister for Foreign Affairs Choi Su Hon, who became the first ever North Korean to be questioned by the Parliament's Foreign Affairs Committee.

The EU's engagement with North Korea began with the provision of aid and humanitarian assistance targeting those at particular risk – children under 7 and pregnant women. The aid was provided through the European Commission's Humanitarian Aid Office (ECHO) and for the period 1995–2005 it amounted to over €344 million. The EU, despite a slow start, has been the largest and most consistent donor apart from South Korea and China. Others – Japan in particular – have

Orphans struggling to survive at Huichon Children's Hospital

General Secretary of the European Parliament Julian Priestly
with Choi Su Hon

used humanitarian aid as a political football, giving it and taking it away to match the changing political environment. On top of emergency food aid, the EU later supplied fertiliser and technical assistance to improve crop yields, and undertook a series of health care, water and sanitation projects. In June 2005, despite the nuclear crisis, the European Commission allocated for 2006 €10.7 million for medicines and equipment.

## Aid at what cost?

Some questioned the value and use of the aid. In 1998, Médecins Sans Frontières (MSF – Doctors Without Borders) claimed food aid distributed through the PDS was discriminatory, with rations determined by political loyalty not aid agency criteria such as gender and age. This was an allegation that Dr Vitit Muntarbhorn, UN Special Rapporteur on the Situation of Human Rights in the DPRK, would later specifically reject. MSF correctly claimed that staff were not allowed random access to PDS and other distribution centres. But NGO pressure had led to notice for visits being reduced to 24 hours, and to no food distribution in counties with no access.

MSF pulled out of its operation in North Korea and instead worked on the Chinese side of the Sino-Korean border providing shelter, clothing, food and medical care to North Korean refugees. They reported that the refugees gave an even bleaker picture of the famine than MSF staff had observed, and that a large majority claimed they had never received food from international organisations. At a US Congressional hearing on North Korea in May 2002, MSF argued:

> anyone who has sat and talked with these refugees would find it difficult to believe the assurances of the World Food Programme, which is reporting that aid is saving millions of lives, and that they have access to the people and know where the aid is going.

However most of the counties that the WFP is not allowed access to, and in which it therefore does not distribute food aid, are in the politically and militarily sensitive area adjacent to the Chinese border, exactly where the bulk of refugees originate. The rest probably either just didn't know or told MSF what they thought staff wanted to hear. The biased sample led to a flawed survey.

Since MSF's noisy departure, five other humanitarian NGOs have departed (Oxfam, Action Contra La Faim (ACF), the Cooperative for Assistance and Relief Everywhere, Inc. (CARE), the US Private Voluntary Organisation Consortium (PVOC), and Médicins Du Monde (MDM). But five others have come in for the first time. These, and those that have been there all the way through, continue to provide help to the most vulnerable, but NGO withdrawals are a convenient stick to beat Pyongyang with.

In February 2003, the Director of the WFP, James Morris, testified to the US House Committee on Foreign Relations and reiterated that WFP staff had access to 85 per cent of the population and 'believes that most food is getting through to the women and children who need it'. Armed with Ronald Reagan's quote 'a hungry child knows no politics,' Morris argued for the separation of politics and aid. The WFP evaluated its engagement positively, reporting that the health condition of children had improved, that little evidence remained of the widespread acute malnutrition seen in the previous years and that attendance in primary schools had risen from 75 to 95 per cent with the introduction of WFP biscuit distribution in schools. In 2003 a UNICEF study confirmed food aid was reaching the most vulnerable, and that between 1998 and 2002, the number of underweight children had dropped by two-thirds, acute malnutrition had been cut almost in half and chronic malnutrition by a third.[9]

In reality the vast bulk of aid was provided through the UN, with NGOs providing only 2 per cent of the total. The WFP did not pretend to have perfect control of every single bag of food, but it claimed to have a 'reasonable degree of assurance that the food provided through WFP gets to those who need it'. Furthermore it refuted claims from US intelligence that food was being diverted to the military. In many senses, that is a red herring. After all, there is no need for the military to divert international food aid as they have the first take, and a sufficient one, on national production. Equally with Chinese and South Korean aid unmonitored, the North could feed the military without WFP supplies.

The WFP argued that time has helped to build confidence between donor and recipient, and that its working conditions improved over the years, with some of its concerns having been addressed by the North Korean authorities. One issue of concern was to augment the WFP's geographical access because of its 'no access, no food' policy. Over the years, the number of counties it has been allowed access to increased from 145 out of the total of 203 counties in 1998 to 161 in April 2004, excluding only 15 per cent of the population. By the end of 2004, it had been allowed to increase its staff and had 50 international staff in Pyongyang and five sub-offices around the country.

While the famine was easing, hunger was still very present. The WFP's 2004 assessment estimated that even with the best harvest since 1995/1996, 37 per cent of young children were still suffering from chronic malnutrition. Despite this Pyongyang announced in August 2005 that it no longer required food assistance from the WFP and other aid groups, and that aid agencies involved in humanitarian work should leave by the end of December 2005, except for those completing ongoing development projects.

Pyongyang was suspicious of the WFP's obsession with wider access to previously closed areas while at the same time, because of a drop in donations, it was cutting assistance to counties already open. The border counties were closed because of security concerns and Pyongyang knows only too well that CIA operatives masqueraded as UN inspectors in Iraq. A further factor was the passage of the UN's human rights resolutions condemning North Korea. This was seen as the United States using humanitarian assistance as an element of its regime change agenda. Even privately, ministry officials dealing with food aid agree that it should be halted if necessary to protect national security, especially as strings-free food donations from China and South Korea continue and food production was improving.

A more positive aspect is that North Korea seems to have come to the realisation that dependence on external sources of food cannot be a long-term strategy for development. The North announced in September 2004 that 'although there is still a need for humanitarian aid they would welcome in the future more technical assistance and more development-oriented support,'[10] entailing assistance in rehabilitation of infrastructure such as irrigation systems and road repairs to allow farmers to transport their crops. As a developmental strategy, putting an end to ten years of dependence on food from the outside and switching to development aid may be a good way to kick-start the economy. The problem is that until the nuclear crisis is resolved there are few willing donors.

## EU aid

The potential short-term effect of ending the food programme for the most vulnerable and poorest people was nevertheless disturbing. The EU pressed to continue with its humanitarian aid. After long negotiations the authorities in Pyongyang gave special permission for the European NGOs to continue their activities through 2006, with the NGOs re-organised as work units under the auspices of the European Commission. These NGOs included Concern World Wide, German Agro Action, Handicap International, PMU Interlife, Premiere Urgence, Triangle and Save the Children.

Pyongyang having made its point, in May 2006 the WFP and the DPRK reached an agreement on resuming aid distribution, with new working arrangements for a two-year operation to combat nutritional deficiencies and boost grassroots food security amongst 1.9 million of the most vulnerable women and young children. The Letter of Understanding provided for ten resident WFP international staff to oversee the operations and four full-time field workers, while others such as the Country Director, Deputy Country Director and Logistics Officer would be allowed to regularly travel to the field. The WFP staff could visit hospitals, orphanages, nurseries, kindergartens, primary schools, PDS and food-for-work sites to assess the impact of assistance and the nutritional status of recipients. The operation was to provide vitamin- and mineral-enriched foods, processed at local factories supported by the WFP, to young children and pregnant and nursing women. Additionally, cereal rations were to be provided to underemployed workers through food-for-work community development projects aimed at rehabilitating agricultural and other community infrastructure. Initial food distribution was to be concentrated in the 30 counties assessed by WFP to be the most food-insecure.

## Solving its own problems

The impact of the famine and food crisis disrupted and devastated the lives of the North Koreans in the 1990s. When the PDS collapsed, people struggled to feed themselves. They abandoned homes, jobs and families to search for food. The black market flourished. The sharp decrease in rations in 1995 meant farmers, who could no longer rely on having their basic needs supplied by the state, gave priority to their own survival. They started to divert production in order to build up their own stocks and spent increasing amounts of time growing crops on their 'illegal' private plots outside the collective. The scale of diversion reached a level where the military was sent to protect the fields from illegal pre-harvesting and, in some cases, to work fields deserted by farmers. Kim Jong Il was forced to appeal to the farming community using the argument:

> if we cannot give them [the military] rice then when the 'Yankees' invade us we cannot defeat them and your sons and daughters will become imperialist slaves once more…It is this logic that must be used to persuade those who hide and smuggle food to regain their conscience.

A consequence of this diversion and moonlighting was the spread of farmers' markets. While at first barely tolerated, the state was forced to turn a blind eye when other sources of food dried up, and eventually reluctantly acknowledge them. With demand totally outstripping supply, and the PDS's consequent inability at times to deliver anything and never enough, there was no alternative but barter and the market. By 2002 farmers' markets became a permanent feature especially in urban areas.

The food crisis drove reform. In March and July 2002, measures were announced 'to improve the management of socialist economy'. The State Price Control Bureau introduced price and wage systems, endorsed 'markets' and granted greater autonomy to farmers and enterprises, setting low targets for delivery to the state with the surplus available for sale. Monetary reform devalued the won 40-fold, salaries were increased 18 times, food prices 26 times, and the exchange rate for the euro, Pyongyang's official currency for foreign exchange transactions, rose by a factor of 70.

With this legalisation, markets grew rapidly in size and numbers. At first, they were rudimentary, consisting of large open-air stalls enclosed by some kind of fencing, and strictly off limits to foreigners. Over time, in Pyongyang and in most of the major cities and towns they have evolved into large, covered, regulated markets, complete with a foreign exchange service at rates substantially better than those of banks or hotels – normally not available to foreign visitors – and stocked with a wide variety of both domestic and imported consumer goods. In Pyongyang, the Tong-il Market is thronged with thousands haggling, selling and buying goods at free-floating prices. On display are a wide variety of products, fresh meat and dried fish, Spanish oranges and North African dates, clothes, shoes, cosmetics and a range

Tong-il Market

of electrical goods from light bulbs to computer parts. The range of imported products now on sale shows the existence of an emerging middle class who can afford to buy previously unobtainable goods.

The market drove productivity. In the agricultural sector, farms and cooperatives, whose sole commitment to the central government was a now easily achievable target for public distribution and whose surpluses could be sold, have shown productivity increases far above those procured with the mere application of fertiliser. For those with capital and enterprise there are enormous benefits from the emerging market economy. Small informal cooperatives appeared, making and selling handicrafts and snacks or repairing shoes or bicycles.[11] Some farmers are getting rich selling their surplus in the markets. An ice-cream making machine on sale for more than two-year's wages in Tong-il market makes an appearance on the pavement next to a block of flats, where an electric cable is connected through a hole in the wall, and an orderly queue waits to buy. Outside of Tong-il, small family-sized businesses and street vendors are everywhere. The urban centres have a litter of new stalls on the streets, and even on rural roads, every mile or so stalls make a colourful punctuation in the monotonous passing landscape.

North Korea went a step further in industrial reform, acknowledging the end of central planning for the vast majority of enterprises with the end of the state's ability to supply the raw materials needed. In 2004, the State Plan was abandoned in most industrial sectors, allowing factories to fire and hire at will and choose their own products and methods of production. However, the prospect of reform in the industrial sectors taking off is poor, as without energy and supplies the only option is to continue to produce nothing, while the new rich's demands are satisfied by sucking in imports in the absence of indigenous supplies.

Where market opening has worked to an extent for the agricultural sector, the manufacturing sector in North Korea is different. The means of production are old and outdated. Managers are unaware of how modern economies work. North Korea, once a developed country with 70 per cent of the workforce in manufacturing, is experiencing a partial re-ruralisation of the economy, with factory managers laying off industrial workers and sending others to grow food. Without reconstruction aid, most factory workers are now free to go hungry.

Reform has its costs. The rate of inflation has exceeded 30 per cent. The ostensible gains from wage reform have been swiftly eroded. Between 3 and 4 million people have fallen into a hunger trap, not earning enough to feed themselves. As months passed and prices ticked steadily upwards, hundreds of thousands of new poor have been created. This underclass finds it increasingly difficult to survive without inputs from family plots, family connections or humanitarian aid. Coal miners, if they achieve their targets, may earn 10,000 won per month; workers in the service sector get 2000 won. The minimum wage for a family of four, in which both parents are working in the service sector, is thus roughly 4000 won, but they need about 90kg of rice to survive for a month. Families can buy at most 45kg of rice at a subsidised price of 45 won per kg (2025 won); the rest has to be bought on the open market at prices an order of magnitude higher. Thus, in the worst-case scenario family income without external inputs can be below the minimum for survival. Pork – rarely available from the PDS at the official price of 75 won/kg – is sold on the market at 400 won.

The PDS was partly revitalised in 2005 as the consequences became clear. Rice and, to a degree, other cereals were taken off the market and PDS deliveries restored although it is not clear if this can be sustained in the long term or whether deliveries are to all groups or often restricted to government employees.

This is just the painful beginning of a long arduous march to a market economy. North Korea is eager for advice. It wants to learn from the West and the rest but it wants to do this in its own way. Together with the Ministry of Foreign Affairs, the European Commission has organised annual workshops on economic reform in Pyongyang since 2004. European experts have presented experiences of economic transition in other parts of the world and outlined a variety of options for reform, including improving the climate for inward investment. The first workshop in September 2004, attended by Kung Sok Ung, Vice-Minister for Foreign Affairs for Europe, focused on a general overview of the economic transition process. The second in October 2005 dealt with more specific issues, including strategies to attract foreign direct investment, restructuring agriculture and the creation of small and medium-sized enterprises. The seminar for November 2006 was postponed in the aftermath of the nuclear test, but a third was scheduled for autumn 2007.

## Reform's rhetoric

*Juche* came to terms with the arrival of millions of tonnes of food aid labelled 'gift' from the EU, United States, South Korea and Japan. *Juche* in practice gave way to a new pragmatism in a country which had been forced to seek a fresh direction and enact reforms that dared not speak their name. Change needed a neutral catchphrase.

## In our own style

With the collapse of the Soviet empire, and China's market reform, North Korea was left standing alone. Initially Pyongyang emphasised difference, with 'socialism in our own style (*Urisik Sahuijuyui*)' setting North Korea's socialist system apart from a failed Soviet Union and a revisionist China. Kim Jong Il blamed the collapse of the Soviet Union and Eastern Europe on weak leadership, poor decision making and loss of faith. He demanded unity at home through stronger social and ideological integration. Facing a changed world, the regime did not bend; it dug in and battened down the hatches. In a speech to senior officials of the Central Committee in January 1992 Kim Jong Il pointed to 'socialist ills' surmising:

> after adopting revisionism, socialism in the former Soviet Union and the East European countries has collapsed one by one. ... The imperialists are attempting to infiltrate bourgeois culture into the socialist world, thus, to paralyse the revolutionary spirit of the people there. ... If the masses are equipped with a firm ideology, then they will be victorious, but if they are ideologically ill, then socialism will face ruin because the superiority of socialist society over capitalist society can be represented by ideological superiority.[12]

The danger was cultural and ideological pollution. Capitalism was a drug that led to addiction and destruction. The job of government was to 'save the masses from the danger of being exposed to the evil drug'.[13] People were to 'live according to our own style, rejecting ideological and cultural infiltration of capitalism'. The anti-capitalist campaign was supported by films, pictures and posters illustrated with stills of former Russian officers selling hot-dogs on the street and the unemployed and the homeless struggling to survive.[14] I have a propaganda poster showing a determined steel worker stoking the furnaces with porn videos and copies of *Penthouse* – obviously not yet up to speed with the spread of DVDs. Capitalism was greed, poverty and crime.

Unfortunately for the North Koreans, 'socialism in our own style' accompanied by the North's further isolation proved an economic disaster. The collapse of the Soviet empire indicated Kim Il Sung had made the right political choice, but the wrong economic one. The Soviet trajectory of *glasnost* and *perestroika* led to collapse and capitalism. However, Kim's political vindication by the collapse of the Soviet empire soon turned sour as the economic consequences finally broke the back of the North's faltering economy. In the midst of the nuclear crisis and rising tension between the DPRK and the United States, Kim Il Sung died. *Juche* as a policy was immediately sidelined, although few outside observers noticed at the time because it

Stoking the furnaces with *Penthouse*

continued to decorate the pages of *Rodong Sinmun* and imbue Party rhetoric. Kim Jong Il's copious writings on the subject had given him the franchise on the term and he soon gutted it of real content. What the KWP's former Ideology Secretary Hwang Jang Yop thought of it all was shown by his escape to the South in 1997, the highest-ranking North Korean ever to defect. When I interviewed him in Seoul in 1999, he was still a true believer. For him Kim Jong Il was a heretic Pope, betraying Kim Il Sung's true legacy. Over time references to *Juche* began to decrease.

With hereditary succession part of 'our style socialism', Kim Jong Il was expected to immediately take the helm. But it was not a good time to be in charge. The country was enduring its worst decade since the Korean War. Kim Jong Il excused himself in December 1996:

> If I concentrated only on the economy, there would be irrevocable damage to the revolution. The Great Leader told me when he was alive never to be involved in economic projects, just concentrate on the military and the Party and leave economics to party functionaries.[15]

The country during its most challenging period was left leaderless and without leadership, while he pleaded the Confucian tradition of three years of mourning.

The response after Kim's death was the strengthening of the military's role in state affairs. Kim Jong Il was rarely seen or pictured other than with senior military figures. Coinciding with the military's growing representation in the ruling elite was the introduction of concepts such as 'military-oriented thought' and 'military-first politics' which shuffled aside previous political rhetoric. The nation was to be a military camp where military requirements took priority over all else. While the military had played a key role before, it was now further extended. Soldiers brought in the harvest and undertook public works. The West Sea Barrage was a military operation. The military became the political, economic and security crisis managers.

Kim Jong Il remained throughout the interregnum Supreme Commander of the Korean People's Army and the Chairman of the National Defence Committee (NDC), but it was not until October 1997 that he finally took the post of General Secretary, putting him in overall charge. Then he blamed the food crisis on certain high-ranking cadres, including Central Committee Secretary So Hwang Hui, all of whom were executed. Military-orientated thought was joined by the 'Red Banner' philosophy of 'unity', 'faith' and 'integrity'. Kim Jong Il showed his 'integrity' by fulfilling his Confucian duty of mourning his beloved father for three years, the Party its 'unity' and 'faith' by his unopposed elevation. The final confirmation came as a relief to North Koreans after so many false dawns when rumours that the transition was about to occur turned out to be premature.

In September 1998 the 10th SPA amended the Constitution and elevated Kim Il Sung posthumously to 'Eternal President'. Kim Jong Il was re-elected as Chairman of the NDC with the position recognised in the new Constitution as the state's most senior post. With Kim Jong Il in post, 'Red Banner' rhetoric exited the scene. After a four-year gap Kim was formally back in charge, though he still avoided taking charge of or responsibility for economic affairs. Cabinet government was introduced and the prime minister was handed this poisoned chalice. The economic crisis was placed at the feet of ministers and Kim warned: 'those who have stood with folded arms during this hard time will have to account for their actions in the future.' Another who was judged to have stood arms folded was Agriculture Minister, Suh Gwan Hee, who was reportedly executed in the late 1990s. The restructuring of North Korea's political architecture centralised power, off-loaded responsibility and strengthened the hand of the military. 'Meeting and greeting' was transferred to Kim Young Nam, Chairman of the Executive Committee of the SPA and now in protocol terms Head of State.

As Kim consolidated his power by the end of 1998, the emphasis started to shift back to the civilian sector with the slogan *Kangsong Daeguk* (A Powerful and Prosperous Nation). It balanced military strength and economic prosperity and was a sign of economic reform to follow. The term first made its appearance in a *Rodong Sinmun* editorial in September 1998 'Let's construct *Kangsong Daeguk* as led by the great leadership of the Party' where the North was to be built into an ideologically, economically and militarily, strong country. It was a sharp change in direction, if not a complete U-turn. *Kangsong Daeguk* came to alternate with *Buhung Kangguk* and *Kangsong Buhung* (Resurgence of a Strong Country).

With the new millennium, the past was formally laid to rest. *Rodong Sinmun*'s New Year's editorial on 9 January 2001 stated:

> we should transcend the old working style and fixed economic framework of other countries in old times. ... It is impossible to advance the revolution even a step further if we should get complacent with our past achievements or be enslaved to outdated ideas and stick to the outmoded style and attitude in our work.[16]

Economic reform 'in our own style' had replaced socialism, while *Juche* had passed the batten to *Kangsong Daeguk*.

*China Daily*, in the post-Deng era, which normally loudly extolled the virtues of the market, privatisation and profit, ran a series of long articles in September 1998 laden with jargon from the 1970s welcoming Kim's taking over the leadership. They were clearly not written for domestic consumption – most readers would barely have understood what they were writing about – but as an act of fraternal solidarity and a quarry for quotes for North Korea's KCNA and *Rodong Sinmun*.

## Factions

Kim Jong Il's bold change of policy direction and rhetoric was going too fast for some. For the first time in decades, policy differences emerged. On 23 September 2004, North Korea's Central Broadcast

| Before 1980 | Juche Ideology (National identity, independence, or Self-Reliance) | |
|---|---|---|
| 1980 | 1980–89 | Mass Movement Anti-imperialism International Solidarity of Socialism |
| | 1989–92 | Superiority of Socialism |
| 1990 | 1990–93 | Confidence and Optimism Our-style Socialism |
| | 1991–95 | Unity and Loyalty Party Leadership |
| | 1995–2000 | Military-First Politics |
| | 1996–97 | Red Banner Ideology |
| | 1996—98 | March under Trial Arduous March for Socialism |
| | 1998–2000 | *Kangsung Daeguk* (a great country that is militarily strong and economically prosperous) |
| 2000 | 2001–03 | Renovation in thinking and in practice |
| | 2001–03 | IT Science and technology-oriented economy |
| | 2001–06 | Resurgent (reconstruction) of a Strong Country Kangsung Buhung/Buhung Kanguk |
| | 1995-2006 | Military-First thought (Ideology) |

Figure 5.1 Change in rhetoric in North Korea 1980–2006

Agency, in support of the 'Party's monolithic leadership system', argued: 'the Party cannot maintain its existence by permitting factions.' This was a response to a 'conversation' no one had previously mentioned. It was then reported in the South Korean newspaper *Joongang* as 'North's political base gets a makeover' (8 December 2004). Triggered by the dismissal in February 2004 of Jang Song Taek, Kim's brother-in-law and Vice Director of KWP's organisation and guidance department – and considered by many to be North Korea's effective No. 2 – and his close associates from their Party posts, there followed a major restructuring and reshuffle of the KWP for the first time since 1994. Kim Jong Il abolished three bureaus of the Central Control Committee – Military Affairs, Economic Policy and Agricultural Affairs – with 40 per cent of the Secretariat reassigned. Jang and two of his brothers, prominent figures in the military, had used their Party base to challenge Pak Pong Ju, the Prime Minister appointed in September 2003, in charge of economic reform. Kim's purge and restructuring ended the Party's ability to interfere in key policy areas. Now military matters would be dealt with exclusively by Kim and the National Defence Committee, and the Cabinet was given free rein to continue the economic, industrial and agricultural reforms.

Jang took heed and learnt his lesson, and a newly repentant Jang was rapidly rehabilitated, re-emerging as the First Director of the KWP's Department of Working People's Organisation and Capital Construction. In March 2006, Jang led a 30-strong group on an eleven-day visit to Wuhan, Guangzhou and Shenzhen. He was charged with learning the lessons from China's reform process that could be applied back home, retracing Kim Jong Il's footsteps and thinking from his January visit.

Seoul and Washington's media spent 2004 speculating about the stability of the regime, with claims of challenges to Kim's rule. Apart from Jang Song Taek's removal, South Korea's KCIA claimed in May that the chemical signature of the Ryongchon explosion was inconsistent with Pyongyang's claim that it had been an unfortunate railway accident when a train laden with chemicals hit a power line. Rather it had been an attempted assassination, with Kim Jong Il returning that day from a trip to China along the same line and through the same station eight hours earlier than scheduled. This account was embellished by reports of the arrest of a group of ten young North Korean pro-Chinese technocrats.

In September, rumours surfaced of a power struggle around the succession to Kim Jong Il with the death of Ko Young Hee, Kim's wife (see below). November saw the *New York Times* (22 November) speculate on Kim Jong Il's deteriorating health and the unsubstantiated claims of anti-Kim Jong Il protests in the North. The accompanying pictures looked suspiciously fake, being graffitied versions of a Kim Jong Il poster I have never seen on display in 15 visits to the North. The article also reported the removal of Kim Jong Il's portrait from some public places (see below). All told, there was a frenzy of media speculation that parleyed into North Korea in danger of imminent collapse. All too late: while Kim had clearly been challenged, by the time it was reported he had clearly come out on top, with no evidence that the regime was ever seriously threatened.

## Reading the signs

Back in the late summer of 1998 there was a fashion, particularly amongst army officers, to display Kim Jong Il badges, with or without the addition of his father. These were read, at the time, as reflections of a factional struggle over Kim's succession. After the 1998 endorsement of Kim as de facto Head of State, the Kim Jong Il badges disappeared. Any planned return of the badges was quashed when Kim Jong Il himself 'urged' people in 2004 to stop producing them and not to wear them during the tenth anniversary commemorations of his father's death. This was a slightly strange request, in that it is difficult to imagine how production would proceed without prior authorisation. This apparent downsizing of the Kim 2 cult has led to speculation of dramatic changes in the power structure, in what is almost certainly a misreading of events.

One Western translator of the Kims' works, speeches and statements working at the Foreign Languages Publishing House in Pyongyang felt emboldened after several years on the job to suggest that one barrier to reading and understanding in the West was the constant and undue repetition of the Kims' honorifics. Permission was given to scale back on their use. Within months, foreign North Korea watchers were reporting a possible leadership challenge indicated by a sharp shift in the levels of reverence being paid to the Kims. Instructions were promptly given to restore the *status quo ante*.

In September 2004 the first EU–DPRK Workshop on Economic Reform was held in the Great Hall of the People in Pyongyang, attended by 20 Europeans and around 60 North Korean Ministry and Banking officials, with the first session opened by Kung Sok Ung, Vice-Minister for Foreign Affairs. We all noticed immediately that in the meeting room Kim Jong Il's portrait was no longer hanging alongside his father's on the main wall but thought little of it. Months later there were major news items in the Japanese and South Korean press based on stories from Russia about Kim's missing pictures, speculating about rising opposition, acts of sabotage, a sign of Kim's imminent demise or worse. Traced back, the only basis for the story was the workshop and a conversation held over a subsequent dinner with the Russian ambassador. As someone who was there, I know it was no act of sabotage. The picture had been carefully removed, with the remaining picture of Kim Il Sung moved slightly to be exactly central on the wall. It might have been a test run preparing for a future succession. Just as in Islam the early tradition of the Caliph's each speaking one step down from his predecessor on the *Khalib* (pulpit) had to stop before they all ended up underground, there is a limit to how many pictures everyone can have on their walls. Nevertheless since the furore there have been no further reports of a one-Kim, as opposed to a two-Kim, picture policy.

## Kim 3

With Kim Jong Il turning 65 in 2007 the question of the succession is back, but this time those who might object to heredity on Marxist principles are no longer there. It is likely to remain a family affair. It had been speculated that Jang Song Taek (61 in 2007) was to be the successor, but his differences with Kim over the reform agenda may have reduced his chances. The fiasco of Kim Jong Nam's (the eldest son) attempted trip to Tokyo's Disneyland in 2001 meant he has been sidelined, although he did return to Pyongyang in February 2007, sparking speculation that his father was gravely ill. His response when buttonholed by reporters in Beijing was 'It's his 65th birthday!' Speculation has shifted to the two sons of Kim Jong Il's late wife, Ko Young Hee. Kim Jong Chol and Kim Jong Un are both in their early 20s and are currently working in the key Organisation and Guidance Department of the KWP. The rumour is that Kim Jong Il considers his second son, Kim Jong Chol, a strong candidate. The choice obviously depends on how quickly Kim Jong Il decides the transition needs to begin. Speculation that there will be an interim collective leadership before any final takeover by a successor would seem to favour one of the younger sons who would most need/benefit from a collective regency prior to the assumption of complete control. In the meantime, Kim Jong Il has other issues to deal with, including North Koreans crossing the border into China and international pressure about human rights in North Korea.

## Flood of refugees?

Triggered by the food crisis, a flood of refugees from North Korea crossed into China. NGOs claim there are up to 300,000 refugees and illegal immigrants in the border areas. These claims are difficult to sustain. Such a number would be equivalent to the largest city in the region, Yanji, which has a total population of 350,000, of whom 210,000 are ethnic Koreans. The reality is that many people cross for short trips

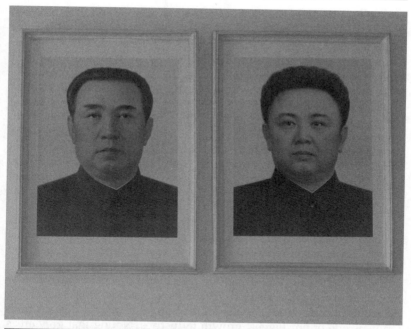

And then there was one

to visit relatives, buy and sell goods or search for food. The Tumen River serves as the border for hundreds of kilometres, and a drive along the road paralleling the river on the Chinese side shows little or no evidence of guard posts on either side of what is, in summer, a river shallow enough to wade across. During the early 1960s and the famine following the disaster of the Great Leap Forward, the traffic was the other way round, with the North receiving and feeding starving Chinese with tens of thousands in the North. Some estimates have suggested that now 25–50,000 indentured labourers are on local farms with no access to even basic health care and education. The South's Ministry of Unification backs that with estimates of up to 30,000 economic refugees. The shortage of women in China in consequence of the 'one-child policy' and emigration to the cities from rural areas means young females are particularly welcome as farmers' wives.

On top of these illegal economic migrants and short-term visitors are refugees and defectors. Defining North Koreans crossing the border is not easy; terms like defector, asylum seeker, refugee and economic migrant are all beset with ambiguity. Politics plays an important role in the choice of description. Returning illegal immigrants to their country of origin has a very different sound from 'deporting defectors to their deaths'. After all, in Europe expelling illegal immigrants is one of our biggest growth industries. Noting that grey areas exist, the terms here are used broadly as follows: a *defector* is someone in a senior position of responsibility in the North who is attempting to flee to South Korea for political reasons; a *refugee*/asylum seeker is someone who has fled a natural or human-made catastrophe, in this case famine or has a 'well founded fear of persecution'; an *economic migrant* is someone who has moved in search of better living standards.

A complication however, is that economic migrants can be turned into refugees. When they set off they are not refugees but they become so when they arrive. This is because North Korea punishes those it apprehends on their return; economic migrants become, according to the UNHCR, *refugee sur place* because of this threat. The Chinese do have sweeps from time to time to round up the more obvious refugees and return them to North Korea. Generally there is a degree of tolerance for local communities to go to and fro, as there has been for decades. This however, very definitely does not extend to Party members and senior officials suspected of trying to defect. Equally, repeat offenders can and will be sent to the camps.

In the past, prior to the serious tightening up of security by the Chinese, refugees travelled to Beijing to seek asylum in foreign embassies. That worked for a while. Nowadays a refugee and defector industry is growing up along the border, where they are preyed on by evangelical Christian groups and criminal gangs. Until 2004 South

Border crossing from China

Korea paid a bounty of $30,000 to each defector arriving from the North as a resettlement payment, but the rapid escalation in numbers created problems for the South Korean government. Upon arrival, defectors are housed in *Hanawon* (hostels) for three months for resettlement training and education. The facilities and the training programmes are now stretched way beyond their intended capacity. The cutting of the settlement grant by two-thirds is intended both to discourage the gangs and to deter those attracted by a resettlement payment that exceeds a lifetime's earning in the North (see Table 5.1).[17] From January 2005, South Korea also tightened up its defector screening process as a way of slowing the flow of migrants claiming defector status. Gangs smuggle the refugees across China into South Korea in exchange for cash on arrival, often from the resettlement money. Much of the rest is taken as a down payment on smuggling the next member of the family out, repeating the process ad infinitum. The evangelicals do the same for souls, as when 468 North Korean refugees were transhipped to Vietnam, where they were eventually put on a chartered plane to South Korea in July 2004, souring both Vietnamese–North Korean and North–South relations in the process. In November 2006, it was the turn of Thailand to play host, while Mongolia is next up.

NGOs and aid agencies rightly criticise Pyongyang for its treatment of those returned from China, which itself is equally criticised for its refusal to grant them refugee status. As part of the EU's human rights dialogue with China, the EU has repeatedly called upon the Chinese authorities to allow the Office of the UN High Commissioner for Refugees to investigate the situation on the Sino-DPRK border. China categorises the arrivals as economic migrants, though it accepts the removal to third countries of those who obtain asylum by gaining entry into foreign embassies and consulates on humanitarian grounds. According to Amnesty International, the Chinese authorities offer rewards, equivalent $240, for information on the whereabouts of illegal North Korean visitors. While the majority are economic migrants, amongst them are those who have a well-founded fear of persecution should they be returned. On the basis of the 1953 Geneva Convention, this minority at least should be granted asylum by China. But China makes no distinction between those who will merely spend a few days in detention and those who will be incarcerated for years or worse.

Yet the most significant barrier to North Korean refugees is Seoul. Under the South's Constitution, all North Koreans are South Koreans. Yanji Airport has seven flights a week direct to Seoul. If it wanted, the ROK would permit all those who wanted to go to travel South, with China taking the attitude of Hungary immediately prior to the collapse of the Berlin Wall in 1989 when it allowed East Germans free passage into Austria and on to West Germany. This prospect horrifies Seoul. The government does not want to precipitate the North's collapse, taking the view – correctly – that the current trickle would become an absolute flood once it became known that North Koreans were guaranteed safe onward passage from China. That would certainly damage relations between Pyongyang and both Beijing and Seoul. Neither the ROK government nor the South Korean public wants the social and

Table 5.1 The number of North Korean defectors arriving in South Korea

| Year | 1991 | 1992 | 1993 | 1994 | 1995 | 1996 | 1997 | 1998 |
|---|---|---|---|---|---|---|---|---|
| No. of defectors | 9 | 8 | 8 | 52 | 41 | 56 | 85 | 71 |

| Year | 1999 | 2000 | 2001 | 2002 | 2003 | 2004 | 2005 | |
|---|---|---|---|---|---|---|---|---|
| No. of defectors | 148 | 312 | 583 | 1139 | 1281 | 1894 | 1387 | |

Source: Data from the Ministry of Unification, Seoul, Korea, 2006. website:
www.unikorea.go.kr

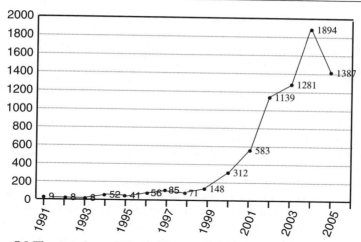

Figure 5.2 The number of North Korean defectors

financial burden. People want their own relatives out, but they certainly don't want everyone else's. North Koreans are viewed in the same way that the West Germans view their Eastern compatriots – 'feckless and idle'. North Koreans find it extremely hard to adjust to the South's complex, competitive and individualistic society. Some, persuaded to come south by criminal gangs in China, feel it was all a terrible mistake. Suicide rates are high and a few have even returned to the North – to what reception it is not clear.

South Korea treats 'defectors' less grudgingly, but they have to come with a story. Until the democratic transition in the South, anyone with something bad to say about the North or officials of the regime was welcome. Today North–South rapprochement means Seoul's enthusiasm has abated and it is embarrassed by the more vocal defectors with their prison camp stories. Since his defection in 1997, Hwang Jang Yop, the former KWP's Ideology Secretary, has been at the forefront of criticising Kim Jong Il's regime, attacking the South's engagement policy and pressing for regime change in the North. On 31 October 2003, Hwang travelled to the United States and testified on Capital Hill before the US Foreign Relations Committee. He is one of many who have trod and who will tread the same path.

## Defectors' world tour

Defectors who have experienced life in prison camps now travel the West retelling their stories. Kang Chol Hwan, the author of *The Aquariums of Pyongyang* (2000), was imprisoned in Yodok Camp from the age of nine. His grandparents were wealthy Koreans living in Japan. They owned a casino in Kyoto and provided substantial financial support to the local Chosen Soren branch. They voluntarily joined the exodus from Japan to the North in the early 1960s. At first, they lived a privileged life in Pyongyang with their own Volvo, a luxury almost unheard of at the time, but it all ended when his grandfather was arrested for treason. The whole family was sent to Yodok, which mainly accommodated returnees from Japan. Kang spent ten years there before the family was released. He went on to university, dropped out and spent a year as a black market trader, living on money sent to him from Japan. Kang finally defected to South Korea and is now working as a reporter for *Chosun Daily* in Seoul. Yet there is a contradiction. Kang Chol Hwan, who went to Yodok prison camp, did not escape from Hell to flee South. It was years before he became an economic migrant. He was released, had a job as a delivery man for his local Office of Distribution, obtained a place at university, dropped out and finally made his way to China and South Korea, to appear in George Bush's office years later as a 'hero'. The co-author of his 'autobiography', Pierre Rigoulot, includes in his CV the fact he is one of the editors of the *Black Book on Communism*. If he'd been a black refugee from Africa few – if any – immigration departments in Europe would have granted him asylum with that history.

Lee Soon Ok, a former general manager of the Chief Product Supply Office, and a senior member of the Party, wrote the evangelical Christian memoir *Eyes of the Tailless Animals: Prison Memoirs of a North Korean Woman* (1999) detailing how she spent seven years in Camp 14, Kaechon, South Pyongan Province, between 1987 and 1993, defecting to the South on her release.[18] She has testified before the US Congress and other international human rights commissions. In her memoirs she reports torture, public executions and biochemical weapons testing on the prisoners. When visiting the European Parliament, Lee took the line that the EU should cut off food aid to North Korea and send bibles instead. Many of the claims are years old. Kang's date back 21 years and Lee's 14 years; both predate Kim Il Sung's death and yet are presented as if they were yesterday.

In February 2004 a BBC documentary was aired that echoed Lee's claims of chemical weapons testing on prisoners in Camp 22, identified from other sources as being in Huiryong, North Hamgyong Province. The claims were based on the testimony of a defector Kwon Hyok who had been, according to the BBC, the Head of Security in the camp. A couple of weeks later, in March 2004, a North Korean delegation led by the Speaker of the SPA, Choi Tae Bok, spoke at a meeting in the House of Commons where he strongly and unsurprisingly denied the allegations of human experimentation. It turns out Bok might just have been right on this occasion.

Kwon Hyok's story was that he defected whilst posted as military attaché to the DPRK embassy in Beijing. After defecting he produced as evidence of human experimentation on prisoners in North Korea a copy of a prisoner's Letter of Transfer stating: 'the above person is transferred from ... camp Number 22 for the purpose of human experimentation of liquid gas for chemical weapons.' Kwon's story soon began to unravel. No one of that name had ever been military attaché in Beijing, and South Korean intelligence identified the letter as a forgery with neither the language nor the seals nor the paper-type matching those used by the North. On 31 March 2004, KCNA carried a report by Kang Byong Sop and his second son Kang Song Hak, who confessed that the whole thing was a money-making scam devised by Kang's eldest son, Kang Song Guk who masqueraded as Kwon Hyok and fabricated the letter in China. Kang Song Guk has disappeared.

When questioned, Olenka Frenkiel, who produced the BBC documentary, said that while she had not seen the gas chambers or prisons, 'the next best thing you have is testimony and what documentary evidence you can find.' New claims continue to arise. In March 2004 a senior chemist from a North Korean laboratory who had defected said he had personally witnessed political prisoners used in chemical weapons experiments. This time at least the South's Ministry of Unification confirmed his status, if not his claims.

The international community is over-reliant on the testimony of defectors. While no one argues there are serious and large-scale human rights problems in the DPRK, defector reports range from credible to incredible – the most extreme claims are then shipped around the world by US neo-con think tanks and lobbies. A meeting organised by the European Parliament's Liberal Group, held at the Parliament on 21 March 2006, illustrated the limitation of defectors' testimonies as a primary tool for evaluation.

The hearing had the selfsame two defectors who had spoken at the neo-con Freedom House Conference in Brussels the day before and came with an entourage of Americans, South Koreans and Japanese, amongst whom were sprinkled European human rights activists. Having previously testified on many occasions in the United States and more recently in France, their manner of testifying was professionally tailored and well recited. This was not a place for questions or critical engagement, but endorsements. Any hint of backsliding from the party line or scepticism had the entourage voicing its displeasure. The hearing was more a political rally than a fact-finding event. The financing behind all of this activity comes from US Christian fundamentalist groups, the Heritage Foundation and monies made available by the North Korean Human Rights Act (see below), pushed through the US Congress by the Republican Right that is bent on regime change in the Iraq style. None of this in itself invalidates the testimonies given; nevertheless opportunities for a serious critical engagement would be more likely if the wheat could be separated from the chaff.

As so often North Korea is its own worst enemy. Politics, like nature, abhors a vacuum. So in the absence of credible reports from Amnesty International and similar bodies, we find substituted the testimony served up by evangelical Christian groups and the United States' more rabid Republicans. North Korea should allow monitoring on the ground. It should provide access to the UN Special Rapporteur Vitit Muntarbhorn. It should also engage in technical cooperation with the office of the High Commissioner for Human Rights and the UN Human Rights Commission. The story they would tell would be bad or worse, but far better than the image Pyongyang allows to grow and take hold in the West.

## North Korean Human Rights Act

The North Korean Human Rights Act of 2004 (H.R.4011, 108th Congress 2nd Session) was passed by the US Senate on 28 September 2004 and signed into law by President George W. Bush on 18 October 2004. According to the House resolution (23 March 2004), the Act is intended 'to promote human rights and freedom in the Democratic People's Republic of Korea and for other purposes'. This was a more elaborate version of the North Korean Freedom Act of 2003, which aimed to: make it easier for the United States to assist North Korean refugees by providing humanitarian assistance to North Koreans inside North Korea; provide grants to private, non-profit organisations to promote human rights, democracy, the rule of law and the development of a market economy; and increase the availability of information inside North Korea, and provide humanitarian or legal assistance to North Koreans who have fled the country. When early news of the North Korean Human Rights Act became public, a number of North Korean economic refugees attempted to seize the opportunity. In Laos a couple ended up in the US ambassador's garden. One later chose to leave. The act was not yet law and so the one who remained, after being put to the test – having to sing the songs of the Great Leader and being checked for absence of dental work – was bundled across the Thai border, given a South Korean passport and dispatched to Seoul.

According to a statement released by the White House on 21 October 2004, the 'Act provides useful new tools to address the deplorable human rights situation in North Korea by focusing efforts to help both those who flee the regime and those who are trapped inside the country.' The Act assigned a budget of $124 million a year and made North Koreans eligible for political asylum in the United States. Freedom

House, a Washington-based neo-con organisation (see above), scooped the funding pool. In May 2006 the US administration reported that it had granted six unnamed North Koreans refugee status.

The Act was seen for what it was by South Korean politicians, particularly by Seoul's ruling Uri Party. For them the Act was more concerned with regime change than human rights, and they believed it would increase tension in the region and damage relations between the two Koreas.

## EU talks about human rights

The EU's response to human rights concerns took a different form, promoting a positive and result-oriented approach through dialogue and cooperation. The historic visit by the EU Troika of May 2001 raised human rights, amongst other issues, directly with Kim Jong Il and he agreed to establish a formal human rights dialogue with the EU, a first for North Korea. The model was to be that of the EU–China Dialogue, in place since 1997.

The first round of talks took place between the EU and officials of the North's Ministry of Foreign Affairs in Brussels in June 2001. There was a frank and open exchange of views on the humanitarian situation in the North, cooperation between North Korea and human rights bodies, and the ratification and application in North Korea of the main human rights conventions. The ministry officials acknowledged the importance of human rights, but argued that they had their own standards and that their priority concerns were the right to subsistence, right to development, and equality. Claiming that universal human rights principles could only be applied taking into account the objective reality of individual nation states, they stressed that principles of equality, mutual respect, non-interference, impartiality, objectivity and non-conditionality should be the basis of future dialogue with the EU.

A second round of talks was held in June 2002. It resulted in the North Korean authorities giving a partial breakdown of figures of those held in 're-education camps' and making amendments to the Criminal Code to reflect international standards. The EU voiced its concerns at the lack of access by UN human rights rapporteurs and NGOs, as well as the absence of any official statistics on human rights issues. The EU reiterated the need for continued and expanded cooperation with the UN. The DPRK expressed uneasiness about visits by NGOs and UN rapporteurs due to previous 'bad' experiences. They claimed that foreign allegations were unjustified, were distorted for political purposes by hostile powers, and should be largely ignored.

Before a third round could be held, the process was derailed by a lack of joined-up thinking within the EU and the activities of US neo-con lobbyists. In 2003 France slid through the Council of Ministers a proposal to table and sponsor a resolution on human rights in North Korea at the UN Commission on Human Rights (UNCHR) meeting in Geneva, with no discussion of the consequences and without either informing the DPRK or discussing it with them. So a draft resolution was presented to the UNCHR expressing grave concerns about the precarious humanitarian situation in the country, noting reports of systemic, widespread and serious violation of human rights. South Korea abstained during the vote on 16 April but the resolution was adopted. The result was all too predictable. The North Koreans announced during the meeting with the EU in December 2003 that they were suspending dialogue. They expressed deep regret that the EU had sponsored the resolution, which had put those who advocated and participated in the dialogue in a very difficult position.

They would have accepted the EU voting for a resolution sponsored by someone else, but felt the EU had gone too far in acting as sponsor, making it an act of confrontation and an obstacle to further dialogue. The Europeans rather disingenuously claimed that the resolution should not be seen in such a light, but rather as an indication of areas where members of the international community believed that progress should and could be achieved. The EU also claimed that there is no fundamental contradiction between a bilateral engagement on human rights and the tabling of a resolution in Geneva.

The DPRK offered to lift the suspension if the EU did not sponsor a new resolution at the next UNCHR meeting. In April 2005, however, the EU did exactly that, this time sponsoring a second resolution jointly with Japan – a provocation in itself. In preparatory meetings, with US Heritage Foundation staff lurking on the fringes, proponents of the resolution used the Catch 22 argument that there must be a second resolution because there was no dialogue, conveniently forgetting that the reason for no dialogue was because of the first resolution. A clear example of the truth of Nietzsche's dictum: 'Madness is rare in individuals, but common in parties, groups and organisations.' The human rights dialogue between the EU and the DPRK remains suspended.

An assessment of the two rounds of dialogue that did take place shows the gap between the two. While North Korea at times seemed to accept international human rights norms and instruments as universal standards, they stressed that implementation must respect local circumstances and cultural differences. At other times, they displayed hardline positions on sovereignty/non-interference in internal affairs, arguing that international human rights standards, especially individual rights, are illegitimate, alien and subversive to the goals of state and party. Sovereignty must be respected and human rights should not be used to constrain other activities or for hostile political motives.

The DPRK dialogue was a part of the EU's broader commitment to promoting universal human rights and democratisation, and was therefore not specifically targeted at the North or intended as a political weapon to be used to 'strangle' the regime.[19] When European Parliament delegations have raised human rights issues at meetings in Pyongyang, initial reactions have been disarmed by passing around copies of the Parliament's two annual Human Rights Reports, the first on human rights in the EU and the second on human rights in the world. Nevertheless, in the light of events, it will take time for North Korea to put its trust back in the EU.

## Things can only get better

The European Parliament on a number of occasions has expressed its concern regarding reported large-scale human rights abuses and urged North Korea to improve its human rights record. The resolutions noted reports of serious violations of civil and political rights and the failure to respect economic, social and cultural rights.[20] They have urged the DPRK to ratify and comply with the convention against torture and other cruel, inhuman or degrading treatment and punishment, to implement the International Covenant on Economic, Social and Cultural Rights and the International Covenant on Civil and Political Rights, and to bring domestic legislation into line with the provisions of these treaties.

North Korea did ratify the International Covenant on Civil and Political Rights in September 1981, yet it has never allowed organisations regular access to monitor the situation. As a part of the Covenant, North Korea is under an obligation to submit reports on its implementation of international human rights standards. It did in 1984, but a second report due in 1987 was never delivered. When pressed for its submission in 1997 by the UN Sub-Commission on Human Rights, North Korea withdrew from the Covenant, the first and, so far, only nation to do so.

The report of the UN Human Rights Committee in July 2001 urged North Korea to improve its human rights condition and regretted that it had not volunteered significant information, particularly on the fate of the North Korean refugees repatriated by China. North Korea finally submitted a report in 2002, but its lack of substance undermined its credibility. The defensive line North Korea usually takes is 'arbitrarily assessing the human rights in other countries and imposing one's will on others is an infringement on their sovereignty and interference in their internal affairs.'[21]

The process of finding a way to restart a direct dialogue is key. Short-term knee-jerk actions which helped get the EU where it is now must give way to a more nuanced approach. The maintenance of credible, candid and sustainable dialogue is the most effective way to bring about tangible improvements in human rights, not regime change agendas masked as human rights resolutions. The promise to the European Parliament visiting delegation in June 2007 that the North might restart the Human Rights Dialogue with the EU is a small step in the right direction.

## Same country, two pictures

North Korean defectors emphasise the dark side of the country, and there certainly is one. Contemporary visitors report a different North Korea with increasing signs of change. The establishment of 'markets' in the emerging grassroots economy in North Korea has been widely featured.[22] Even the US delegations to North Korea in 2004 confessed they found considerable evidence that North Korea is committed to moving toward a market economy.[23] China and Vietnam's success in market reform and regime stability has provided the North with an alternative vision to that of the Soviet experience. As a result the system has been radically changed. With the state unable to deliver daily necessities sufficient for survival, this change seems irreversible. Now shops have goods on the shelves and the restaurants on Changgwang Street are open and serving. Commercial billboards in Pyongyang proudly advertise PyongHwa automobile company's cars produced in Nampo by this North–South Korean joint venture company. Things are moving. Colour is bleeding back into North Korea's cities.

East Asia is now one of the most vibrant parts of the world. China's impressive economic growth over the past three decades has brought about increasing liberalisation and decentralisation in its society, at the same time as 400 million Chinese have been lifted out of poverty. Its economic success is making it a world power. Taiwan, despite the stand-off with China, has made the transition to democracy. Indonesia, the world's fourth largest country and the largest Muslim state, finally consolidated its democratic transition in 2004 with its first-ever peaceful transition of power. After decades of totalitarian and authoritarian governments, economic success enabled South Korea to make the leap. Who would have imagined South Korea's former foreign minister (Ban Ki-moon) as the UN Secretary-General even a decade ago? All these prefigure the long march that North Korea has just begun.

# 6 WMD paranoia rules

## Introduction

North Korea has been cited alongside Islamic fundamentalism as a major threat to world peace. The US neo-cons, with the ear of Bush and Cheney, claim that North Korea is so dangerous that the United States has no alternative but to engineer regime change. Consequently, North Korea is labelled by President Bush a 'rogue state', 'outpost of tyranny' and a founding member of the 'axis of evil'. The security threat posed by the North with its nuclear weapons and missile programme is real, but woefully exaggerated.

The United States is responding by deploying, in conjunction with Japan, a theatre missile defence (TMD). Here the very name is a contradiction in terms. TMD is offensive. It gives the United States the ability to launch a pre-emptive strike against the North and defend South Korea, Japan and its bases in those two countries. In the meantime, the United States is pressing the North to abandon its military and civilian nuclear programmes and curtail missile research, development and demonstration. North Korea's response is that the 'hostile US policy toward the DPRK' is the reason for its decision to develop nuclear weapons and continue its missile programmes. So, who is a threat to whom?

## Team America

Since the end of the cold war, US film makers – and more worryingly, the US military-industrial complex – has been combing the globe for new enemies. *Deterrence* (1999) told of a second invasion of Kuwait by Iraq, followed by a nuclear showdown. In *Rules of Engagement* (2000), Americans met with a terrorist attack in Yemen. More recently *Team America: World Police* (2004) has Kim Jong Il meeting his match. The plot is simple and straightforward. A special operation unit of US Intelligence undertakes a mission to foil a series of terrorist attacks. They discover that the brain behind it is the North Korean leader, who has supplied Al Qaeda with weapons of mass destruction and is in fact choreographing the global war of terror. The United States' vigorous response is hampered by the 'bleeding heart liberals' of the Film Actors Guild (FAG), who protest that pre-emptive attacks on terrorist targets with massive civilian casualties are only creating thousands of new terrorist recruits. Kim Jong Il organises a World Peace Conference attended by all the world leaders, while planning to unleash a global wave of terrorist attacks at the culmination of the event. Team America tries to stop him, but its members are captured. The central character, a new recruit who left the team with a troubled conscience, re-enters the fray, and rescues his colleagues. Team America is saved. The world is saved, though Kim Jong Il escapes, leaving room for a sequel. The actors are puppets and the story line politically illiterate, but then so is the 'axis of evil' myth, the manufactured threat from the North and the deeply counterproductive response of the United States, which has done more to prevent than provide a resolution of the crisis on the peninsula. It is based on a combination of arrogance and ignorance.

## Military perception

That North Korea is a military regime on a semi-permanent war footing since the early 1960s should not be a surprise; it is still technically at war with the world's pre-eminent military power. The military is essential to North Korean society, and national defence has always taken a central role. The Korean People's Army, founded on 8 February 1948, is under the command of Kim Jong Il. It is the world's fifth largest army, with 1.2 million troops in uniform and 7 million in reserve, plus 100,000 Special Forces designed to operate behind enemy lines during wartime. In effect, with a population of 22.3 million, the military, including reserves, comprises the male population between 17 and 50.

But look through the other end of the telescope. North Korea is no match for the military might of the United States, with 2.26 million personnel (including reserves) and a budget of $441.6 billion (€331 billion), 3.7 per cent of its GDP. That is larger than the military budgets of the next 20 biggest spenders combined, none of which are 'rogue states'. The US military is also the most technically advanced, with multi-billion dollar research programmes maintaining its technological edge. North Korea's military budget may be 25 per cent of its GNP, but it is less than 0.4 per cent of that of the United States, Japan and South Korea combined. South Korea alone has a military budget four times larger than that of the North, with 686,000 highly trained military personnel reinforced by 68,000 US troops based in the South and Japan. Japan's image, engendered by its imposed Peace Constitution, belies reality. Japan spent $44 billion (€35 billion) in 2006 on its military. Further, Japan's Prime Minister Shinzo Abe established in January 2007, for the first time since the end of the Pacific War, a fully fledged Ministry of Defence to replace the Self Defence Agency and announced plans to massively augment the military budget in future years. North Korea's military would be a serious obstacle to any invasion from the South but its offensive threat is close to zero.

## WMD

After the collapse of the Soviet Union and its empire, Pyongyang became more insecure and paranoid. It had lost Moscow's protection. North Korea genuinely feels there is an external threat to its very existence. Its military planning, which had already shifted from invasion to hopeful scenarios of intervention during mass civil unrest in the South in the 1970s, moved on again to deterrence. From the mid-1990s the economy was in meltdown and the only viable exports were missiles and military technology. Pyongyang was and is in an overwhelmingly inferior position compared with potential aggressors. It has neither the resources to modernise and upgrade its conventional forces, nor any access, if it wanted, to sources of modern technology. It has made, in its own terms, the entirely rational choice to opt for the development of nuclear weapons and the creation of its own nuclear umbrella as a deterrent, with the knock-on benefit that this will allow the eventual release of hundreds of thousands of conscripts back into civil society to kick-start an emerging market economy.

Pyongyang has probably engaged in chemical and biological weapons research, but even that is not certain. If it has a programme, little is known about its capability or reliability. North Korea possesses the technological capacity to produce early-generation chemical and biological weapons. That does not need much more than a basic laboratory and a degree in chemistry or microbiology. The United States claims that North Korea maintains a significant arsenal of modern chemical and biological weapons, and has sufficient expertise, infrastructure and capability to produce and utilise such weapons in the event of a war. A CIA assessment from February 2002 stated:

> North Korea has acceded to the Biological and Toxic Weapons Convention [in 1987], but nonetheless has pursued biological warfare capabilities since the 1960s. Pyongyang's resources include a rudimentary (by Western standards) bio-technical infrastructure that could support the production of infectious biological warfare agents and toxins such as anthrax, cholera, and plague. North Korea is believed to possess a munitions-production infrastructure that would allow it to weaponize biological warfare agents and may have biological weapons available for use. ... Like its biological warfare effort, we believe North Korea has had a long-standing chemical warfare programme. North Korea's chemical warfare capabilities include the ability to produce bulk quantities of nerve, blister, choking, and blood agents, using sizable, although aging, chemical industry. We believe it possesses a sizeable stockpile of

these agents and weapons, which it could employ should there be renewed fighting on the Korean Peninsula.[1]

Unlike the United States, which China and North Korea claim tested its biological weapons on them during the Korean War, North Korea has never demonstrated its capability. All military planners like to test their technologies in the heat of battle. Despite numerous military assistance programmes to dozens of countries, and reports of North Korean troops directly participating in military campaigns around the world, there is not a single report of the deployment and use of biological or chemical weapons.

It is true that the North Koreans have not signed the Chemical Weapons Convention. There are claims that it has two chemical weapons factories, one in Kanggye and one in Sakchu. Dramatic reports of the use of political prisoners for testing chemical weapons were broadcasted in the BBC Documentary *Access to Evil* (2004), but later revelations that the allegations were a money-making scam have not received the same coverage.[2] Such weapons would only be a military threat if deployed during fighting on the Korean Peninsula. It is conceivable that they could be used as a threat to Japan's civil population, but it is difficult to imagine their use being authorised, as the retaliation would be totally disproportionate to any short-term advantage.

## Nukes

The only remotely serious threat would come from nuclear weapons and missiles. After the 2002 nuclear crisis was used by the United States to abrogate the Agreed Framework, the North announced it would produce plutonium-based weapons from its Russian-designed graphite-moderated reactor at Yongbyon. Pyongyang unfroze the plant at the end of that year and reprocessed the fuel rods, with an only partially successful underground test following in October 2006. North Korea continues to deny it has a parallel heavily enriched uranium (HEU) nuclear weapons programme.

Pyongyang has the capacity to launch intermediate-range ballistic missiles with a range encompassing all of South Korea and most of Japan. It is developing ICBMs which, depending on the payload, may have a range sufficient to strike the outer peripheries of the United States. The United States makes great play with the prospect of the North putting weapons and delivery systems together, or of its potential to sell either or both to any willing buyer. Its previous track record in sales – $3.5 billion worth of Hwasong and Rodong missiles to Iran, Pakistan, Syria and Libya – is used to prove the point. However, the difference is that any future sale to a terrorist group would inevitably be intended not as a deterrent but rather for immediate use against the United States, a rather different proposition that is enough to concentrate anybody's mind.

As recently as 2002, Charles Kartman, then Head of KEDO (Korean Peninsula Energy Development Organisation) said, 'the number of proven weapons is zero'. Yet a combination of ill will and bad faith, poor crisis management and incompetence by the United States has transformed that situation to one where the North has enough plutonium for half a dozen bombs and has become the world's ninth nuclear state after the United States, UK, France, China, Russia, Israel, India and Pakistan. While earlier US claims that Pakistan had conducted a nuclear weapons test for North Korea in May 1998 in the Kharan desert were the product of an over-active imagination, the October test demonstrated without doubt that North Korea had a nuclear device.[3]

How did this all happen? North Korea's nuclear programme had its origins back in July 1955, when a delegation from the North Korean Academy of Sciences attended a conference on nuclear energy in Moscow. The next year Pyongyang and Moscow signed an agreement allowing North Korean scientists to be sent for training at Dubai Nuclear Research Institute. In 1959 the North signed a second agreement on nuclear cooperation with Moscow and a first with Beijing. Following China's nuclear test in 1964 Kim asked Mao for the bomb. Presumably Moscow had already said no. Mao made it unanimous. The lessons of Kim's Korean War had been burnt deep.

Moscow gave a little. In the early 1960s Pyongyang had established a Nuclear Scientific Research Centre near the Kuryong River at Yongbyon, 100 kilometres northeast of the capital, and in 1965 Moscow sold Pyongyang an IRT-2MWe pool-type research reactor while Soviet scientists provided on-the-job and on-the-spot training to Koreans. At this stage there was no evidence the North was trying to produce nuclear weapons.

A decade on from the initial request, Kim again unsuccessfully requested Chinese assistance with a weapons programme as Seoul had started its own preliminary research. But it was not until the late 1970s that the North established its own programme. Its key figures had trained in Japan, the United States, Germany, the USSR and Pyongyang, while its leader was Lee Sung Ki, Kim's scientific advisor, and the inventor of Vinalon, a synthetic fibre made from coal which for several decades clothed many North Koreans.

In 1980 North Korean nuclear scientists, with Soviet help, started the construction of a 5MWe experimental graphite-moderated reactor in Yongbyon. It finally went critical in 1986. This reactor was capable of producing weapons-grade plutonium, and had from a North Korea perspective the enormous advantage of making the country self-sufficient as it neither required heavy water nor enriched uranium, which Pyongyang could not obtain easily. Instead it used natural uranium available from domestic mining. The North Koreans also constructed a fuel fabrication plant, a short-term spent fuel storage facility and a reprocessing facility to extract plutonium. After the collapse of the Soviet Union no fuel supplies were delivered for the IRT-2MWe reactor and it is only run intermittently to produce iodine-131 for thyroid cancer radiation therapy.

By the early 1990s Yongbyon was also the site for a 50MWe graphite-moderated reactor, while a 200MWe reactor was under construction at Taechon, 20 kilometres northwest of Yongbyon. Neither of the two ever became operational. Construction was frozen as part of the 1994 Agreed Framework. The Taechon site is currently derelict, while the 50MWe reactor, which at the time of the freeze was only twelve months from completion, has badly deteriorated in the interim.

Both the KGB and CIA believe the world came closer to a nuclear war in 1994 than at any time since the Cuban Missile Crisis of 1962. Both security services informed their governments that the North Koreans had up to five nuclear weapons, made from diverting plutonium from their reactor at Yongbyon. The KGB had speculated that they might have a nuclear weapon as early as 1990. Because the reactor was built with Soviet assistance, Moscow pressed Pyongyang to sign up to the Non-Proliferation Treaty (NPT) and submit to IAEA inspections. The North finally signed in 1992 and consequently allowed the IAEA to conduct on site inspections. Between May and November 1992, four rounds of ad hoc inspections took place. The inspections confirmed that the Yongbyon plant had a plutonium extraction facility, although the North Korean's authorities placed off limits two sites where the IAEA inspectors believed plutonium reprocessing might be taking place. Any inspections would have been able to verify whether significant amounts of plutonium had been diverted to establish a nuclear weapons programme.

International pressure grew on the DPRK to open up these sites for inspection, for which under the NPT it had no basis for refusing access. In March 1993 Pyongyang announced it was withdrawing from the NPT. It used as its get-out clause Article 10(1) of the treaty, specifying that a country can withdraw at three months notice if its 'supreme national interests are jeopardised'. Although clearly within its rights, North Korea was the first country to utilise the withdrawal clause. This triggered a major crisis in the United States and South Korea, with claims the withdrawal proved North Korea either had or was about to obtain nuclear weapons. In retrospect all it probably proved was that the North Koreans neither wanted to be caught cheating by diverting plutonium nor wanted the IAEA as surrogates for US intelligence crawling all over sensitive military sites.

Three months later, and the day before its withdrawal from NPT became operational, North Korea agreed to suspend the process in exchange for direct negotiation with the United States. Inspections resumed in March 1994 only to immediately run into yet more problems. Pyongyang wanted to unload fuel rods from the Yongbyon reactor without supervision, destroying in the process evidence of any earlier plutonium reprocessing. When the IAEA confirmed that spent fuel was being removed in May 1994 the crisis threatened to spiral out of control as the Clinton administration threatened military action. Plans for pre-emptive strikes on all the North's nuclear facilities were prepared and approved by President Clinton.[4] F-111 aircraft in Okinawa were fuelled and ready to fly. In response Pyongyang threatened to turn Seoul into 'a sea of fire'. The North's attempt to hide its efforts was an intelligent move. It was only the uncertainty about the completeness of the intelligence on the Chinese programme that had prevented the United States from authorising a pre-emptive military strike to prevent Mao from acquiring nuclear weapons in 1968.

A decade later, in January 2005, I interviewed one of the key US players, Bill Perry, Clinton's Secretary of Defence (1994–97) who confirmed pre-emptive strikes were planned and prepared, and who then said rather incredulously he 'now' believed that the North Koreans felt genuinely threatened by the United States – though apparently never realising that ten years earlier when the planes were warming up on the runways.

## Framing an agreement

The situation was rescued by the maverick intervention of former President Jimmy Carter, who was invited to Pyongyang at the height of the crisis. He met at length with Kim Il Sung and negotiated an unauthorised 'package deal' with the DPRK involving further direct US–DPRK talks and compensation. Announcing his deal publicly on CNN forced the Clinton administration's hand, despite serious reservations in some quarters.

Negotiations took place in Geneva from 23 September to 21 October and produced the Agreed Framework signed by both parties. This promised Pyongyang two proliferation-resistant 1000MWe light water reactors (LWRs) by 2003 in exchange for freezing their Yongbyon reactor and halting construction of their two new reactors at Yongbyon and Taechon. It is not impossible to produce weapons-grade nuclear material from LWRs, but it is several orders of magnitude more difficult than from graphite-moderated reactors and well beyond the North's technical knowledge and its resources.

In the interim, before the LWRs were completed North Korea would get 500,000 tonnes per annum of heavy fuel oil (HFO) to compensate for the shortfall in energy supply notionally caused by the loss of output from the mothballed reactors.[5] Actually, if they had gone on line the North's rudimentary and ageing electricity grid would almost certainly have been unable to cope. Washington promised to lift the almost half-century-long economic embargo imposed after the Korean War and normalise relations with the North. When the reactors were ready to come on line and not before, the North Koreans would permit the requested inspections to establish whether and how much plutonium had been diverted, and allow the spent fuel rods to be exported for permanent storage abroad. It seemed a perfect technological fix to a political crisis.

Whether the United States ever seriously intended to deliver on its promises seems unlikely. The Agreed Framework was signed in bad faith by the United States. For Washington it was just a way to buy time until North Korea collapsed. The US administration saw the regime inevitably following their fellow Communists from Central and Eastern Europe well before the delivery date for the LWRs. If it did not happen quite to timetable, construction could always be slowed on one pretext or another. Ambassador Robert Gallucci, Clinton's chief negotiator, certainly believed and worked on the assumption that the United States would never have to deliver. When asked privately about the difficulties of delivering the LWRs, Gallucci at the time assured questioners that they need not worry since the North was disintegrating. He was not alone in his thinking. Declassified documents from the National Security Archive, show a CIA panel of experts concluding in 1997 that North Korea was likely to collapse within five years.[6] Conveniently, South Korea would, on taking over subsequent to the North's collapse, find itself with the foundations for two nuclear reactors it could slot in later.

Unfortunately for the United States, North Korea was much more resilient than expected and it weathered the crises of the 1990s. North Korean 'communism' was not of the same brittle variety imposed by the Soviet empire on Central and Eastern Europe, a Communism that collapsed once Gorbachev's reforms in the Soviet Union removed the crutches that supported it. North Korea's ideological superstructure, in contrast, was deeply rooted in Korean history, experience and culture. Marxism-Leninism had mutated into a version of the Japanese emperor cult, with Kim Il Sung as philosopher-king. Unlike in Eastern Europe, there has been no internal surrender by the North Korean people. The United States failed to recognise the difference between the imposed regimes of the Soviet empire in Europe and the indigenous character and deep historical continuities of Kim's deeply heterodox communism.

Whatever the intention, the United States never delivered on 1994's promises. Economic sanctions against North Korea were never lifted. Coca-Cola did very publicly ship a container across the border at Sinuiju for the benefit of media. But a lorryload of Coca-Cola wasn't enough. Nor did the promised normalisation of relations take place. The KEDO project, which became the operational arm of the Agreed Framework tasked with building the two LWRs by 2003, proceeded at a snail's pace. The North Koreans complained of the slow pace of work and demanded compensation as early as April 2001.[7] The United States then threatened not to allow the delivery of key nuclear components until after the IAEA 'completed' its inspections, in contradiction to the initial agreement.

HFO was delivered fitfully. This was the only portion of the Agreed Framework to be paid for by the United States, small change compared with the billions of dollars South Korea and Japan were to pay for the construction of two LWRs. Almost before the ink was dry, however, the United States was offering Russia a share of the Korean and Japanese contracts for KEDO in exchange for abrogating its nuclear contracts with Iran. Whether Seoul and Tokyo knew, or were informed, is not known. When Clinton lost control of Congress in the 1995 mid-term elections, the new Republican majority blocked the funds for the HFO. By the end of 1997, the EU had joined the Executive Board of KEDO alongside the United States, Japan and Korea, partly to honour an earlier promise to provide political cover for the Japanese Socialist Prime Minister, Tomiichi Murayama (1994–96), who was trying to hold together a shaky coalition with the right wing Liberal Democratic Party (*Jiminto*).

With Korean and Japanese contributions ring-fenced for the nuclear project, the EU ended up picking up the HFO bills whenever US funds were delayed or unpaid. A member of the European Parliament's then Energy, Research and Technology Committee, I was at the time the committee's rapporteur for the Commission's proposal to join and fund KEDO. Members of the European Parliament do not often get phone calls from their prime minister's office. Yet on this occasion, I received a call from 10 Downing Street saying Clinton had asked Blair to ensure the EU signed up, enabling them to pay for HFO. My report endorsing EU membership went through the Committee and Parliament, and KEDO got its money. By then Japan's coalition had fallen apart, but the White House was happy. The legal basis for the Commission's request was limited to nuclear projects, so funding KEDO itself was no problem but payments for HFO were probably of dubious legality. But as it was in nobody's interest to ask the question, nobody did.

The United States was a serial discoverer of secret nuclear programmes in the North. In the late 1990s, satellite reconnaissance identified an underground chamber near the village of Kumchangri, which was immediately assumed to be an underground nuclear weapons facility. The United States demanded the right to inspect. After some months of argument, an assistance programme was traded for a US inspection in 1999. It was a political debacle. The suspected nuclear site turned out to be secure storage for use during wartime to prevent the destruction of holy artefacts, namely Kim Il Sung statues and other icons.

After they came to power in 2000, Bush's people were determined to find another North Korea secret nuclear weapons programme. In the October 2002 meeting between James Kelly, US Assistant Secretary of State for East Asian Pacific Affairs, and Kang Suk Ju, the North Korean First Vice-Minister for Foreign Affairs and someone known to be close to Kim Jong Il, Pyongyang was confronted with evidence that it had a uranium-based programme and enough plutonium for at least two nuclear weapons. According to the United States a furious Kang responded saying 'Your President called us a member of the Axis of Evil. ... Your troops are deployed on the Korean peninsula. ... Of course, we have a nuclear programme.'[8] This was taken as a confession of a secret HEU programme. The reality was more ambiguous. Kang's 'confession' was not on record, with neither tape nor transcript available. The North Koreans angrily retorted that the Vice-Minister had been misinterpreted and that what he really said was that North Korea had the right to a programme – not that it had one.[9] It was an interpreter's nightmare. There is a subtle but crucial difference between 'is entitled to have (*kajige tui-o-itta*)' and 'has come to have (*kajige tui-otta*)' even for Korean speakers. The US heard what they wanted to hear.

The immediate response from the United States was to suspend deliveries of HFO. Not that that was a great surprise to the North Koreans; their faith in the US commitment to the Agreed Framework had been fatally undermined earlier when the expected HFO deliveries failed to materialise in the coldest months of the year when the electricity supply in Pyongyang was going on and off like Christmas lights due to lack of fuel. This suspension was the final nail in the coffin. Promises of normalisation of relations, lifting of the embargo, two LWRs by 2003, and interim deliveries of HFO had finally dribbled away to nothing. North Korea had no alternative. It is not clear whether it had the components of a nuclear weapon before the end of 2002, but now it made a dash for the bomb. For North Korea believed the lesson from the US-led invasion of Iraq was that the problem was not having WMD rather than having them.

## Nukes II

A combination of cock-up and conspiracy by the Bush administration created a situation that destabilised northeast Asia and threatened a new arms-race and the prospects of war – accidental or deliberate? The North put the Yongbyon plant back on line and completed its withdrawal from the NPT in January 2003. Claiming again that its 'supreme national interests [were] jeopardised', Pyongyang had a point. Bush's new strategic doctrine of pre-emptive deterrence plus the 1994 plans for a pre-emptive attack on North Korea's nuclear facilities fitted the bill. The reopening of the plant enabled the North to reprocess the 8000 fuel rods and extract enough weapons-grade plutonium to produce five or six nuclear weapons, approximately 45Kg of plutonium, with the potential to produce a further 5Kg of plutonium per year.

The apparent indifference of the Bush administration led Pyongyang to organise a visit to Yongbyon by a private US delegation that included the nuclear scientist Dr Siegfried Hecker in January 2004. Hecker, the former Director of the Los Alamos National Laboratory, was shown what was claimed to be 200 grams of plutonium and an empty storage pool where spent fuel rods may have been stored. Giving a talk at the Asia Pacific Research Centre at Stanford University in 2005, Dr Hecker confessed that he had been able neither to verify the authenticity of the plutonium nor to determine whether all the fuel rods had been reprocessed. His impression was that North Korean scientists were keen to show they had the technical skills, facilities and capacity to undertake reprocessing and to produce weapons-grade plutonium. On 10 February 2005, North Korea declared it had now become a nuclear-weapons state. North Korea's Head of State, Kim Young Nam, went on record saying that its 'nuclear deterrent force' was purely for self-defence and that there would be 'no first use' of nuclear weapons.

The United States' creation and response to the crisis had shown the tactical skill of General Custer at Little Big Horn. It turned North Korea into a nuclear weapons power in barely two years. While North Korea denied it had a parallel highly enriched uranium (HEU) weapons programme, even if it did have, it would have been six to ten years, if ever, before enough HEU could have been produced to make a bomb. Worse, uranium weapons are heavier and more difficult to mount on missiles than plutonium. Thus North Korea has obtained nuclear weapons that serve its purposes better and more quickly than would have happened if HFO deliveries had continued. The cost was not a factor either. Even at current oil prices, 500,000 tonnes of HFO cost less than $200 million, six months' running costs for one US aircraft carrier.

North Korea had certainly acquired the blueprints for an HEU programme from the entrepreneurial efforts of Pakistan's nuclear scientist A. Q. Khan, who sold his secrets to Libya, Syria and Saudi Arabia, as well as North Korea (the only two states where he didn't hawk his nuclear secrets seem to have been India and Israel). Khan visited the North a total of 13 times. Pakistan almost certainly gave Pyongyang some – possibly up to 20 – first-generation high-speed centrifuges, warhead designs and weapons testing data from Pakistan's own nuclear tests in return for missiles and missile technology.[10]

Yet North Korea never even obtained the highly specialised materials required, let alone the components, nor does it have the quantity and quality of electricity (100–200MWe) for any serious HEU programme, which requires enough electricity to run a medium-sized city with a totally unvarying current. Not a feature of the North's normal electricity output where lights constantly flicker, if they don't go out. Any HEU facility would require a large plant capable of holding a minimum of 1000 centrifuges arranged as a cascade to produce enough fissile material for one to one-and-a-half bombs per annum, situated near a railway siding, with access roads and a major power station.

North Korea certainly attempted to obtain quantities of the special aluminium alloy necessary to construct some gas centrifuges but the cargo shipment of 214 aluminium tubes destined for North Korea was intercepted in Hamburg in April 2005.[11] But even if it had plans it was not necessarily for HEU. The North's experience of US backsliding provided good reasons in the late 1990s for them to seek a capability for uranium enrichment. The LWRs, unlike the Yongbyon plant, required enriched uranium to run, thus making the North dependent on imports of nuclear fuel. A capacity for enriching uranium to a sixth to a tenth of the level required for nuclear weapons, at around 93 per cent, would have provided an indigenous source of fuel to allow the North's reactors to continue to function if an embargo was placed on fuel imports. The decision to go ahead occurred when Pyongyang thought that the United States would be an unreliable long-term partner, but would at least deliver on the LWRs.

When Iraq was labelled as reviving its nuclear programme it was because it was trying to buy 60,000 aluminium tubes, while in Iran the Natanz project was to employ 50,000 centrifuges in a very large facility in order to produce several weapons a year. The United States failed to provide any hard evidence of North Korea's HEU programme, and should therefore have found the international community sceptical. Even voices in the US State Department became increasingly sceptical over time. In March 2007 the *New York Times* finally reported that the United States had downgraded the likelihood of a North Korean HEU programme from 'probable' to 'possible'. It had all the hallmarks of the Iraq intelligence fiasco over again. The Bush administration admitted they got it wrong. With the prospect that after the agreement at the six-party talks earlier in the month that North Korea would re-open its doors to international weapons inspectors, the US intelligence community faced the prospect that their assessments would once again be compared with what is actually found on the ground. Now talk is of a possible uranium enrichment operation.

The intelligence was based on ambiguous satellite photos and claims that the North Koreans brought and tried to buy thousands of non-specialised aluminium tubes in the early 2000s. As with Iraq those purchases were considered proof positive of plans for uranium enrichment. It turned out the tubes were unsuitable for purpose and were so harmless that they were not controlled by global export authorities and gave no indication of a nuclear programme.[12]

As we have seen above, North Korea carried out an underground nuclear test on 9 October 2006. The test was conducted in the mountains near Kimchaek City in northeastern North Hamgyong Province. The blast was equivalent to an earthquake registering 4.2 on the Richter scale, and radiation was detected subsequent to the test. It was a fizzle rather than a bang, yielding a blast equivalent to only 1000 tonnes of TNT, a quarter of that forecast to the Chinese when North Korea gave China a couple of hours notice of the test. The failure was caused by the nuclear explosion reaching criticality before the fission was optimally compressed, resulting in the plutonium assembly being driven apart before a significant portion has undergone fission. However, it showed that the North has the material and the technology to build a nuclear bomb. Already, as the Chinese put it, they have a nuclear device. There is the prospect that any future test would prove that the North has a full, even though unreliable, capability.

Any bomb produced after such a test would take a minimum of six to twelve months to produce, and would be too bulky to deliver by missile or aircraft; there would be a significant chance that it would not detonate. North Korea's did not even test properly, while a minimum number for testing and maintaining a deterrent would be seven deliverable bombs. Putting Pyongyang's nuclear power in context, the United States has 100,000 times more nuclear firepower in its Trident fleet alone than Pyongyang demonstrated with its October 2006 test. The United States has a total of 9300 nuclear weapons, with a single Bravo 83 weapon 1200 times more powerful than the North's total capability as demonstrated by its test.

When China tested its first unclear weapon with a 20-kilotonne blast in October 1964, President Johnson's response was:

> I was not concerned for the immediate future. A long and expensive road separated setting off a nuclear blast and developing the power and accurate missiles to carry nuclear weapons across seas and continents. Some future President would have to face the question of how to deal with this situation.

## Nuclear club

North Korea has just about joined the Nuclear Club, but claiming that this sets a dangerous precedent for the NPT misses the point. The bulk of global proliferation has come from one country, Pakistan, which, like India and Israel, refuses to sign the NPT. Pakistan has actively engaged in proliferation conducted by its nuclear establishment, which is riddled with Al Qaeda fellow travellers. As one US commentator put it: 'right now, the most dangerous country in the world is Pakistan. If we're incinerated next week, it will be because of HEU that was given to Al Qaeda by Pakistan.' Pakistan had a flourishing nuclear programme in the 1980s when it was working closely with the United States to undermine Afghanistan's Communist regime and its Soviet support troops. But by the mid 1990s, the United States' enthusiasm for Pakistan had cooled and the country was in deep financial trouble. To maintain the arms race with India, Pakistan continued to import North Korea's missile technology, with Pakistan and Khan trading nuclear know-how for missiles.

Even Pakistan itself has recognised plutonium's superiority to HEU. Initially it looked at plutonium but then threw everything into the HEU option. But recent satellite photos of Pakistan's Khushab nuclear site showed what appears to be a partially completed heavy-water reactor, which when completed would be capable of producing enough plutonium for 40–50 nuclear weapons a year, giving Pakistan the ability to produce plutonium-based bombs that are lighter and simpler to mount on missiles than its 30–50 current warheads. This development is likely to trigger a new nuclear arms race in Southeast Asia.

Nor is the connection made between the West's collusion with Israel's nuclear weapons programme and the drive by Iran, a competing regional power, to emulate it. It is only a nuclear North Korea that threatens world peace, not a nuclear Pakistan, India or Israel – a nuclear power since 1966. The United States has insisted on sanctions against North Korea since its missile and nuclear weapons test in 2006, yet it has now lifted all financial and other sanctions imposed on India and Pakistan following their nuclear weapons tests in 1998. The Bush administration even signed a cooperation deal with India legitimising its nuclear weapons programme. For the United States some proliferations are more acceptable than others. After all, back in the 1960s the United States pondered whether to encourage Indian nuclear proliferation as a counter weight to the 'Chicoms' (Chinese Communists) bomb.

## Missiles' reality

The other two security issues are the North's missile programme and its general arms sales. Yet neither is illegitimate or particularly extensive. Development of North Korea's ballistic missile technology owes a debt to both the former Soviet Union and China. In the early 1960s, North Korea relied on technology transfers from the USSR. Moscow supplied surface-to-air missiles and unguided artillery rockets, along with engine and guidance designs. North Korea obtained Soviet Scud-B missiles in the 1970s and again between 1985 and 1988, from which it produced the reverse-engineered Hwasong-5 and Hwasong-6. China also assisted North Korea's early missile development efforts with the transfer of surface-to-air missiles and anti-ship cruise missiles. A joint Chinese–North Korean programme was initiated in 1975 (East Wind 61) to develop a mobile ballistic missile with a range of 600 kilometres. The programme was cancelled in 1978, but provided North Korean engineers with training in missile development, engine design and production processes.

North Korea subsequently refined these Soviet and Chinese designs with Soviet missile technology bought – illicitly in some cases – from Egypt, Iran, Libya, Pakistan and Syria. It is said that a number of Soviet Scud-B missiles were re-exported to the North from Egypt between 1976 and 1981, and North Korea entered into a joint programme with Egypt to develop ballistic missiles after the collapse of the Soviet Union. The involvement of Russian mercenary missile experts in North Korea's programme, after the collapse of the Soviet Union, has proved invaluable.

North Korea now has several hundred Hwasong missiles that are capable of hitting South Korea, Rodong medium-range missiles (up to 1500 kilometres) carrying a payload of 700kg and capable of striking most of Japan, and the unproven Taepodong missiles that are theoretically capable of hitting the fringe of the United States. No other 'rogue state' has such an indigenous capacity. Iran's Shehab missiles are based on incremental improvements to North Korea's Rodong. Interestingly, in November 2004 US intelligence reported Iran was trying to modify them to be capable of carrying a nuclear warhead, implying that they currently lacked the ability to do so. Pakistan's Ghauri is a copy of Rodong, and the promised Ghaznavi is a clone of Taepodong-1. Both countries are still dependent on North Korea for technology and expertise. Syria is standing pat with the earlier Hwasong-6 which, with a range of 500 kilometres, has all the range it needs in its standoff with Israel. Libya's Al-Fatah missiles contain elements of Rodong technology.

Yet reliability and capacity are not impressive. Both Iran and the United Arab Emirates, who purchased the North's missiles, were disappointed by the unreliability of the Hwason-5. During the second phase of the Iran–Iraq War, the 'War of the Cities' in 1988, Iran fired 77 of these missiles, with 10–15 per cent exploding on launch. Despite its reported range of 1500 kilometres, Rodong managed a mere 500 kilometres when it was launched in May 1993, while an Iranian test in 1998 saw the missile self-destruct after 1000 kilometres. The same year saw an apparently successful Pakistan test in April with no indication of achieved range. Late in his regime Saddam Hussein unsuccessfully tried to purchase missiles from the North.

It was the Taepodong series that created the 2006 crisis, with the United States claims that it has a range of 6200 kilometres in its two-stage variant, sufficient to strike Hawaii and Alaska, and all of the United States in a three-stage variant. In practice the situation is rather different. There have been two Taepodong launches to date. The first was the attempt to put the satellite *Kwangmyongsong* into orbit on a three-stage Taepodong platform on 31 August 1998. Its trajectory went over Japan but the third stage failed to ignite, scattering debris across the Pacific. Citing email correspondence from an unidentified staff member of the Senate Defence Appropriations Subcommittee at the time, Gordon Chang claims in *Nuclear Showdown* that debris was found in Alaska. The failed satellite launch illustrated that Pyongyang was further along with its missile development than Washington and Tokyo had suspected. It proved a perfect opportunity to tint the threat from Pyongyang in even darker colours.

## Born on the fourth of July

The second long-range missile test was provocatively timed for 4 July 2006, American Independence Day (5 July, Korean time), when the North fired seven missiles, including a Taepodong-2 which crashed into the Sea of Japan after only 43 seconds. With the first test falling 8000 kilometres short of Washington and the second 11000 kilometres, it was hardly an impressive show of technological progress. Even if Taepodong had worked perfectly, its payload would be barely capable of carrying the 59 volumes of the *Complete Works of Kim Il Sung* to the US mainland, let alone a nuclear weapon. The simultaneous Rodong and Hwasong tests were more successful. Testing six short and intermediate-range missiles, the real core of North Korea's missile capacity, allowed the military to assess current capabilities. With increasing sales resistance due to growing concerns about reliability, it may well be that in financial and technological terms these were the more important tests. In August 1998 potential buyers observed Taepodong's launch. Whether the same was true on 4 July is not known.

At the end of Clinton's second term, the administration came very close to a deal to buy out the entire medium and long-range missile programme but the US defence industry, which wanted an excuse to deploy Star Wars technologies, and robust neo-cons, who wanted a US empire enforcing regime change, ultimately choked off any agreement. An added bonus of North Korea's continuing nuclear and missile programme is that it threatens to sabotage Chinese economic development; Beijing will have to switch resources from the civilian sector, where it is attempting to cope with the crisis in the countryside, into the defence sector as it is forced into a new arms race. The absence of a missile deal means North Korea continues to deploy and export its missiles, and maintains its R&D.

The bottom line is that, as with its HEU programme, North Korea's capabilities are overstated, misreported and constantly rounded up to transform possibilities into probabilities and probabilities into inevitabilities. The Taepodong series of missiles and space launch vehicles the United States estimates, when finally developed, will have a range of 10,000 kilometres and be capable of hitting Washington (*sic* – actually 11,000 kilometres from North Korea) with a 1000kg warhead. One British minister, as early as 2004, justified the UK's support for the US hardline position on North Korea by claiming Pyongyang would have the capacity to hit the UK with its missiles within 18 months

While North Korea does produce, deploy and export missiles with a range of between 300 and 1500km, getting a missile to travel nearly 9000km would require a significantly more powerful booster rocket than was used in Taepodong-2. In addition, the missile would require an onboard computer to calculate its trajectory, as well as other electronic circuitry to improve targeting accuracy. The North needs to develop a warhead that is not only light and small enough to fit within the space and payload available, but strong enough to withstand atmosphere re-entry. North Korea could in theory obtain some of these technologies by modifying commercially available devices. Currently Rodong does have enough accuracy to target Japanese cities in coastal areas near the Sea of Japan, but Pyongyang does not have the necessary high-tech electronic parts or precision-guidance technology to make the Taepodong-2 capable of credible targeting. It is incapable of a pinpoint attack and any launch would be not much more than a 'hail Mary' suicidal lob into the West. Any scenario that had Pyongyang picking out the UK after bypassing the United States and Japan has to be fantasy land.

### Star Wars

The supposed threat of North Korea's missiles, married with its nuclear weapons potential, conveniently serves to justify the deployment of theatre missile defence (TMD) and terminal high-altitude missile defence (THAAD) by the United States and Japan as part of the wider US National Missile Defense (NMD) system.[13] Since the 1998 satellite launch, North Korea has been presented by Japan's Conservative politicians as a major threat to the country's security. Japan is rapidly enlarging its 'defence' capabilities and has engaged in joint research with the United States on TMD. The public is being dragged unwillingly into a series of programmes to defend against the supposed missile threat, with Aegis cruisers at sea, AWACS in the air, Patriot surface-to-air missiles and THAAD on land. While Patriot has a proven track record in Gulf War I, and Japan already has 24 operational missile launch pads near urban centres and airbases, THAAD technology is unproven, untested and designed for US rather than Japanese needs.

The real threat to Japan is not Taepodong but Rodong, which has been around since its first deployment in 1993. However, talking up North Korea's missile capacity and capability serves the purposes of Japanese neo-cons, who desperately need a credible threat to justify writing out from the 1947 US-imposed Constitution Article 9 which limits the role of Japanese armed forces to self-defence.

The missile threat provides the United States with a justification for continued spending of tens of billions of dollars on NMD. Once in place TMD and THADD will allow a pre-emptive strike against a nuclear North Korea with a limited number of nuclear-tipped missiles. If any North Korean missiles not destroyed in the initial attack were launched, they could be intercepted before striking Japan and its US bases. The 1998 North Korean launch missed mainland United States by thousands of kilometres and cost a few hundred million dollars. In response, the United States plans to spend 200 times as much – nearly ten times North Korea's annual GNP – without any guarantee of security. The Bush administration came into office armed with a determination driven by economics and ideology to push ahead with NMD, in the face of opposition from around the world. The idea originating with the Reagan presidency was, with the Heritage Foundation's High Frontier programme, a technologically appealing one of erecting over the United States an impenetrable umbrella of anti-ballistic missiles that would give the United States immunity from ICBMs tipped with nuclear warheads from the Soviet Union. This has now been transformed to defend against a threat from the world's current list of rogue states – Syria, Iran and North Korea – that none are capable of exercising. While the Soviets had around 1500 ICBMs, the grand total for all three 'rogue states' combined is zero. Equally, the proposed missile shield in Poland is supposedly aimed at Iran, not Russia.

NMD is the answer to a problem that no longer exists. With the collapse of the Soviet threat, Britain, France, Russia and China are the only countries capable of firing ICBMs at the United States. For Star Wars/NMD to have any justification, the United States needs an enemy that is a state entity. It is just all too difficult to justify deploying against the Taliban, Al Qaeda and their fellow travellers, whose weapons of choice are the terrorist bomb and the suicide attack.

The simple idea is more complex in practice as test after test fails, while the tills of the US military-industrial complex continue to ring merrily. During the Presidential election in 2000 both Bush, enthusiastically, and Gore, less enthusiastically, supported developing NMD technologies prior to a final decision to deploy. It would cost a minimum of $40 billion and possibly up to $100 billion, and would provide 'cost plus' profits for the defence industry – explaining why the US presidential elections cost billions and why the US defence industry showers funds on both Democrats and Republicans alike.

Meanwhile, those sounding the warnings about the technological absurdity of Star Wars were being silenced. When the Republicans took control of Congress, they immediately abolished the highly respected Office of Technology Assessment (OTA), which produced independent evaluations of complex scientific and technological issues for Congress. The OTA had offended neo-con Republicans by publishing some of the most damning and authoritative indictments of the technology behind Star Wars since its inception in the early 1980s. Simultaneously the White House silenced any 'in house' critical evaluations by forbidding government scientists from serving on outside expert panels without permission, stressing that when they do they must always represent government policy rather than their own opinions.[14]

The claim that there is uncontrolled proliferation either of weapons of mass destruction or the vehicles for their delivery has an absurd element to it. NMD makes little strategic sense and its arguments do not hold up to close inspection. It is by no means certain that the North Koreans plan to use ICBMs for delivery of nuclear warheads. That is neither the only nor the best way. When did the North Koreans sign an agreement to deliver nuclear weapons, or for that matter biological and chemical weapons, by ICBM? Even if subsequently Pyongyang favours missiles, initially, North Korea's military nuclear development seems to have been directed towards free-fall airdrop weapons, rather than warheads. Now that TMD systems are deployed in Japan, with THAAD following, Pyongyang would anyway re-evaluate its options.

North Korea's missiles have neither the size nor the payload to deliver nuclear weapons even if Pakistan's foreign minister claimed, in a self-serving comment that argued Pakistan's help had not really been necessary, that they are further along the road to nuclear miniaturisation than suspected. The Hwasong is too small to carry a nuclear weapon and the Rodong would struggle to cope with early-design plutonium weapons let alone the heavier and larger HEU weapons. Ballistic warheads would require a design sophistication they currently lack. Until its missile technology shows significant progress, the North is scarcely capable of delivering nuclear warheads to Japan let alone further afield. Even if it had the technology to do so, launching a strike would be foolish in the extreme. The best option would be to use either decoy aircraft creeping under NMD's umbrella or unconventional means such as a cargo ship flying a false flag. Or they might even try DHL from the facility in the Koryo Hotel in Pyongyang.

Ballistic missiles have an indelible return address and a guarantee that state actors are centrally involved. Missile launches and their point of origin are impossible for US satellites to miss; therefore swift and terminal retaliation is inevitable. The scenario of the North Koreans firing a couple of hopeful ICBMs in the direction of the United States, using missiles that have proved to have neither the range, reliability nor payload capacity to carry the required distance, tipped with untested warheads based on a single nuclear test that was only partially successful, followed by North Korea being wiped off the face of the earth by the US response, seems to stretch extrapolation beyond any sane limit. The North's claim that it is a deterrent rather than a pre-emptive threat makes a whole lot more sense. Perhaps less convincing is the North's commitment to 'no first use' in response to any military action on the peninsula.

Bush rejected the Clinton approach to NMD, which aspired to hit the speeding missiles in flight, in favour of striking during the launch-phase. The new emphasis was on boost phase technologies when, immediately after launch, the missiles are accelerating up out of the atmosphere before they can deploy multiple independent targetable re-entry vehicles (MIRV). This is technologically simpler, but inherently prone to costly and maybe fatal mistakes since there is only a matter of minutes in which to make the right call and act accordingly. A trigger-happy Pentagon would have had four or five minutes, at most, to decide whether the launch of Taepodong in August 1998 was a pre-emptive strike or an attempted satellite launch on a trajectory over Japan dictated by geophysics that had an electronic and visual signature identical to that of an ICBM. Taking out the satellite – for that is what it was – would have precipitated the very conflict NMD was intended to prevent.

Security in northeast Asia is worsened, not strengthened, by NMD and the reinforcement of the US–Japan Defence Guidelines. NMD deployment turns a less than plausible threat into a real one, possibility into probability. It virtually forces North Korea to behave badly. With the United States deploying for a pre-emptive strike, it is impossible for a paranoid North to accept that US intentions are benign.

Japanese deployment of TMD and especially THAAD neutralises China's ICBMs and triggers a regional arms race. China, as mentioned above, judges that North Korea is being used as a scape-goat to justify Sky Wars developments. These will impel China to shift funding from civilian to military projects, shifting tens of billions of euros to develop and deploy hundreds of new ICBMs to give them a capacity to swamp NMD and to restore the *status quo ante*. Beijing currently has only around 20 ICBMs, but would have to increase that number up to 200 in the belief that Japan and the United

States see TMD simultaneously as both a deterrent against China and an offensive deployment against North Korea. In addition, developing MIRVs to enable strikes against multiple targets from single launches virtually neutralises all but launch-stage NMD technologies. Multiple warheads, mixed with decoys that deploy separately once the missile is outside the atmosphere, complicate re-entry defence by an order of magnitude and more, far beyond any defence currently available or projected. Threatened by this escalation from China, the domino effect of China and North Korea would mean that they would be joined in short order by Taiwan, South Korea and Japan as new nuclear powers.

NMD neither defends against a 'rogue state' that is other than idiotic in its military planning, nor against Russia nor – when it adds new banks of ICBMs – China. If that is the United States' intention then it is the twenty-first-century equivalent of the Maginot Line in France. The only purpose it serves well is offensive.

Deployment of TMD in Poland and Japan, ostensibly to defend against Iran and North Korea, will in fact simultaneously provide a preemptive counterforce capability against Russia and China. The United States has steadily improved its 'counterforce' capabilities – those nuclear weapons most effective at targeting an enemy's nuclear arsenal. Keir Lieber and Daryl Press in the July/August issue of the *Atlantic* magazine explain that as China currently has 18 ICBM silos, one Trident submarine with its highly accurate missiles would have a 97 per cent chance of destroying every single silo in a pre-emptive strike. The US keeps at least two of these submarines on 'hard alert' in the Pacific at all time, meaning they are ready to fire within 15 minutes of a launch order. What this might mean for North Korea, Iran, China and Russia, along with US plans for pre-emptive deterrence, is self-evident. It can only encourage military adventurism in the White House.

**Comrades-in-arms**

The notion that Pyongyang makes a substantial contribution to the world's arms market is equally exaggerated. Although its customers are those *persona non grata* in Europe and the United States, overall North Korean arms sales are a minute fraction of the global arms market. Its annual sales are less than 0.4 per cent of those of the United States and bring in less money than those renowned military powers Australia, Canada and Sweden. Yet the only rationale behind the supposed security threat posed by North Korea is its readiness to export arms to any willing buyer. North Korea's arms sales do contribute to acerbating civil and regional conflicts, as well as assisting authoritarian governments to maintain their control over their populations. But in the context of the international arms market, North Korea is a minor irritant, not a global threat. The North's arms exports began in the 1960s as a part of assistance in the form of military equipment, training and local advisors to national liberation movements throughout the third world. The full extent of North Korea's involvement is hard to estimate, but lack of resources limited assistance to comparatively low-cost training and advice programmes. According to the US Library of Congress Country Report, by 1990, North Korea had provided military assistance and training to groups in 62 countries – 25 in Africa, 19 in Central and South America, 9 in Asia, 7 in the Middle East and 2 in Europe – training more than 5000 foreign personnel back in the North and dispatching over 7000 military advisers, primarily from the Reconnaissance Bureau, to 47 countries.[15]

In Africa, during the 1970s, support and some modest quantities of military equipment were provided to Polisario in the Western Sahara for its fight to end Moroccan occupation, as well as to governments or revolutionary groups operating in Angola, Benin, Burkina Faso, Congo, Ethiopia, Ghana, Madagascar, Mozambique, the Seychelles, Tanzania, Uganda, Zambia, and Zimbabwe. In the 1980s, North Korea equipped and trained the Zimbabwean army's Fifth Brigade for counterinsurgency and internal security duties. Pyongyang provided almost all the equipment and about $18 million worth of small arms and ammunition. The result was not entirely successful. By 1986 the Zimbabwean government had the unit retrained by British military instructors. North Korea provided Malta with an unspecified amount of arms plus military training for its forces in 1982. Officially a generous gesture to strengthen DPRK–Malta friendship and solidarity in the 'common struggle against imperialism', this was simply a donation to a country whose GDP per capita was higher than its own as a *quid pro quo* for Kim Jong Il's year-long residence on the island to learn about the West.

In South America and Central America, North Korea provided similar assistance to anti-government groups operating in Argentina, Bolivia, Brazil, Chile, Guatemala, Mexico, Nicaragua, Paraguay, Peru and Venezuela during the 1970s. Documents seized during the US invasion of Grenada in 1983 revealed plans for Pyongyang to provide small arms, two patrol boats and ammunition. The North provided Nicaragua's Sandinista government with patrol boats and other unconfirmed assistance. Yet money talked louder than politics, and by April 1986 North Korea was selling small arms to the Peruvian government to help put down the previous recipients of its aid, the Maoist insurgents Sendero Luminoso.

North Koreans are suspected of being involved in military operations in the Middle East. There are reports that North Korean pilots flew Egyptian aircraft during the Yom Kippur war of October 1973, and as many as 100 North Korean pilots and aircrew were in Libya training pilots on Soviet-supplied aircraft from 1979. North Korean support to the Palestine Liberation Organisation (PLO) began in the late 1970s and continued until the early 1990s.

By the early 1990s North Korea was capable of supplying a much wider range of weapons. Although support of leftist revolutionary movements remained a significant component of military assistance, the political dimension was superseded – as in the case of Peru – by the need for hard currency. Military sales expanded to include missiles, tanks and armoured vehicles, self-propelled and towed heavy field artillery, and naval vessels. North Korean weapons technology is far from state of the art, but has the two advantages of cheapness and availability to those with no alternative source of supply. Although North Korea's missile programmes are definitely second rate, it has been exporting missile technology to the world's less fashionable regimes for decades. For instance, $3.5 billion worth of Hwasong and Rodong missiles were delivered to Iran, Pakistan, Syria, Libya, the United Arab Emirates and Yemen – though none to Iraq. The recent rapprochement between Libya and the West has put Libya back at the top of the target list for Western arms dealers, so Pyongyang has lost one market.

North Korea's development and sales of missiles were all perfectly legal even after the 1994 Agreed Framework, for it included no provisions regarding missile testing, deployment or sales. Pyongyang never signed any agreement restricting its missile programme or the export of missiles. Nor was it against international law. In December 2002, a joint US–Spanish operation in the Indian Ocean intercepted a North Korean ship, the *So San*, carrying Rodong missiles to Yemen; however, the United States was forced to allow the ship to continue its voyage when the Yemenis demanded delivery of the goods they had bought and paid for. At the time, there was no provision prohibiting the ship or the cargo. This, however, changed after the North Korean missile test of July 2006. The UN Security Resolution of 15 July 2006 interdicted future missile sales from the North and legitimised future stop and search operations to intercept missile deliveries. The resolution prohibited UN member states from trading with North Korea on missile-related goods and technology. The prospect was for a future incident along the lines of the Cuban Missile Crisis, with a North Korean ship sailing towards US, Australian or Japanese vessels intent on interception and inspection, with a pregnant pause to see who blinked first. Whether recent developments will allow Pyongyang to recommence its arms sales is unclear. Might is right and the North may learn to live with rules that do not apply elsewhere.

## Security perception or reality

The question of what is fair or logical seems irrelevant. Why is nuclear development in some countries – Iran and North Korea – a threat to world peace while the equal dangers posed by Israel and Pakistan to the Arab world or India are elided by the US administration? The priority for North Korea is regime survival, which suits South Korea and China. It certainly suits the million that would die in a new war on the peninsula or the hundreds of thousands that would probably perish in any economic collapse. The North wants a negotiated solution. The US neo-cons want regime change. A pragmatic regime faces a dangerously ideological counterpart. A few are confused about which is which. Compensating North Koreans in the short-term for abandoning their only flourishing export trade in missile technology and their nuclear programme is no different, in principle, from the United States paying the Taliban $40 million in June 2001 for limiting opium production. It's just a mite more expensive. Providing, at the same time, assistance to establish new export industries based on the North's mineral wealth as a substitute for weapons exports makes good sense. The EU and China should supply the political impetus to overcome the US opposition, while South Korea, in its own best interests, and Japan as a part of the settlement of the legacy of the Second World War, could provide the bulk of the financial resources required.

# 7 Negotiating its place

## Introduction

Generations of diplomats and military officials have been trapped in endless negotiations with Pyongyang. Even former allies now claim that they never really understood their partner.[1] This lack of understanding stems not only from the Communist–capitalist divide and the cultural chasm between Asia and the West, but also from failing to recognise North Korea's obsession with sovereignty independence and autarky.

Globalisation and the end of the cold war have seen a new world order with the emergence of new networks, alliances and trading blocks. The fall of the Soviet Union and the rise of a new China owing more to the market than Marx ended Pyongyang's traditional relationship with these two allies. Inter-Korean relations after the arrival of Kim Dae Jung and the 'Sunshine Policy' provided some breathing space for the North, yet heightened tensions with Japan and the United States threatened the very survival of the regime. At the same time, the emergence of the EU as a global player provided an opportunity for the North to redefine its relationship with the West. Pyongyang is struggling to understand the dynamics of multilateral politics and to find a niche in the New World Order. The status quo is not an option. It has no alternative but to break the chains that lock it to the past, the product of itself, its friends and its enemies.

## Traditional allies

The fall of the Berlin Wall in 1989 and the subsequent collapse of the Soviet empire in Eastern Europe effectively marked the victory of the West in the cold war, with only mopping up operations left to do. Gorbachev's attempted reforms merely exposed 70 years of mismanagement and the reality that the Soviet economy had been forced by the arms race to live a lie, devoting disproportionate resources to the military at the expense of the civilian, with the consequent impact on standards of living and morale. The 1988 Olympic Games in Seoul showcased South Korea's economic success to the world. The Soviet Union and China both established trade partnerships with Seoul, and South Korea's bilateral trade doubled with China and tripled with the Soviet Union between 1987 and 1989. The Soviet Union announced the establishment of full diplomatic relations with the Republic of Korea on 30 September 1990.

Further developments worsened Pyongyang's woes. China followed the Soviet example and established diplomatic relations in August 1992. Yet the shock of this betrayal was nothing compared with the impact of the disintegration of the Soviet Union and the collapse of empire.

The Soviet Union crumbled and fell in 1991. The old Soviet system was abandoned and an attempt was made to transform the political, economic and social systems into 'Western' style democratic capitalism. It didn't work. Instead crony capitalism emerged, and Russia's economy got worse before it got better. In the early 1990s the first Russian President, Boris Yeltsin, wrote off North Korea in favour of the South. The economic consequences were dire. China and the Soviet Union had historically competed to buy influence by providing oil and other goods at 'friendship' prices. With the fall of the Soviet Union, it became a seller's market. Trade between Russia and the North effectively stopped, going from $3 billion (€2.6 billion) in 1989 to $40 million (€30 million) in 1999 – barely 1 per cent of the earlier figure – as hard currency replaced shoddy goods as the means of exchange. Losing generously subsidised imports of food and energy as well as captive markets for increasingly poor-quality counter traded goods left the North economically marooned. In addition to oil deliveries that ceased in the absence of hard currency, the deal that Konstantin Chernenko had made with Kim Il Sung in the mid-1980s to provide four nuclear reactors was cancelled. China followed Russia's line. For the first time since Mao's victory, China began demanding payment in hard cash.

Russia was no longer a superpower and was neither politically inclined nor economically able to prop up the North. This situation was exacerbated by the United States diplomatically sidelining Russia to the point where it played no part in the resolution of the 1994 nuclear crisis. That was ironic, considering the reactors which were the source of the crisis had been supplied by the Soviet Union. Russia was further marginalised when the United States ignored Moscow's proposals in 1997 for multilateral talks and instead proceeded with four-party talks with the two Koreas, and China. Russia's eventual response was to try to rebuild its bilateral relations. President Vladimir Putin went to Pyongyang in 2000, and Kim Jong Il made a return visit to Moscow in July 2001. Relations between the two warmed, with the prospect of mutually beneficial projects like a railway linking South Korea to Europe via the North and Russia. The Russian approach paid off. In 2003 Russia was invited to participate in the six-party talks. It may have been helped by the Russians agreeing to install in their Pyongyang embassy Krypton-85 detection equipment from the CIA to detect North Korean nuclear activity. Nothing was found. But the Koreans, always suspicious, believe it may explain the UK's eagerness to open an embassy in Pyongyang.

As Russia fell, China rose. Annual growth rates of 9 per cent plus for 30 years in succession have transformed China into today's global economic and financial power that for the first time is now flexing its political muscles. Chinese industry now threatens to kill off in short order what remains of the European textile, footwear and plastics industries. As for the United States, Wal-Mart does more trade with China than does the United Kingdom. Estimates have the United States losing, by 2014, 14 million jobs to China with its low-wage skilled labour. Financially the Chinese have bought so many US bonds that the United States now owes more than it owns. Presently China is choosing to let its peasants carry the US middle class on their backs, leaving the United States exposed to a financial crisis at a time of China's choosing.

The world cannot cope with 1.3 billion Chinese with US levels of energy consumption, but how can it, morally or physically, prevent China buying Iranian oil or Zimbabwean nickel and chrome to help lift 300 million of its people out of poverty when consumers in the United States spend more on pet food than these people earn? China's military is on the move, even without the EU lifting the arms embargo. China's January 2007 destruction by ground-based missile of one of its own satellites was a telling riposte to Washington's abandonment of the Anti-Ballistic Missile Treaty to pursue Star Wars. China is an emerging player demanding a new economic and political order. China's leap into the global political pond is making waves.

China's policy towards the two Koreas has become more balanced over time. The issue of refugees and asylum seekers shows Beijing torn between its anxiety not to endanger its relationship with either, while concerned about its own image in the run-up to the 2008 Olympic Games. China does not want to see Pyongyang collapse, not because it cares deeply about the current regime but because any collapse threatens military adventurism by the North, millions of refugees and ultimately US troops directly across the Yalu/Amnok river. Military conflict on the peninsula would trigger a global economic crisis that would devastate China's growing economy. Regional stability in northeast Asia is essential to China if it is to maintain the flow of foreign direct investment and the continued economic growth to enable it to meet its 2020 goal of $3000 (€2250) GDP per capita.

China is desperate not to let North Korea and Kim Jong Il threaten its long-term interests. Without a comprehensive solution to the crisis the knock-on effects will force China into an arms race with Japan and the United States. Such an arms race would inevitably threaten continued economic and social development. However, China has had plans to intervene in place for at least five years, which will be dealt with more fully in Chapter 8.

Sufficient to say here China wants peace and stability. But that requires two things at minimum – a solution to the nuclear crisis and major systemic reform in the North. The Chinese authorities have taken the horse to water. General Secretary Jiang Zemin visited Pyongyang in September 2001. After the 2002 crisis both the Vice-Minister for Foreign Affairs, Dai Bingguo, and the Chairman of the National People's Congress, Wu Banguo, met Kim Jong Il and succeeded in convincing Pyongyang to participate in the proposed six-party talks, joined by the United States, South Korea, Japan and Russia. At the same time they did all they could to reinforce his reformist tendencies. Kim took the train from Pyongyang to Beijing in May 2000, January 2001, April 2004 and January 2006. He should have bought a season ticket.

During his 2001 visit, Kim undertook a 'study tour' to Shanghai and Fudong, which are showcases of the success of China's own reforms. He was impressed and the response was instant in the *Rodong Sinmun*: 'China has achieved a unique socialist development with social unity and stability under the leadership of the Communist Party, and as a result, the status of China is continuously elevating in the international stage.'[2] The same month *Rodong Sinmun* began a regular feature highlighting the achievements of Chinese reforms, a significant move for a newspaper conspicuous for previously only mentioning economic reform in the context of state collapse in Eastern Europe. Kim returned to the same region in January 2006, and as mentioned earlier in March sent a 30-strong fact finding mission, led by his brother-in-law and potential successor, Jang Song Taek, to Wuhan, Guangzhou and Shenzhen, the heart of China's economic powerhouse.

North Korea's slow pace of reform and its limited success outside agriculture still worry the Chinese leadership. Recognising that external economic inputs are vital and that direct economic assistance from South Korea – while welcome – is inadequate and not entirely reliable, while other potential sources of funding such as 'compensation' from Japan will not be available until the current crisis is settled, Vice-Minister Wu Yi signed a multi-billion dollar trade deal in Pyongyang in 2005. This was reaffirmed with President Hu Jintao's visit later in the year.

### Inter-Korea relations

The South Korean engagement with the North experienced a step change when Kim Dae Jung, running for the fourth time, won the South Korean presidential election in 1997. With the 'Sunshine Policy' the new administration abandoned previous hard-line positions on national reunification.

After his narrow and almost certainly fraudulent defeat in the 1992 Presidential Election, Kim Dae Jung took a sabbatical from the daily grind of South Korea's political infighting. He went to Cambridge University to study the lessons of German unification for Korea. His research gave him serious pause for thought. West Germany had found East Germany a huge mouthful to swallow, to the extent it threatened its economic stability. Bonn had failed to fully appreciate exactly how dire the East's economy was: the standard of living in the East, estimated to be 40 per cent of that of West Germany, turned out to be much lower. The industrial infrastructure was virtually scrap, with the industrial landscape littered with factories so out of date and uncompetitive that modernisation and rehabilitation was more expensive than levelling the sites and starting again.

The situation on the peninsula was worse. The comparative sizes of the two parts presented even greater disadvantages to the South, more than West Germany had faced. The standard of living in North Korea was less than a tenth of the South's, with no industrial infrastructure worth saving. When the South Korean economy belatedly took off, the North's failed to follow. North Korea never made the transition from heavy to light industry. Consequently, the cost of reunification had over time spiralled exponentially upwards, to a point where it threatened to bankrupt South Korea. Future fusion would have put South Korea's fragile democracy under enormous strain, with millions of destitute refugees heading south to look for family and future. Kim was forced to look again at the whole drive for unification that had obsessed the political class in the South. 'How', became 'how not'. Now the need was to stop a 'shotgun' marriage of the North and South triggered by a Northern collapse.

Kim Dae Jung took unification off the agenda. The 'Sunshine Policy' replaced it with 'one nation, two countries, two systems'. North Korea, for which Korean unity was almost a *raison d'etre*, was initially deeply resentful and suspicious. After decades of flirting, playing hard to get while desperately wanting to get married, it was an enormous shock to find the intended had suddenly chosen celibacy. The 'Policy' was presented by the North as a subversive new approach, designed to make the North economically dependent so as to facilitate later absorption. However, when Kim Dae Jung's lobbying in Washington for an easing of sanctions led to that policy being recommended in the October 1999 Perry policy paper, Pyongyang was impressed and despite itself began to warm to the 'Sunshine Policy'.[3] To prove its commitment to improving inter-Korean relations, North Korea announced in September 1999, just before the Perry report was officially released, that it was suspending missile testing. Then came the 'bombshell' of a North–South summit in Pyongyang.

On 15 June 2000, Kim Jong Il greeted Kim Dae Jung on the tarmac of Pyongyang airport. The image of the two leaders hugging each other went around the globe and transformed perceptions of the North in Seoul. The summit appeared a resounding success, with a five-point joint declaration in which the two leaders acknowledged common ground in their approach to unification, pledging to work 'independently', to 'promptly resolve humanitarian issues', to 'consolidate mutual trust by promoting balanced development of the national economy'. All these were to be delivered through 'dialogue between relevant authorities' and a return visit to Seoul by Kim Jong Il 'at an appropriate time'.

The June Declaration produced results: by March 2004, there had been 13 rounds of inter-Korean ministerial talks, a meeting of defence ministers, numerous economic talks, six rounds of talks on the reunion of separated families; and an agreement that led to athletes from North and South entering Sydney's Olympic Stadium during the opening ceremony as a single team with a single flag. Despite its domestic critics, Kim Dae Jung's 'Sunshine Policy' gave a momentum to reconciliation, cooperation and exchanges between South and North.[4]

Yet after the initial burst of enthusiasm, inter-Korean cooperation stumbled on sharply different interpretations of the June Declaration. For the North, the South's commitment to work 'independently' meant the removal of US troops, a view not shared in Seoul. Inter-Korean relations from 2001 were also affected by regime change in the United States, with Bush replacing Clinton and a six-month hiatus in policy formulation followed by the new administration's harder line. The events of 9/11 further toughened the US attitude to the North, with intelligence twisted and spun to promote a new nuclear crisis. All this left the 'Sunshine Policy' out in the cold. The result was the opening up of differences between Washington and Seoul, with the ROK taking an increasingly independent line from that of Washington, backed by a previously suppressed anti-Americanism amongst the Southern public that was finally able to speak its name. It carried over into domestic politics with the shock victory of the former dissident lawyer Roh Moo Hyun in 2003, succeeding Kim Dae Jung and continuing his policies with regard to the North, but re-labelled 'peace and prosperity'.

The radical generational shift in the Roh government, made up as it was of those active in the opposition to the authoritarian governments of the 1980s, pushed the rapprochement with the North even further, forcing further re-evaluations of the South's relationship with the United States and Japan. Despite the nuclear crisis, inter-Korean exchange and cooperation accelerated. Inter-Korean travel and trade soared, with economic and cultural cooperation and exchange expanding massively. Regular governmental working-level meetings have led to progress on inter-Korean projects such as construction of the Kaesong industrial complex (an area the size of Manhattan), reconnection of rail and roads, promotion of Mt Kumgang Tourism, and the building of a reunion centre for separated families. Government and NGO humanitarian aid consists largely of food aid (rice, corn, wheat, flour and dried milk), support for agricultural rehabilitation (fertiliser, seeds and pesticide) and medicine. The South is making its contribution to ensuring regime survival.

Pressure from the United States has stopped neither the donation of large quantities of food aid with few or no strings attached, nor the offer in June 2005 of 2000 megawatts of electricity to the North, equivalent to the abandoned KEDO LWR programme, as compensation for halting its nuclear programme. The Kaesong industrial complex is moving on to its second phase with a joint North–South Korean office opened there. Hyundai is moving to develop Mt Paektu Tourism, while separated families are re-united by video conferencing.

The pain of the Korean War, ideological conflict and mutual hostility are all fading in the face of rising 'One-Korea' nationalism. A survey by the conservative *Chosun Daily News* in 2004 revealed the United States was perceived as a greater threat than Kim Jong Il. Asked which country most threatens Korea's security, 39 per cent named the United States and only 33 per cent the North. The difference was greater still for the younger generation. Among people in their 20s, it was a 58–20 split.

In South Korean schools, in a sharp contrast to the past, textbooks now paint the North as the good guys and the United States the bad. The half-century-long US–ROK alliance is under threat. These attitudinal changes in South Korean society are reflected in Seoul's cinemas and bookshops. Films are pouring out, to box office acclaim, endorsing 'One Korea' nationalism, anti-Americanism and anti-Japanese sentiments. *Heaven's Soldiers* (2005) has North and South Korea signing a pact to jointly construct nuclear warheads, but the plan is leaked, leading to a tense stand-off with the United States. A combined unit of North and South Korean soldiers disobey the order to destroy the warheads and try to prevent their seizure. In the process they are transported back in time to 1597 when the Choson Dynasty was under attack from Japan. The new arrivals join Korea's defenders, fighting in the Imjin War's naval battles, bringing victory. *Heaven's Soldiers*, marketed as a sci-fi comic-thriller, contains 'one Korea' nationalism as strong as anything in the North's ideological play-books. Kim Chin Myung's novel, *The Rose of Sharon has Blossomed* (1993), had a similar theme, and became the South's best selling book ever, with 4.5 million copies sold.

## Sleeping with the enemy

North Korea's relations with Japan and the United States have fluctu-
ated between deep freeze and mild thaw since the 1990s. After the
collapse of Communism, North Korea had very pragmatic motives for
an attempted rapprochement with Japan – money. Japan had paid
'compensation' for its occupation when it normalised relations with
the South in the 1960s. A similar normalisation with the North was
worth as much as €10 billion at contemporary prices, equivalent to
€5000 for every man, women and child.

The first crack in the ice appeared when in March 1989 Japanese
Prime Minister Noburu Takeshita apologised in the Diet, expressing
'deep remorse' for the excesses of Japan's colonial rule on the Korean
Peninsula, and called for the North to open talks. A delegation of
Japanese Diet members representing both the ruling party, Jiminto,
and the main opposition Japan Socialist Party – later Japan Social
Democratic Party – visited Pyongyang six months later in September
1990, leading to eight rounds of talks on normalisation between
January 1991 and November 1992. Pyongyang proved greedy,
demanding additional compensation for the post-colonial period, a
claim too far for Japan. Talks broke down, officially over the allegation
that a Japanese woman had been abducted and forced to train terrorists, but the real deal breaker was that the United States – opposed to
any possible rapprochement – had the CIA inform Tokyo of
Pyongyang's nuclear ambitions. All further initiatives have met with
sabotage. A series of incidents – some real, some imaginary – have
allowed Japanese conservatives to prevent a rapprochement that does
not suit their political agenda.

In August 1998, North Korea launched over Japan a three-stage
rocket, with the *Kwangmyongsong* satellite on board, which crashed in
the Pacific when the third stage failed to ignite. In Pyongyang the
authorities claimed *Kwangmyongsong* had been successfully placed in
orbit, circling the globe every 165 minutes broadcasting 'The Song of
General Kim Il Sung' and 'The Song of General Kim Jong Il'. Tokyo's
Self Defence Agency (since January 2007 Ministry of Defence) claimed
this was a ballistic missile test. At a technical level, the argument was
irrelevant, but at a political one it was rather different. Whether satellite or missile, the incident served as a clear demonstration of the
North's potential capacity to launch and deliver warheads over long
distances. Subsequently the Japanese authorities misled the media, the
press whipped up the public, and the aftermath halted the prepara-
tions for a re-opening of normalisation talks agreed the year before. In
truth, *Kwangmyongsong* with its *Taepodong* platform was an irrelevance
for Japanese security. North Korea has long deployed around 100

Rodong missiles with ranges capable of reaching almost any part of Japan. *Taepodong* was designed to impress Washington not Tokyo, and in the event of a conflict it would certainly not be wasted on intermediate range targets in Japan.

Dialogue did resume, after an eight-year hiatus, in April 2000 but was suspended in December 2001 when Japanese coastguards chased a North Korean spy ship out of its territorial waters, sank the boat and captured the crew. Japan, at great expense, recovered the vessel in September 2002 and put weapons and espionage equipment on display. In March 2003 the Japan Coastguard, through the public prosecutors office, charged the ten crew members with attempted murder and other counts. While one cannot defend North Korea's clear breach of international law, the incursions were all too common and were normally ignored by the Japanese. The choice was made at the highest levels of government to create an incident that would again block prospects of better relations.

Even without these convenient incidents, 'normalisation talks' would have had two major obstacles to surmount. One is North Korea's harbouring of terrorists. On 31 March 1970, nine members of the Red Army faction of the Japanese Communist League, an armed terrorist group founded by Fusako Shigenobu hijacked a Japanese Airliner carrying 129 passengers and crew. They ordered the pilot to fly to Pyongyang. The journey became a peregrination. First they flew to Fukuoka, where some of the hostages were released, then to Seoul, where the South Korean authorities had fooled the hijackers by flying North Korean flags around Kimpo Airport. Here, the remaining hostages were freed. Finally, the hijackers flew to Pyongyang, where plane and crew were released. The hijackers were granted political asylum. They have remained in the North for the last 37 years, with Pyongyang refusing to return them to Japan. However the North would be only too delighted to see them return voluntarily and this is being gently encouraged by regular family visits.

In Japan the sensitivity is such that a planned visit to Pyongyang by the Socialist International's (SI) Asia-Pacific Committee led by the then leader of the Japanese Social Democratic Party, Takako Doi, was cancelled because on the return leg from Pyongyang to Beijing, she would have had to travel on the same flight as the mother of one of the hijackers. Seven years on the SI visit has still not taken place. Behind-the-scenes attempts by Pyongyang to obtain an informal commitment that should the hijackers return any prison sentences meted out would be comparatively lenient have been rebuffed. This was not an insensitive request. After all the hijacking resulted in no deaths and their return would remove one obstacle to normalisation of relations with Japan and simultaneously strip away the United States' last excuse for keeping the North on its terror state list. The refusal is perhaps not surprising, showing a Japan that can say no, when it suits its purpose.

The most important issue that impedes progress is Japan's insistence on placing centre stage the issue of Japanese abductees. Japan's longstanding claim, dating back to the breaking off of bilateral talks in 1992, is that the North had kidnapped a number of Japanese citizens and used them to teach Japanese language and culture to the Korean Special Forces. In May 1997 the Japanese police registered seven cases involving ten Japanese nationals, dating from 1977 and 1978. Since then the numbers have kept creeping up. The abductions were orchestrated through the infamous Operations Department of the Central Committee of the KWP in charge of South Korean Affairs. For more than a decade North Korea denied the allegations. Back in Japan it became an emotive public issue. From the late 1990s it was top of Japan's agenda, and Japan's diplomatic activity has ensured it is on everybody else's agenda as well.

After the spy-ship incident died down, Japan–North Korea relations seemed to be back on track when in September 2002 Prime Minister Junichiro Koizumi announced he would have a summit meeting in Pyongyang. At the summit Kim Jong Il, to everyone's surprise, acknowledged the abductions and apologised that 'rogue' North Korean intelligence agents had abducted 13 Japanese nationals in the 1970s and 1980s.[5] Koizumi was immediately taken to an adjacent room where he found five of the abductees. All five travelled to Japan after the summit, officially for a short visit although none subsequently returned to the North; the pressure to stay was enormous.

The revelation was badly prepared and was mishandled by both sides. What should have been a triumph for Kim and Koizumi turned into a PR disaster. Kim's confession proved counter productive. It did not satisfy Japanese public opinion whipped up by the media. Nor did it provide closure. There were just too many unanswered questions about the fate of the eight abductees who remained unaccounted for. According to Pyongyang two had died in separate accidents on the same day, and several bodies had been 'washed away' in floods. Since then things have gone from bad to worse. The North returned the remains of the most famous abductee, Megumi Yokota, but DNA analysis failed to verify her identity. In Japan there has been a ratchetting up of the number of claimed abductees which has grown from the initial ten, first to dozens and then towards a hundred, with conservative factions of *Jiminto* quoting up to 80 abductees. As of March 2007, Tokyo's official number has climbed from 16 to 18; this includes the five already released, leaving twelve outstanding cases.

The only positive outcome, although this was more the resolution of a Japan–US problem than a Japan–North Korea one, has been that the husband and children of one of the abductees, Hitomi Soga, have been allowed to join her in Japan. Charles Robert Jenkins, the husband, was a US military deserter who fled to the North in 1965. He met Hitomi in North Korea, married her in 1980 and they had two children. His reunion with his wife was delayed by an arrest warrant for him issued by US military authorities. He eventually travelled to Japan via Jakarta with his children. In Tokyo, he was court-martialled and sentenced to a symbolic 30 days in the stockade before being dishonourably discharged.

The abduction issue was a key aspect of Prime Minister Abe's European tour in January 2007, with Japanese Cultural and Information Centres attached to embassies previewing *Abduction – the Megumi Yokota Story* in cooperation with the American film distributor Safari Media to invited politicians. How the Japanese government expects to find a solution is difficult to understand, with constantly moving goal posts and with the public 'loss of face' for Kim Jong Il that their very public campaigning will inevitable cause. The tactics of public confrontation are most likely to prevent a solution, rather than find one.

While the US–South Korea relationship is increasingly problematic, the Japan–US relationship is growing closer again. For a period, emerging Japanese nationalism meant an increasingly independent line. That has changed, with the two now like 'lips and teeth', as the Chinese used to say of their relations with Pyongyang. The new generation of Japanese politicians is far more self-assertive than their predecessors who experienced Japan's defeat and US occupation. Since the early 1990s the demand for a 'normal' Japan has grown in political circles. Ryutaro Hashimoto's (Prime Minister of Japan 1996–98) *Vision of Japan: A Realistic Direction for the 21st Century* (1994) talked of a 'normal' Japan, while opposition leader Ichiro Ozawa's *Blueprint for a New Japan* (1994) positively screamed the same thing. Prime Minister Koizumi was wish made flesh, aggressive, nationalistic and outspoken. He was no US lackey, but rather the new self-confident voice of Japan that had come to shared conclusions independently. This identity of views with the United States coupled with a rising Japanese assertiveness has put increasing strains on bilateral relations with China and South Korea.

Tokyo is therefore as hawkish regarding Pyongyang as Washington. In some senses more so. Regional fears of a new Japanese militarism have been revived as Japan's ruling party, *Jiminto*, now under the control of conservative factions, attempts a revision of Japan's US-imposed Constitution that would remove Article 9 prohibiting the external use of force by Japan. Tokyo finds North Korea a convenient justification of the abandonment of pacifism for remilitarisation and the long-term possiblity of developing nuclear weapons. Koizumi's gratuitous incitement of the victims of Japan's imperial ambitions, with his serial visits to the Yasukuni Shrine during his time in office, reveals the new nationalist face of Japan. His visit in August 2006 was particularly provocative as it followed the publication of the diaries of a former head of the Imperial Household Agency that revealed that Emperor Hirohito, who had last visited the shrine in 1975, refused to visit it again after the shrine added to its role of honour in 1978 the 14 Class A war criminals from the Second World War.[6] Whether Prime Minister Shinzo Abe, who believes that the Tokyo War Crimes Tribunal of the Far East was victor's justice, will visit Yasukuni is unclear, but he has gone out of his way to donate to the shrine. His political orientation is, if anything, to the right of Koizumi, and factions sharing his thinking have firmer control of the *Jiminto* than ever before.

Other causes of rising tensions with China and the two Koreas are the revision of textbooks to write out of history Japanese atrocities like the Nanking Massacre and the activities of Japan's biological and chemical warfare Unit 731 based in Harbin, plus Japan's territorial disputes with South Korea and China. The North pours fuel on the fire with stamps series picturing the disputed Tokdo Island and an article in *Democratic People's Republic of Korea,* its glossy English language monthly, explaining that the last time Japan claimed and occupied Tokdo in 1910, it was the prelude to Japan's occupation of the whole country in 1910.[7] It looks unlikely that relations will improve in the absence of a comprehensive settlement.

## Broken promises

The first opening of US–North Korean relations came in the late 1980s when the Reagan administration eased trade restrictions and encouraged people-to-people exchanges. They feared an isolated North Korea abandoned by its traditional partners would be more dangerous than one engaged with the international community. North Korea asked for bilateral talks and the first US–DPRK meeting took place on 5 December 1988. During the five years that followed, the two sides met 34 times. North Korea's agenda focused on US troop withdrawals and the need for a peace treaty, while the United States pushed for progress in inter-Korean relations, the North's nuclear programme and its missile exports as well as disavowing the use of terrorism. The talks were upgraded to the under-secretary level in January 1992. The thaw did not last long.

Clinton, elected in November 1992, was immediately faced with a North Korean nuclear crisis mimicking the Cuban Missile Crisis of the 1960s, which escalated to a point where military confrontation seemed inevitable and imminent. It was at the point of conflict when Jimmy Carter's renegade intervention allowed both sides to climb down, and negotiate a solution. The 1994 Agreed Framework led to visits of high-level officials, bilateral negotiations on missiles and the prospect of a visit by Clinton to Pyongyang.[8] North Korea froze its civil nuclear programme in exchange for two proliferation-resistant light water reactors (LWRs) to be constructed by 2003, and 500,000 tonnes per annum of HFO to compensate for the notional loss of energy supply between the freezing of the North's facilities and the LWRs going on line. The Agreed Framework committed the United States to abandon its half-century-long trade embargo and normalise diplomatic relations.

Momentum slowed as incompatible agendas bedevilled the talks. The United States proposed that South Korea should join the negotiations, and in April 1996 President Clinton and ROK President Kim Young Sam formally proposed four-party talks to include both Koreas, the United States and China. The North reluctantly accepted in exchange for a shift in focus to deal with the food crisis that was beginning to devastate the country. Talks were constantly hampered by external events: the 1996 DPRK submarine incursion into South Korean waters; the US NRO's discovery from satellite photos of an underground chamber at Kumchangri, which the United States claimed was a nuclear weapons factory in 1997; and the launch of *Kwangmyongsong* over Japan in August 1998.

Clinton's engagement was given a new impetus in 1999 with a report by William Perry, a former US Defence Secretary. Perry visited Pyongyang in May and convinced Kim Jong Il of the United States' willingness to find a negotiated solution to its concerns on missile development and sales. Initial discussions were positive, with Pyongyang willing to end not only missile exports but its missile development programme in exchange for financial compensation. A first step saw the DPRK suspend missile tests in return for a promise extracted by Kim Dae Jung to lift US sanctions under the Trading with the Enemy Act. Things were moving. Vice-Marshal Jo Myong Rok, the North's number two, visited Washington, where he was received by Clinton in the Oval Office. In the joint communiqué of 12 October 1999, Jo and Secretary of State Madeleine Albright declared: 'North Korea and the United States would no longer have hostile intent towards each other.'

To pave the way for a presidential visit, Albright was sent to Pyongyang to meet with Kim Jong Il and see if a deal was on the table. Time ran out. In the end, there was no meeting between Clinton and Kim Jong Il and no missile deal. With Florida's hanging chads dooming the Democrats, the North lost its enthusiasm. With no guarantee that any last minute deal would be honoured by an incoming Bush administration, Pyongyang was unprepared to gift much to Clinton's legacy. Clinton, torn between pushing yet another peace plan for the Middle East or North Korea, chose the former in an unsuccessful late run for a Nobel Peace Prize nomination. In retrospect, it was a serious mistake. Both problems remained unsolved, and with North Korea left to Bush's and Cheney's tender mercies all the slow painful progress was jettisoned.

North Korean policy came under immediate review. The Perry Report went out of the window. The Agreed Framework was to follow. The Republicans in Congress had fought Clinton all the way on implementation, blocking funding of HFO year on year. A sign of the way the wind was blowing was Bush's 'rogue state' remark in February 2001 only days after his inauguration. When South Korean President Kim Dae Jung suggested resuming talks with the North, Bush expressed deep scepticism of Kim's 'Sunshine Policy'. In June Bush did offer talks with the North, but whether the offer was serious was never put to the test. Events conspired against them. US foreign policy priorities were completely transformed by 9/11 and North Korea was blown off the agenda. By January 2002 President Bush's speechwriter, David Frum, in search of a 'killer phrase', confirmed Bush's first thoughts as Iraq, Iran and North Korea became the 'Axis of Evil' in his State of the Union Address. The comment united North and South. The North was outraged, while the South felt betrayed by a US president whose search for a telling sound bite had put the peninsula at risk.

The United States played hardball. When in September 2002 Japan–North Korea relations seemed to be on the verge of a breakthrough with the Kim Jong Il–Koizumi summit in Pyongyang, the Bush administration deliberately sabotaged the rapprochement by triggering a new nuclear crisis, claiming in October that the North had a secret weapons programme based on highly enriched uranium (HEU).[9] This was part of a pattern. Similarly, when during the visit to Pyongyang in 2001 by Swedish Prime Minister and President in Office of the European Council Göran Persson, Javier Solana, High Official for Foreign Common Security Policy, and Chris Patten, European Commissioner for External Affairs, were to meet with Kim Jong Il, the CIA informed the Japanese authorities that Kim's son, Kim Jong Nam, was travelling to Tokyo on a Dominican Republic passport. The Japanese, then in one of their more accommodating phases, detained Kim, who was heading for the dubious pleasures of Tokyo Disneyland accompanied by his four year-old son and two women. He was held incommunicado until after the EU troika had departed and was then expelled. Any premature announcement would almost certainly have led to the cancellation of the EU visit. One consequence was that the following year France refused to grant Kim Jong Nam a visa to travel to Paris.

At this point, the construction of the LWRs was running late, very late. All the North Koreans had for their efforts were two large holes in the ground and several thousand tons of concrete. The United States had neither normalised relations nor lifted the embargo. Worse, the United States strong-armed its KEDO partners into first suspending shipments of HFO and then killing KEDO. The North was thus left empty-handed: no LWRs, no HFO, no lifting of the embargo, no normalisation of relations and their Yongbyon plant frozen. With no viable alternative the North re-opened Yongbyon and started the clock ticking again for withdrawal from the NPT. Within weeks it began reprocessing the fuel rods and within months had enough plutonium for five to six nuclear weapons, a situation it would not have achieved for a minimum of three or four years even if it had had a fully functioning HEU programme. The United States' short-sighted reaction transformed tomorrow's crisis into today's. Yet for some neo-cons, like the American Enterprise Institute's Nick Eberstadt, who believes the military option is the only way forward, and the sooner the better, it was a perfect result. It was almost perfect amalgam of cock up and conspiracy.

## KEDO

The construction of two proliferation-resistant LWRs by 2003, promised as part of the exchange for the nuclear freeze, was to be under the auspices of the Korean Peninsula Energy Development Organisation (KEDO). The North Koreans would have been their own worst enemies, save for the United States. The KEDO project, the heart of the Agreed Framework, was subject to a seemingly endless series of political, financial and administrative hold-ups and delays that opened a yawning financial credibility gap almost before the project started. The North wanted no truck with the South's nuclear industry and held up progress until a suitable comprise was achieved, one that was as much about terminology as technology. Then Japan put the political brakes on for the first time after the failed *Kwangmyongsong* satellite launch in August 1998; that led to the suspension of work and put the project back twelve months. The Japanese were furious, yet formally Pyongyang was perfectly in order. The Agreed Framework says 'no dubious nuclear power stations', not 'no dubious rocket launches' and the North needed to sell rockets for rice. The North Koreans contributed to the ill feeling with disputes over the desecration of pictures of Kim Il Sung by irreverent South Koreans on the Kumho site – where the two plants were to be constructed – and the pitiful wages paid to North Korean contract workers. As a result the North withdrew all but 100 workers from the site – delaying construction until KEDO replaced them with Uzbekis at close to the wage levels the North Koreans had demanded for their own workers.

The US, having brokered the initial deal, expected someone else to pick up the hefty tab. The very nature of complex high technology projects means they overrun and costs escalate. Nevertheless KEDO was in a class of its own. Delays doubled the total costs from the initial $4.6 billion (€3.4 billion). That turned the financial gap into a chasm, widening by the day with delay. The South Koreans had little option and took up 70 per cent of the burden while the Japanese agreed to pay a fixed $1 billion (€0.75 billion). It was a cheap price to pay for conflict prevention in the region. Geographical proximity to North Korea and the presence of US troops both in South Korea and in Japan meant that in the event of conflict with the United States they would both inevitably be targets. The initial funding gap of $380 million (€284 million) was to be filled by contributions from the EU and others. The EU was invited to join the KEDO Executive Board and contributed $123 million (€93 million) through Euratom (the European Atomic Energy Community). The rest of a motley crew of contributors ranged from Argentina to Uzbekistan, chipping in anything from $14 million (€10.5 million) (Australia) to $10,000 (€7,500) (Hungary).

The grand total of all contributions between 1995 and 2006 was $2.5 billion (€1.8 billion). Neither a Bush administration nor a Republican Congress were going to dig into their pockets for North Korea. In fact

Jacques Santer, former President of the European Commission, at the KEDO site

they were headed in exactly the opposite direction. The North Koreans proved a convenient scapegoat to justify NMD. The White House wanted to renegotiate the whole agreement – a proposal that understandably found no favour in Pyongyang. In retrospect, KEDO died in October 2002; it just wasn't buried until 2007.

Three months before the LWRs were supposed to come on stream, with North Korean demands for compensation growing louder, and just after the Japan–North Korea summit, the United States conveniently 'discovered' in October 2002 that the North had an illicit HEU nuclear weapons programme. US negotiator James Kelly reported that North Korean First Vice-Minister for Foreign Affairs Kang Suk Ju had admitted that it had a second nuclear weapons programme during a meeting in Pyongyang. This was immediately claimed as a clear breach by the North of the 1994 Agreed Framework.

When James Kelly, Assistant Secretary of State for East Asian Pacific Affairs, met and confronted Pyongyang in October 2002, he was given an explicit brief by US hardliners that left no room for manoeuvre, and was minded by the State Department's senior adviser David Asher, who was against even talking to the North. Asher's job was to wreck the agreement. He did it exceptionally well. Immediately the United States took the position of 'no negations without the programme's abandonment', before anyone even confirmed it existed. A second nuclear crisis ensued.

First the United States fixed the KEDO Executive Board. South Korean President Kim Dae Jung, at the end of his term and with his party's candidate for president, Roh, lagging badly in the polls, had little option but to support the suspension of HFO deliveries that had so far cost \$380 million (€285 million) and the KEDO project itself. Then Japan, after a visit from senior Bush administration officials, joined the 'consensus'. The Europeans were on their own in resisting precipitate action. The EU's reluctance led to a one-month delay, before it was pressured in the interests of solidarity to fall in line with the other three Board Members. The HFO deliveries stopped at the end of 2002. The construction of the LWRs was initially suspended. At that point the project was officially a third complete,[10] although this was mainly hardcore rather than hardware, with no key nuclear components delivered (with only a third completed in eight years the project would not have been completed until the early 2020s, two decades late). Two of the Executive Board Members, South Korea and the EU, wanted KEDO to continue, but Japan, increasingly hard-line, sided with the United States.

Suspension was, in fact, a weasel word for termination. The United States made clear from the outset that in its view suspension was indefinite. Formally the Executive Board endorsed a confirmation of the suspension in November 2004 for a further year, but by then the United States was refusing to even fund its share of KEDO's administrative costs, let alone suspension costs. The Executive Board in November 2005 decided in principle on termination but wanted first to look at termination cost sharing, disposal of KEDO assets and legal issues involving outstanding contracts. On 1 July 2006 the Executive Board officially announced KEDO's termination. The reactors had cost South Korea $1.46 billion (€1.1 billion) (70 per cent), Japan $500 million (€374 million) (24 per cent) and the EU €123 million (6 per cent), although some was siphoned off to pay for HFO when Congress refused to deliver. The United States contributed scarcely 1 per cent ($25 million) for KEDO administration. In the end, the only positive outcome of KEDO was that it delayed North Korea's acquisition of nuclear weapons by a decade.

Legally KEDO continued to exist until its secretariat closed in the middle of 2007 to safeguard the ownership of the materials on the Kumho site valued at $500 million (€374 million), This Pyongyang will have to repay in any final accounting. Certainly Japan will require its full KEDO costs to be paid back in any financial settlement that will accompany a future normalisation of relations. The Korea Electric Power Corporation (KEPCO), the prime contractor for the LWR project, has offered to take over all KEDO's liabilities and assets. This might prove rather lucrative should anything come of the hinted South Korean–Chinese–Russian intervention to construct proliferation-resistant nuclear reactors of Russian design as an addendum to any settlement package.

## Six-party talks

After the crisis broke Bush argued a peaceful resolution was possible. However there were forces around the White House that were merely looking for a pause for breath after Iraq. In the meantime the knock-on effect of a nuclear North Korea destabilised regional security, becoming a particularly serious threat to China and a threat/opportunity for Japan depending on one's perspective. The US administration tried and failed to build a consensus for sanctions against the North. Japan did restrict money transfers from Chosen Soren, an important source of hard currency for Pyongyang, while South Korea did little and China less.

Getting the United States and North Korea back to the table was never going to be easy. Neither trusted the other, and they both had a point. The United States proclaimed it would not reward 'bad behaviour' by engaging in bilateral talks. With the US refusal, China, whose economic successes were beginning to translate into political influence, took the initiative and proposed a multilateral framework of six-party talks. The United States unenthusiastically acquiesced, and under enormous pressure from friends and foes alike the North signed up to participate alongside South Korea, United States, Japan, Russia, and the hosts, China. The first round of talks was in Beijing in August 2003. North Korea would have accepted a new freeze in exchange for a restoration of HFO deliveries. This would have stopped the flow of plutonium to the North's nuclear weapons programme while a comprehensive step-by-step solution was pursued. But there was to be no deal. The United States, rather than concede it had erred in cutting HFO, preferred to accept the prospect of North Korea becoming a fully-fledged nuclear state, instead of one that just might have a small handful of 'orphan' weapons that could neither be replaced nor added to and which, with the passage of time, would become unusable.

The North wanted 'security guarantees', a 'non-aggression pact' and assistance with its energy supply. The United States demanded unconditional complete verifiable irreversible dismantlement (CVID) without compensation, having just reneged on the compensation built into 1994's Agreed Framework. This was an impossibility, as Hans Blix said in the context of South African nuclear disarmament: 'there is inherent difficulty in verifying the completeness of an original [nuclear] inventory in a country in which a substantial nuclear programme has been going on for a long time.' It was a 'nothing for something' ultimatum to the North, and Pyongyang gave nothing for nothing. Bush neither would nor could sign a non-aggression pact with North Korea. He 'loathed' Kim Jong Il as he had told journalist Bob Woodward and the world, and even if he had undergone a religious change of heart, opposition from the Republican majority in Congress would have made it impossible. It was wishful thinking to suppose that the United States, technically still at war with the North, could demand deeply intrusive inspections of all military facilities in exchange for a note from Bush with no legal standing saying the United States had no hostile intentions. The demand was naïve and provocative. Certainly the North was not going to surrender its nuclear programme without a compensating indigenous energy supply. The single most important factor contributing to the North's current economic woes was the crippling shortage of fuel and energy. The United States insistence on CVID first and the North's demand for security guarantees and energy ensured a stand-off. The talks went nowhere.

It was not until the North had been given two years to initiate and build its nuclear arsenal that the United States moved and the breakthrough appeared to come. In September 2005, at the end of the fourth round of talks, an outline agreement was announced. The four rounds of talks between August 2003 and September 2005 threatened to become an end in themselves, with little evidence that sharp divisions of interest between the participants were narrowing. At one point the North dallied in the hope that John Kerry, who supported engagement, would win the Presidency. He didn't, Bush did – and this time without the help of Florida's flawed voting and the Supreme Court. On 19 September, the six parties announced an agreement. The major points are summarised below.[11]

First, the six parties unanimously reaffirmed that the goal of the six-party talks was the verifiable denuclearisation of the Korean Peninsula in a peaceful manner. The DPRK (North Korea) committed to abandoning all nuclear weapons and existing nuclear programmes and returning at an early date to the treaty on the non-proliferation of nuclear weapons (NPT) and to IAEA safeguards. The United States affirmed that it has no nuclear weapons on the Korean Peninsula and has no intention to attack or invade the DPRK with nuclear or conventional weapons. The ROK reaffirmed its commitment not to receive or deploy nuclear weapons in accordance with the 1992 joint declaration of the denuclearisation of the Korean Peninsula while affirming that there exist no nuclear weapons within its territory. The 1992 joint declaration of the denuclearisation of the Korean Peninsula should be observed and implemented. The DPRK stated that it has the right to peaceful uses of nuclear energy. The other parties expressed their respect and agreed to discuss at an appropriate time the subject of the provision of light water reactors to the DPRK.

Second, the six parties undertook, in their relations, to abide by the purposes and principles of the Charter of the United Nations and recognised norms of international relations. The DPRK and the United States undertook to respect each other's sovereignty, exist peacefully together and take steps to normalise their relations subject to their respective bilateral policies. The DPRK and Japan undertook to take steps to normalise their relations in accordance with the 2002 Pyongyang Declaration, on the basis of the settlement of unfortunate past and the outstanding issues of concern.

Third, the six parties undertook to promote economic cooperation in the fields of energy, trade and investment, bilaterally and/or multi-laterally. China, Japan, the ROK, Russia and the United States stated their willingness to provide energy assistance to the DPRK. The ROK reaffirmed its proposal of 12 July 2005 concerning the provision of 2000 MWe of electric power to the DPRK.

Fourth, the six parties are committed to joint efforts for lasting peace and stability in northeast Asia. The directly related parties will negotiate a permanent peace regime on the Korean Peninsula at an appropriate separate forum. The six parties agreed to explore ways and means of promoting security cooperation in northeast Asia.

Fifth, the six parties agreed to take coordinated steps to implement the aforementioned consensus in a phased manner in line with the principle of 'commitment for commitment, action for action'.

It looked good on paper. The problem was implementation with the promise of simultaneous step-by-step progress. North Korea agreed to abandon its nuclear development programme in exchange for US promises to rule out pre-emptive military action against it or attempts to promote regime change, accompanied by the provision 'at the appropriate time' of an LWR and development aid to kick-start the economy. For the United States the 'appropriate time' was closer to never than now, while for the North the 'appropriate time' was prior to its final surrender of nuclear weapons. Thus for the North there would be no civil nuclear power for the foreseeable future, but instead electricity would be fed in from the South with the off-switch firmly under Seoul's finger. That might be acceptable as an interim measure, but was a deeply unattractive long-term solution for a country where autonomy, self-reliance and *Juche* have been the watchwords. The reality is there is no alternative to nuclear power that gives the North any modicum of energy independence. Their experience of the 1994 Agreed Framework had burnt deep into Pyongyang the lesson that the United States was not to be trusted to deliver fuel or future promises.

As it turned out the ink was barely dry before, from Pyongyang's perspective, the United States demonstrated their bad faith. They forced the North's bank of choice in Macao, Banco Delta Asia, to freeze North Korean accounts on the grounds they were being used for money laundering, the claim being that Nigerian gangs were dumping around Asia counterfeit $100 bills produced in the North. In light of September's joint statement, screwing it up for $25 million – small change for organised crime in any major US conurbation – was stupidity or conspiracy. The North chose to interpret it as the latter.

For Pyongyang to engage with the prospect of CVID, two minimum conditions were necessary. First, a serious menu of economic development had to be on offer that included an indigenous electricity supply, and second, trust had to be built. Hanging over the fifth round of talks convened in November 2005 was Pyongyang's feeling that the first condition was not going to be met and the second not to be relied on after the Macao farrago. The United States and the DPRK sparred over the freezing of the bank accounts and whether the first stage of denuclearisation was a freeze or full disarmament. No progress was made. Ground and good will was lost as the two sides talked passed each other. The North walked.

This failure to build on the Joint Declaration did not disappoint everyone. It left the US neo-cons confident that they now had the North Koreans exactly where they wanted them – no KEDO, no nuclear power, and the country effectively embargoed by the West. Pyongyang would be bound to respond to the provocation. And, it did – the North is notoriously bad at not responding – and regime change was back on the agenda.

## Back to square one

North Korea was left in limbo, even as the United States held out to Iran the prospect of direct negotiations over its nuclear programme. There was a six-month hiatus before North Korea overshadowed the lift off of the space shuttle *Discovery* on US Independence Day by provocatively test firing a cocktail of missiles, as described earlier. This even included a long-range Taepodong-2, further aggravating the deteriorating relationship with the United States and Japan. The launch was a failure. Although Taepodong-2 is credited by the United States with a range capable of reaching the US mainland, after 42 seconds it fell into the East Sea. Peter Hayes, executive director of the Nautilus Institute, a US-based think tank, stated the US tests each of its new types of missiles more than 40 times before deploying. In the past eight years North Korea has test-fired Taepodong-2 missiles twice. At this rate it would take the country another 160 years before it was ready to deploy a Taepodong-2 in anger.

The failure did not stop the test playing into the hands of Japanese conservatives and strengthening the position of US hawks. The US neo-cons had driven North Korea into a corner by their intransigence at the six-party talks, yet they expressed synthetic indignation over the missile tests. After four years of crisis triggered by the United States over a programme that doesn't exist, it was back to hysteria and hyperbole. Japan and the United States called for an immediate meeting of the UN Security Council and then unilaterally before it met imposed sanctions on the North, committing themselves to a further strengthening of TMD. Japan suspended the Wonsan–Niigata ferry link and banned all charter flights to North Korea. The Security Council saw divisions open up between the trio of Japan, the United States and Britain who wanted a resolution adopted under Chapter Seven of the UN Charter allowing for the use of military action to ensure compliance, and China and Russia who demanded weaker language. China threatened to use its veto to block mention of Chapter Seven.

After ten days of difficult negotiations a compromise was hammered out on 15 July. Security Council Resolution 1695 prohibited member states from selling material or technology for missiles or weapons of mass destruction to North Korea, and from receiving missiles, banned weapons or technology from it.[12] The resolution urged Pyongyang to return to the six-party talks stalled since its

November walkout. North Korea's UN Ambassador Pak Gil Yon rejected the Resolution, reiterating that 'the Korean People's Army will continue with missile launch exercises.' Once again the North reacted. Pyongyang conducted an underground nuclear test on 9 October 2006. Beijing was not well pleased. UN Security Council Resolution 1718 followed five days later calling for additional sanctions.

The nuclear test demonstrated the failure of US policy. Rather than stopping the North in its tracks, it had given it cause to join the nuclear club. The six-party talks were proving incapable of finding a consensus to resolve the dispute. It was a blow to China's first attempt at global diplomacy and South Korea's commitment to engagement. To show their displeasure, albeit temporarily, both lashed out by suspending all assistance to the North.

After the test, China put Pyongyang on the rack. Hu Jintao sent a special envoy to meet Kim Jong Il, who agreed to postpone further tests and return to the talks after learning the United States had agreed to the simultaneous establishment of a bilateral working group that would lift the freeze on the Macao bank accounts. Talks resumed in December 2006 and the third session of the fifth round of the six-party talks two months later concluded with an agreement on 'Initial actions for the implementation of the joint statement'.

February 2007 took the world back close to where it was when the music stopped in October 2002. The DPRK agreed to freeze plutonium production and reprocessing at Yongbyon and allow the IAEA inspectors to monitor and verify this freeze, with the provision of 50,000 tonnes of HFO within 60 days. Then in a second phase the DPRK will make 'a complete declaration of all nuclear programmes' and disable all existing nuclear facilities, including graphite-moderated reactors and reprocessing plant. In exchange economic, energy and humanitarian assistance up to the equivalent of 1 million tonnes of HFO, which includes the initial shipment, will be provided to the DPRK at a cost of approximately €210 million, and there will be talks on normalising relations with the United States and Japan. All seemed fairly simple and straight forward, a barely distorted echo of the 1994 deal, at least in its initial phases. From the North Korean perspective, all was predicated on a lifting of the freeze on its money in the Banco Delta Asia. It seemed a done deal, although even that got complicated as the United States found a most convoluted means of delivering its commitment, which to the North broke the spirit if not the letter of the agreement. In the end the transfer of money expected in days took four months. The second stage will prove problematic. This involves the North 'kissing and telling' the US about all its nuclear programmes. This will require difficult judgements and decisions by North Korean leader Kim Jong Il and a level of some trust by Washington. Neither will be easily achieved.

At the moment there are signs of drift in Pyongyang of the ability to be open and truthful. Circumstantial evidence suggests Kim is recovering from heart surgery. There was a recent prolonged visit to Pyongyang by a team of German heart surgeons, accompanied by features in the North Korean media extolling the virtues of their own heart surgeons. It was not until July 2007 that Kim was seen in public with the visiting Chinese Foreign Minister Yang Jiechi. But even if Kim comes clean about his health he may not be believed or his statement accepted. One problem is Iran. Pyongyang and Tehran are close. The North has supplied Iran with its missile technology right from the deployment of the not entirely successful North Korean 'Hwasong' missile in the 'War of the Cities' during the Iran–Iraq War. The Iraqis took their revenge on the North Koreans by ensuring that one of the first victims of the early bombing raids was North Korea's first and only oil tanker, which was moored off Kharg Island. Iranian observers were present at the launch of North Korea's putative ICBM Taepodong in 1998 and reportedly at the 9 October nuclear test. The US concern that is not covered in the action plan is the threat of ping-pong proliferation. After last November's state visit to Tehran by Kim Young Nam, the North's formal Head of State, the feeling is that even if Pyongyang gives up all its nuclear materials and signs up again to the NPT, until Iran's nuclear programme is neutralised it will only take one phone call to Tehran in the future for everything to be back on course again in the North.

The third phase looks worse. Five working groups were set up:

1. US–DPRK relations.
2. DPRK–Japan relations.
3. Energy and economic aid.
4. Armistice and security issues.
5. Denuclearisation of the Korean Peninsula.

It is unclear where some of the red flags that neo-cons in the US wave will be discussed and resolved. Missile testing and sales would fall under 4, but would be dependent on 3 and 5. Counterfeiting, money laundering and drugs fit nowhere. Within weeks Japan was refusing to provide any financing without progress on the abductees, and urging the United States not to remove the North from its 'terror state' list, with Pyongyang responding that Japan should withdraw from the whole process if it was already reneging on the agreement. In Working Group 3 the North Koreans will not be satisfied with any long-term solution that does not provide them with high levels of energy self-sufficiency, which would appear to take the whole discussion back to LWRs again.

The working group that may break new ground is group 4. Denuclearisation will be a step-by-step process in which Yongbyon will be the penultimate step for final demolition and Pyongyang's nuclear weapons the ultimate. To get to that final point may require an institutionalisation of working group 4 into some permanent body which may be able to provide guarantes to the North that the United States will fulfil its intentions. Aid will be expensive, but cheaper than conflict. The EU will again be asked to contribute disproportionately. As Javier Solana's spokesman said in the European Parliament's Foreign Affairs Committee in February 'we want to be players, not payers,' a sentiment consistent with Parliament's earlier position in March 2005 of 'no say, no pay'.[13] This position was once again expressed in the Parliament's Foreign Affairs Committee on 27 March 2007 when, voting on its report on the Common Foreign and Security Policy (CFSP), it asked the EU to seek active involvement rather than confine itself to financing. The EU's goal on the nuclear weapons, missile testing and sales is identical to that of the United States. But Parliament, Commission and Council are becoming irritated at being seen in Washington as a convenient 'cash cow'. The five countries that were invited to go to the North to assess the energy situation did not include the EU, which will be expected to contribute, but did include Japan, which said it would not. Given the absence of EU strategic interests on the Korean peninsula, the EU could even play, along with China, a role as mediator. The EU should have a place at the table and must seek to be involved in working groups 3 and 4. The former will distribute the largesse and the latter oversee the peace process and reassure the North Koreans against threats of externally promoted regime change. It will be a long, winding and bumpy road with many setbacks and reversals, as even the initial months have shown. The question is whether everyone is in for the long ride, or whether some will get off at the first stop.

## New partner for dialogue

That the EU will become a player on the peninsula and in the region is the logical outcome of its industrial and economic integration playing out in the emergent CFSP. When it first became engaged in the late 1990s the EU took a line of 'critical engagement' with Pyongyang, in opposition to the confrontational approach of the United States and to a lesser extent Japan.

Under pressure from the US administration and its human rights lobby, EU policy has publicly shifted closer to Washington's, yet the EU continues to provide more than just humanitarian aid. It has rehabilitation projects for water sanitation and donates seeds and farm machinery. That the EU would become an important partner for the North was hard to imagine until a decade ago. The member states' early involvement had been less than positive. Out of the 15 pre-2004 enlargement members, six had sent troops and three more had sent hospital facilities and medical staff during the Korean War.[14] In the 1970s, Pyongyang borrowed up to $3 billion (€2.25 billion), of which two-thirds was from European banks, for industrial investment. The 1973 'oil shock' meant the timing was far from ideal and the projects all failed more or less spectacularly. By the end of the decade, the North had stopped paying its debts. It was bankrupt.

At my initiative in 1984, the European Parliament's then External Economic Affairs Committee drew up a report on 'Trade Relations with North Korea'.[15] Frankly, the conclusion was that there weren't any. Total trade was around $7 million (€4 million). The report suggested a possible way of recovering some of the debt by utilising Pyongyang's new joint venture legislation or by European companies counter-trading, swapping European technology for non-ferrous metals like gold, silver, zinc, copper and lead. When the report was debated in January 1986, Commissioner Peter Sutherland, subsequently head of the World Trade Organisation, stated that the Commission was 'generally in favour of any increase in trade with North Korea while noting the high risks associated'. An indication of the state of relations between the North and the EU was that despite the standard demand that the report be sent to Pyongyang, this never happened. Eighteen months later bemused North Korean diplomats in Paris clearly had no idea what I was talking about when I asked about their reaction to the report. I asked the Parliament's administration why no copy had been forwarded. The official response was 'we didn't have an address'.

On the political side this ignorance was compounded by history, a lack of strategic interests in the Asia-Pacific region and geographical distance. Up until 1997, there was no channel of communication between the European institutions and the North. Only five out of 15 member states had diplomatic relations with the DPRK. Finland, Sweden and Denmark had opened formal diplomatic relations in 1973, all encouraged by the North–South Joint Statement of July 1972. Austria followed suit in 1974, and Portugal in 1975 after its own 'Carnation Revolution'.

The need for more active involvement became evident in the aftermath of the 1994 nuclear crisis when Europe was presented with the threat posed by North Korea to global security with its developing nuclear weapons and its missile sales to 'countries of concern', particularly in the Middle East. The emergence of the EU's CFSP in the mid to late 1990s, with the EU's distinct positions on Iran, the Middle East and the Korean Peninsula, inevitably increased the need for engagement.

Direct practical involvement came with food aid and humanitarian assistance programmes after the floods of 1995 and 1996.

The EU channelled its aid through the UN's World Food Programme and various NGOs, with food targeted at those at particular risk – namely children under seven and pregnant women – and undertook some rehabilitation programmes. Humanitarian assistance expanded to include winter clothes, medicine, plus sanitation and hygiene projects. Europe was pressured to do more. It joined the KEDO Executive Board that had a €118 million price tag attached. Other EU assistance, humanitarian and food aid and food security in the same period totalled €344 million, making a grand total of €452 million.[16]

The EU warmly welcomed Kim Dae Jung's 1997 election in South Korea, making as it did the first democratic transition of power in the South's history, and his 'Sunshine Policy'. Kim's goodwill encouraged Europe to play a bigger role. As a result, in December 1998 an official EU–DPRK dialogue started which continued through the next two years. The spin-off of this was a series of resolutions in the European Parliament calling for the establishment of diplomatic relations, a human rights dialogue similar to the one already in place with China, and further aid programmes.[17] The political momentum of the June 2000 inter-Korean summit was such that almost all EU member states were dragged in its wake to establish diplomatic ties with Pyongyang. Italy had jumped the gun in January 2000, but the UK started the rush in December that year. On the eve of the ASEM Summit (Asia-Europe Summit) in Seoul, Blair and his Foreign Minister, the late Robin Cook, took the decision en route to open an embassy in Pyongyang. Within three months, six other EU member states followed suit (see Table 7.1).

Göran Persson, the Prime Minister of Sweden, and at the time President in Office of the European Council, travelled to Pyongyang urged on by Kim Dae Jung, who had been stung and disappointed with his meeting with Bush, who had expressed scepticism, if not open hostility, to the 'Sunshine Policy'. As a result, Persson led the delegation from 2–4 May 2001 accompanied by Javier Solana and Chris Patten. Patten's impression of Kim Jong Il was of someone highly intelligent, articulate and very much in control, but totally obsessed by the United States.[18] Kim asked the Europeans to explain the U-turn on policy between Clinton and Bush, why Bush was being so gratuitously offensive with his personal name calling, and why the United States was threatening Pyongyang. On 14 May the European Commission agreed to establish diplomatic relations with the DPRK to facilitate aid, reform and reconstruction.

In December, Kim Dae Jung addressed the European Parliament in Strasbourg. He expressed his appreciation of the EU's efforts and asked for continuing support for his engagement policy:

Table. 7.1 Timetable of diplomatic relations between EU member states and the DPRK

| Decade | State | Date |
|--------|-------|------|
| 1940s | Poland | 16 Oct 1948* |
| | Romania | 26 Oct 1948* |
| | Hungary | 11 Nov 1948* |
| | Bulgaria | 29 Nov 1948* |
| 1950s | | |
| 1960s | | |
| 1970s | *Malta* | *30 Dec 1971* |
| | *Sweden* | *7 April 1973* |
| | *Finland* | *1 June 1973* |
| | Denmark | 17 July 1973 |
| | *Austria* | *17 Dec 1974* |
| | *Portugal* | *15 April 1975* |
| 1980s | | |
| 1990s | *Lithuania* | *25 Sep 1991* |
| | *Latvia* | *26 Sep 1991* |
| | *Cyprus* | *23 Dec 1991* |
| | *Slovenia* | *8 Sep 1992* |
| | *Czech Republic* | *1 Jan 1993* |
| | *Slovakia* | *1 Jan 1993* |
| | Estonia | 5 May 1994 |
| 2000s | Italy | 4 Jan 2000 |
| | UK | 12 Dec 2000 |
| | Netherlands | 15 Jan 2001 |
| | Belgium | 23 Jan 2001 |
| | Spain | 7 Feb 2001 |
| | Germany | 1 Mar 2001 |
| | Luxembourg | 5 Mar 2001 |
| | Greece | 5 Mar 2001 |
| | Ireland | 10 Dec 2003 |

Note: Countries in italics established diplomatic relations before joining the EU. Countries marked by * established relations under Communism.

The EU has been taking part in the Korean Peninsula Energy Development Organisation (KEDO) and has offered a range of humanitarian and economic assistance to North Korea. It is also pursuing an array of diverse activities, including techno-logical assistance and training programmes, for the North Koreans. Many EU members are actively supporting our efforts for peace on the peninsula by establishing diplomatic relations with North Korea. In May this year, when the inter-

Korean relationship experienced a temporary setback, an EU delegation, led by Swedish Prime minister Göran Persson and including EU Commissioner for External Relations Chris Patten, visited North Korea and helped us resume our dialogue. The EU is an important supporter of peace on the Korean Peninsula and exchanges and cooperation between the South and North. You, the Members of the European Parliament are genuine friends of the Korean people. I earnestly hope that your unsparing support will continue until the day when peace is settled and the first ray of unification shines over the Korean Peninsula.[19]

By the end of 2001, 13 out of the then 15 EU member states – the exceptions being France and Ireland – had diplomatic relations with the North. Ireland followed in December 2003. With the enlargement on 1 May 2004 it became 24 out of 25, and on 1 January 2007, 26 of 27 (See Table 7.1), with France being the only formal hold-out. The official reason given by the French was human rights in North Korea. The rumoured reason was more mercenary, with France initially putting pressure on South Korea for a bigger slice of KEDO contracts for its nuclear industry. Chirac was certainly furious with Blair's preemption on the eve of Seoul's ASEM Summit. Officially, KEDO's position was that they would be awarded in proportion to KEDO contributions, a position not entirely tenable in that it would have excluded the United States and certainly would have precluded the United States' offer of KEDO contracts to Russia as a 'sweetener' for breaking its nuclear links with Iran in 1994. France's public logic is difficult to follow. If the issue is human rights, why are there French embassies in Turkmenistan, Burma and Saudi Arabia?

Even France has some North Korean diplomatic presence with a DPRK General Delegation Office in Paris. The leadership of the French Socialist Party visited North Korea in 1981. A couple of months prior to Mitterrand's election as President, he, Pierre Maurois and Lionel Jospin took time out to travel to Pyongyang. After Mitterrand's victory the incoming government quickly approved the establishment of the General Delegation Office. Seven EU embassies (Bulgaria, Romania, Sweden, Germany, UK, Poland and Hungary) are currently in Pyongyang, while other member states are variously represented by their ambassadors in Beijing and increasingly Seoul.

Since the Commission's decision in 2001 to establish diplomatic relations, France has consistently blocked implementation. Immediately after the North Koreans began house-hunting in Brussels, the EU designated its then ambassador to Seoul, Dorian Prince, as its ambassador designate to Pyongyang. It never happened. France's refusal to budge, and the rest of the Council's lack of courage to overrule it, left the issue in limbo for more than six years. It may require President Sarkozy to move the French Foreign Office. Certainly Bernard Kouchner the new Foreign Minister may not be sympathetic.

# 8 Changing regime or regime change?

## Introduction

Regime change is high on the US agenda, centred on but not limited to neo-cons, but exactly what it means is unclear. The North Korean Human Rights Act implies the North should be driven along the path of Russia and the former Soviet empire into, at best, liberal democracy or, at worst, corrupt crony capitalism. Yet, this conveniently misses a Korean reality that has unification hanging over Seoul like the sword of Damocles. The only regime change that would not precipitate such a disaster for the South would be either Kim Jong Il's removal by internal *coup d'etat* or having the regime 'tweaked' by Chinese intervention. The problem with the first is that what internal opposition there is rails against Kim Jong Il's drive for economic reform. The opponents are in the same ideological camp of those behind the 1991 coup in the Soviet Union who wanted to restrain *glasnost* and *perestroika* rather than accelerate it. They are the right-wing conservatives of Pyongyang not radical reformers. To look to them for relief does not make a lot of sense. Kim is the reformer, not the brake on change. If anyone should be out to get him it should be the conservatives.

There are voices in the United States arguing for engagement, but they come either from Democrats or from Republicans well outside the Bush–Cheney camp. It is only the unfolding debacle in Iraq that has prevented more robust ideas from taking hold. From 2002–07 the United States used its supposedly superior intelligence to intellectually and politically intimidate the rest of the world into following where it led. But with Iraq's civil war getting worse and the Iranian nuclear crisis, a few voices now sing from a different hymn sheet. Christopher Hill, the US chief negotiator at the six-party talks, has been given a last chance to find a peaceful solution before the United States looks towards a military option.

China stayed outside the global consensus, despite its fury with Pyongyang from time to time, while Russia sang to the right tune but with harmonies reflecting its own self-interest. It was Seoul that took a more independent line as both the progressive government and conservative opposition realise that Bush's approach is 'I bomb, you die, he falls.' The EU's constructive engagement was downplayed as it was brought into line after the October 2002 nuclear crisis, although even after that from time to time it muttered dissent. As said before, if it wasn't for the United States – and Japan – North Korea would be its own worst enemy. Pyongyang's provocations are heaven sent for those who want to fan the flames of world opinion. Rethinking North Korea requires an appreciation of post-war history leading up to the current crises and Kim Jong Il's boldness in driving forward economic reform.

## Kim's regime

North Korea's ruling regime is not one anyone should admire. It is a brutal dictatorship with, in Western terms, a deplorable human rights record. North Korea is possibly the most closed, isolated and tightly controlled society in the world. Only Burma, Turkmenistan and Saudi Arabia run it close. Except at the highest levels of the Party and the military, North Koreans have no access to anything but the state-controlled media. The Internet, foreign books and magazines are off limits. Travel at home requires hard-won permission, while travel abroad is limited to the elite.

The North Korean economy began faltering in the mid-1970s and early 1980s as the over-emphasis on heavy industry and the remobili-sation of the economy to provide almost a third of GNP to the military began to seriously distort production. The collapse of the Soviet Union and its empire in 1991 plus a series of floods, droughts and hurricanes in the first half of the 1990s, drove the economy into meltdown. The consequence was a hidden humanitarian disaster as bad as anything seen in the last quarter of the twentieth century. Up to one in eight of the population, about 3 million people, died of starvation.

Currently the North's only saving grace is that it is seriously engaging in the first stages of economic reform. The problem is that these attempts are both overshadowed and hindered by the security crises on the penin-sula. Headlines are about nuclear weapons and missiles, not about Pyongyang taking the road to Chinese or Vietnamese-style Market-Leninism or cult capitalism. In the current circumstances no entrepre-neurs in their right mind, apart possibly from the Korean 'family' where non-economic factors play a major role, are going to invest in the North. While successful reform would benefit Koreans, North and South, north-east Asia and the global community, it is being sabotaged by a US admin-istration blind to what it cannot or will not see, because it doesn't fit the United States' preconceptions and agenda.

There are some serious double standards in the world. Almost all nuclear proliferation over the last quarter of a century has originated with Pakistan, not North Korea. The North's arms sales are a fraction of 1 per cent of the global arms trade. Turkmenistan's former President Niyazov had a personality cult that ran the Kim dynasty close, coupled with an equally dire human rights record. Yet oil, gas and land borders with Afghanistan and Iran mean that in his case the *Turkmenbashi* ('Father of Turkmen') got drawn into dialogue rather than discord.

Kim Jong Il and the regime are bad, yet that doesn't mean we have to believe the worst. A number of human rights horror stories have turned out to be fabricated rather than exaggerated. North Korea and its ruler are not insane. They are rational actors who face a real and present danger that the United States is acting to promote regime change. Their actions are in their own terms perfectly rational. Pyongyang is willing to negotiate away its nuclear weapons and more. Its nuclear weapons, military and missiles are now defensive, not offensive.

## Nuclear crisis I

After the Sino-Soviet split in 1963, Pyongyang walked a delicate tightrope between its two Communist neighbours, leaning first to one side, then to the other. The KWP Plenum of December that year endorsed the slogan 'Arms in one hand and a hammer and sickle in the other!' Military spending went within five years from 6 per cent of GNP to 30 per cent. After 1962 and the Soviet backdown over Cuba, Pyongyang increasingly felt the need to go it alone militarily. From 1992 onwards there were suspicions that North Korea had a clandestine nuclear weapons programme based around the diversion of weapons grade plutonium from its Russian-built graphite-moderated reactor in Yongbyon. When in 1993 under pressure from the United States, the International Atomic Energy Agency (IAEA) demanded inspections of the plant, the North Korean response was to cite 'supreme national interests' in article 10(1) of the NPT to justify its withdrawal from the treaty. The ensuing crisis lasted well over a year. The United States prepared plans for pre-emptive strikes against the North's nuclear sites, but the last-minute unscripted intervention of former US President Jimmy Carter led both sides to the negotiating table.

The Kim Il Sung–Carter meeting brought the two sides back from the brink and led to the signing of the Agreed Framework in October 1994. As discussed earlier in the section on 'Framing an agreement', this broke the impasse by offering the North proliferation-resistant LWRs and interim supplies of HFO in exchange for freezing the Yong-byon programme – a perfect technological fix to a political crisis.

The fundamental flaw in the 1994 Agreed Framework was that the US negotiators assumed that the North Korean regime was doomed to a rapid collapse, failing to recognise that the DPRK was not an imposed regime like those in Eastern Europe, but instead a deeply rooted indigenous system that reflected Korean culture, history and society. It was therefore a profound shock and disappointment to the

United States to see it survive the collapse of the socialist bloc, the death of the Great Leader, severe economic difficulties, and food and energy shortages that led to mass starvation.

Consequently, it was hardly surprising that the Agreed Framework was honoured by the United States as much in the breach as the delivery. Washington failed to construct two LWR plants by the end of 2003. The United States threatened, in breach of the Agreed Framework, to halt the delivery of key nuclear components until after the IAEA 'completed' its tests on the North's reactor. The United States finally killed the project, initially suspending KEDO then using the de facto US veto to terminate it. The promised deliveries of HFO by the United States to tide over North Korea's flickering power system were sporadic, as Republicans in Congress blocked funds. The North's suspicions were compounded by the incoming Bush administration's new strategic doctrine of pre-emptive deterrence. The deeply suspicious, isolated and authoritarian regime in Pyongyang concluded that they were just being played for time and that the United States was not looking for a solution, but rather merely juggling the sequencing to Iraq, Iran, North Korea.

## Nuclear crisis II

Clinton had passed the baton to Bush. As mentioned in the earlier section on 'KEDO', the United States had no intention of bailing North Korea out, but rather of using the crisis to justify the continued development and deployment of national missile defence (NMD) and its regional variant theatre missile defence (TMD). After all, with the end of the Soviet empire, were the US wargamers going to target Moscow's stock exchange? Bush signalled provocatively that he wanted to renegotiate the whole deal downwards, a proposal that found no welcome in Pyongyang and just reconfirmed US perfidy.

This time apparently it was not just intelligence but a confession that triggered the convenient crisis. The United States claimed to have hit the jackpot when negotiator James Kelly reported that during his meeting in Pyongyang in October 2002 the North Korean First Vice-Minister for Foreign Affairs, Kang Suk Ju, confessed that North Korea had an alternative nuclear weapons programme using HEU. Kang immediately denied the allegation, saying he had been misunderstood. Whether he was misinterpreted or not, the timing was perfect. The revelation sabotaged the ongoing rapprochement between Japan and the North that had been signalled by the Koizumi–Kim summit only the month before, and let the United States off the KEDO hook. Only two months before the first nuclear plant was due on line – it was running years late and a North Korean claim for compensation was pending – Kang's confession was interpreted as a clear breach by North Korea of the 1994 Agreed Framework, even if the letter of the agreement was much more ambiguous on the point. North Korea denied everything.

The outcome was like watching a train wreck in slow motion. It was self-evident that ending HFO deliveries would lead to the unfreezing of Yongbyon and a dash for nuclear weapons. The HFO deliveries were the only remaining fig-leaf the North Koreans had left from the Agreed Framework. The promise of normalisation of relations, lifting of the embargo, two LWRs by 2003, and interim deliveries of HFO had dribbled away to nothing. Pyongyang had no alternative but to unfreeze the reactor and complete its withdrawal from the NPT. The re-opening of the plant enabled Pyongyang to reprocess the fuel rods and extract enough weapons-grade plutonium to produce five to six nuclear weapons, with the potential to produce enough fresh material for another bomb every few months.

The United States' October surprise turned North Korea into a nuclear weapons power in months rather than years. North Korea continued to deny it had a parallel HEU nuclear weapons programme, but even with one it would have been years, if ever, before enough HEU could have been produced to make a bomb. Worse, uranium weapons are heavier and bulkier and so more difficult to mount on missiles compared to plutonium. Which explains why Pakistan, the arch exponent and exporter of HEU, is now looking at the plutonium route. North Korea has obtained nuclear weapons that serve its purposes better and more quickly than would have happened had HFO deliveries continued.

Finally, in February 2007, the six-party talks got the United States and North Korea back to where they started, as explained in the previous chapter. HFO deliveries were to restart at the cost of more than €200 million per annum; some of these can be traded in for humanitarian or other aid, but not cash, and Pyongyang will provide a full inventory of its nuclear programmes and make them available for IAEA inspections. In parallel the United States slowly and painfully lifted the freeze on Pyongyang's bank accounts in Macao, and US intelligence confessed that maybe the whole HEU story had been an over-suspicious interpretation of the data. They were just as wrong about North Korea as they were about Iraq. A negotiating detour that meant the United States now had to negotiate away North Korean nuclear weapons rather than deter the North from developing them, 13 February was a pyrrhic victory indeed.

**Reform rules**

While the world focused on the fantasy threats of North Korean pre-emptive nuclear strikes against the mainland United States and neo-con fairy tales from Langley and the NRO, the ongoing reform programme in the North that, if supported and reinforced, can metamorphose the North was ignored.

The food crisis in the 1990s disrupted not only the economy but society. When the Public Distribution System (PDS) that had provided basic necessities virtually collapsed, the population struggled to feed themselves. People had no option but to engage in illegal transactions on the black market, and in the worst cases abandoned homes, jobs and families to search for food. This necessitated the state turning a blind eye to the establishment of 'farmers markets', which were later adopted as established parts of the economy. Kim Jong Il saw the writing on the wall. After his formal accession to power in 1998, he began to inch the North away from his father's notion of self-reliance or *Juche*. Kim travelled to Beijing in May 2000 and liked what he saw. During a further visit in January 2001, he was taken on a 'study tour' of Shanghai and Fudong, showcasing the success of China's economic reforms. He was impressed by the 'social unity and stability' of this 'unique socialist development', and the rising prestige of China on the international stage.[1]

Thought became action. The same month Kim urged: 'we should transcend the old working style and fixed economic framework of other countries' in earlier times with a 'renovation in thinking and in practice [that] is needed to meet the demand of the new era.' A revolutionary call for reform. *Rodong Sinmun* began to regularly highlight the achievements and successes of China. We have already noted how radical a move this was for a newspaper whose previous mentions of reform had framed it as a precursor to, and harbinger of, state collapse in Eastern Europe.

In July 2002 the State Price Control Bureau introduced a new price and wages system that cut state subsidies, endorsed the 'market' and granted greater autonomy to farmers and agricultural and craft enterprises, setting new low and easily achievable targets for delivery to the state, with the surplus for private sale in the markets. The result was, as the Vice-Chair of the State Planning Commission said when I met him, 'agricultural reforms proved better than fertiliser at raising productivity.'

Reform was not without opposition. In February 2004 Jang Song Taek, Kim's brother-in-law, who was believed by many to be the regime's effective number two, was removed from his post after clashing with Pak Pong Ju, the champion of economic reform in the cabinet. Subsequently, Jang's power base, the KWP, was restructured, with key Committees dealing with military, economic and agricultural policy abolished, hamstringing the KWP's ability to interfere and signalling Kim Jong Il's commitment that the Cabinet would continue to push ahead with reform. Reform continued. In June 2004 it was announced that for 90 per cent of industry, 'The Plan' had been abandoned. As explained to the first EU–DPRK workshop on economic reform in Pyongyang four months later, now that the state could no longer provide the necessary inputs of energy and raw materials, industrial enterprises had been freed to choose their own processes and products, and given the ability to hire and fire at will. The initial result was a lot more firing than hiring and a partial re-ruralisation of the economy. Work teams from industrial enterprises were sent out to grow food. As the Ministry of State Planning explained, the state would continue to own the means of production, but the groups entrusted with their management had the responsibility to maximise profits. The unanswered question was where this profit was to go. Some even believed that the opposition got physical with an assassination attempt: the April Ryongchon railway station explosion in April 2004. Whatever the truth about Ryongchon, the extent and existence of opposition can be gauged by *Rodong Sinmun* publishing an editorial in September 2004 explaining: 'the Party cannot maintain its existence by permitting factions.'

Kim had visited Beijing, Shanghai and Fudong again in April 2004 and Wuhan, Guangzhou, and Shenzhen in January 2006. By 2006, Jang Song Taek had learnt his lesson and learnt it well. He was rehabilitated, emerging as the First Director of the Department of Working People's Organisation and Capital Construction of the KWP. In March 2006, Jang led a 30-strong group on an eleven-day visit to retrace Kim's January itinerary. Jang appeared to have taken over responsibility for economic affairs.

## Reading the signs

Opening up the market has worked in the agricultural sector, where essential inputs outside sheer manual labour are comparatively small. In the manufacturing sector however, in the absence of energy and raw materials, any boost in demand merely sucks in imports. The means of production are old, tired and outdated. Managers are completely untrained in how modern economies work. Without reconstruction aid – and little will arrive in the absence of a comprehensive settlement – many factory workers are merely being given the freedom to go jobless and hungry.

Marx's slogan 'from each according to his ability, to each according to his need' is being replaced by 'from each according to his work, to each according to his productivity'. Tong-il Market is a hive of activity. Initially a farmers' market where people applied to the Market Management Committee to be able to come and sell their surplus goods for two or three days at a time before rotating out, it now provides for every daily need and beyond, even into conspicuous consumption. Cereals, but not rice since 2005, meat and fish are plentiful, as are domestic and imported cigarettes, alcohol and clothing. Also available are North African dates, Spanish oranges, palm trees and palm tops. Around 90 per cent of imported industrial goods come from China. All this is a revolution away from goods sourced from the local farming community. The shops in downtown Pyongyang also now have a variety of goods for sale, with the Number 1 Department Store under Chinese management and the restaurants on Changgwang Street, Pyongyang's pale equivalent of Tokyo's Ginza, are open and serving. For street decoration, the colourful and contentious ubiquitous propaganda posters have been joined by commercial adverts and large poster boards for the North–South joint venture PyongHwa automobile company's cars on the approach to Pyongyang airport and along the highway to Nampo.

All the secondary signs of economic success and the market are beginning to show. On the fringes of Tong-il loiter numbers of 'unsavoury' characters on the make, prepared to pay a 10 per cent premium and more on the official 'grey market' rate for the euro and the dollar, and in the evenings on the more travelled routes in Pyongyang prostitutes wave down passing cars. Other problems are more serious. Inequality is growing. While those working in agriculture are benefiting financially from the reforms, the same is not true of those on fixed incomes in urban areas. Inflation is running at 30 per cent, and at one point reached 400 to 500 per cent per annum for free-market rice until in 2005 the state resumed and stepped up PDS rice distribution and banned the sale of rice on the market. There are millions whose earnings barely enable them to feed themselves. As much as the reforms have created a middle class that thrives and survives on its own wits, they have also created an underclass that finds it increasingly difficult to survive without inputs from family plots, family connections, access to 'informal foods' (tree bark, roots and weeds) or humanitarian aid. In isolated industrial towns, particularly in the urbanised northeast where the climate is much harsher and alternative sources of food more limited, hunger has returned for the many if not the few. There is a harsh downside to a long process of reform that without external encouragement may end up strangled at birth.

For long-term economic development, North Korea is seeking to expand trade and increase foreign inward investment and development assistance. Currently those wanting a 'strong and prosperous country' (*Kangsong Daeguk*) seem to be winning over the 'military-first' faction. Korea is focusing on building a new economy. Kim Jong Il, after seeing China rising, wants to leapfrog several technological stages of development and jump straight to information technology.

The North has set up a number of institutions to cater for those with outstanding computer skills and is introducing computers into workplaces and schools. In a relatively short period of time, it has produced a large number of skilled IT professionals and developed products both for the local market and for export. Local products include a Korean version of Linux, translation software and Korean character handwriting recognition and voice recognition; export production includes games for mobile phones, PCs and PlayStations. The North's computer software for 'Go', an Asian board game, won the world championship. There are a number of small joint ventures in the IT sector, particularly in the field of *Anime* and games software.

Considering the closed nature of the society, where information flows are strictly controlled, this 'catching up' strategy may prove over ambitious. Nevertheless, the North has become an offshore destination for a growing number of clients from Japan, China and South Korea for software design, driven mainly but not exclusively by price.

Other reforms include new laws governing foreign investment and trade and a renewed emphasis on the development of special economic zones (SEZ). The North's first SEZ was opened up in 1992 close to the triple meeting point with Russia and China on the northeast coast, Rajin-Songbong. The joint venture laws were models of good practice, but the political, economic and geographic environment was less favourable. The Rajin-Songbong SEZ continues to function, although the most substantial foreign enterprise is a Chinese-built and run casino, accompanied by a few lonely South Korean joint ventures. The second SEZ, announced in 2002, was to be around Sinuiju, a town on the Chinese border, where 600,000 people were to live and work in an exclusive enclave under the rule of China's controversial billionaire entrepreneur Yang Bin. The plan was stillborn. China showed its displeasure with venue and viceroy within days of his name being made public in October 2002 by arresting him for tax evasion, despite his Dutch citizenship. He was later sentenced to 14 years in prison. Yang Bin's replacement was named as the Chinese-American businesswoman Julie Sa, but nothing happened on the ground, and the planned SEZ was officially abandoned in 2004.

After the limited success of Rajin-Songbong and the failure of Sinuiju, Pyongyang's third attempt was a success. The Kaesong industrial complex adjacent to the DMZ couples a Southern infrastructure of modern four-lane roads, electricity and water with disciplined, docile, low-paid workers from the North. Kaesong's SEZ was to be developed in three phases, with a final workfare of 300,000 North Koreans. Phase one is complete, with 36 South Korean and one Japanese company manufacturing saucepans, clothes, shoes and watches. Korean consumers have already demonstrated that they are prepared to pay a premium to cook with North Korean kitchenware. Phase two is underway and one potential development may be 'call centre' work for the South Korean service sector, at least in its less sensitive areas like railway timetable enquiries. The United States is doing what it can to impede progress, trying to argue that export restrictions imposed against the North prohibit the transfer of computers into the complex. North–South road links have opened up with the new land route to Mt Kumgang. However, the promised re-opening of the rail link between North and South, abandoned since the Korean War, was long delayed. At one point the project was suspended before being declared on again in February 2007. Finally in April 2007 two trains travelled respectively North and South. These events were greeted with a degree of euphoria in Seoul, but merely factually reported in the North's media, indicating an uncertainty as to what next steps to take.

The US point-blank refusal to include the Kaesong industrial complex within the scope of its ill-fated Korean–US Free Trade Agreement (FTA) just re-emphasised its opposition. The EU's own FTA negotiations with Seoul, which opened in May 2007, have not seen Commissioner Mandelson impose the same restrictions. The issue of the SEZ has not been formally raised in negotiations with the EU, but it is likely to take a more conciliatory line, particularly if it can negotiate a satisfactory compromise on the very sensitive issue of automotive exports from the ROK to Europe. President Roh hopes to initial the agreement with the EU by the end of 2007.

Pyongyang has sent a number of economic fact-finding missions to China and Vietnam above and beyond Kim Jong Il's well publicised visits. The evidence is that the regime, for all its crimes and misdemeanours, would like to open up and start the long march towards an 'in our own style' variant of Market-Leninism (i.e. a gradual and controlled shift to open markets that allows Kim and the KWP to keep power). Kim is stepping outside his father's political paradigm. Reforms hold promise and peril. The economic reform measures are feeding inflation and social hardship, while in the industrial sector the results have been disappointing. Opening up the country to allow market activities inevitably means a partial loosening of political and social control. The pace of change in the North is erratic and uneven; however, the direction is clear and the process fundamentally irreversible, which can only be welcomed. After all, a rising tide floats all ships.

Yet North Korea simply does not have the resources to rebuild its agricultural, industrial and infrastructure base alone. What it desperately needs is advice and development assistance to help it to help itself. The European Commission and the Ministry of Foreign Affairs have been holding annual workshops in Pyongyang (with the next in October 2007) that have seen North Korean officials presented with studies of economic transition in Eastern Europe and specific strategies for restructuring the agricultural sector, creating small and medium-sized enterprises and attracting foreign direct investment (FDI). More extensive training in market economics and business management, plus greater exposure of senior DPRK cadres to the outside world, will accelerate the transformation process already underway. The outside world has a choice: it can help and encourage the reform process, or it can block it, forcing the North into a corner with all the consequences that follow. While US actions have consistently acted to hamper and damage the reform process, the question is whether others like the EU are prepared to join the South and follow a very different path. Skinning a tiger claw by claw has little to recommend it.

## EU: payer or player

The North Korean prime focus is 'regime survival'. Since 2000 Kim has committed himself to economic reform 'in our own style', but the ongoing nuclear and missile crises have completely overshadowed the introduction of the mixed economy. Worse, they have directly and indirectly sabotaged the process. In these circumstances who in their right mind is going to invest in the North when China is next door? Pyongyang is aware that the men and women in Washington who gave the world Iraq War II want the regime swept away. So the only basis for any settlement must be the guarantee of non-intervention by the United States, something close to energy self-sufficiency – in other words, nuclear power stations – and a serious package of economic aid. But someone else will have to pick up the bill for the aid.

The most helpful Western intervention has come from the EU. In 2001 the EU began to look closely at the North's economic development during the preparation of a technical assistance package. In its view, the North's advantages are its large, educated labour force, low costs and technical capacity. Its disadvantages are its lack of energy and infrastructure, plus the need for capacity building and changes in the legal framework. The EU drew two main conclusions. First, North Korea's economic structure is more industrial than agricultural and is closer to that of Eastern Europe than Asia. Important as it is to modernise agriculture to increase food security, agriculture will not be the motor of economic development. Instead effort had to be concentrated on reviving industry, partly in heavy metal mining, but also in the production of manufactured goods for home consumption and export. Second, Pyongyang has to make a strategic choice as to whether to aim at an export-led growth strategy based on cheap labour assembling/outward processing or to work towards skill-based quality production identifying specific niche markets and attracting high-quality foreign investment.

On the basis of the assessment, the EU prepared an Action Plan with an initial indicative budget of €15 million covering three years (2002–04). *The Country Strategy Paper 2001–2004*, focused on three areas: 1) institutional support for capacity building, with training programmes to strengthen key institutions to enable them to adopt international economic practices and build relations with the international community; 2) management of the energy sector to allow for the rational and efficient use of energy resources; 3) creation of a reliable and sustainable transport sector to support the rehabilitation of agriculture.

In March 2002, a high economic delegation led by the North's Foreign Trade Minister toured Belgium, Italy, Sweden and the UK, with a series of industrial visits in each. The delegates also had meetings with EU Commission officials and took part in a number of economic seminars. As a result two pilot programmes, offering training in the principles of the market economy and in raising efficiency in the energy sector, were prepared and ready to go.

The Action Plan's programmes were the first casualty of the October 2002 nuclear crisis. Despite the Plan's suspension, the EU has encouraged reform, promoting contacts between Pyongyang and international financial institutions. The Commission and member states have run small-scale training and capacity building projects, mainly in economies of transition, international finance and trade, environment management and language courses.

Public has been joined by private, with the European Business Association Pyongyang (EBA), founded in April 2005, fostering ties between European and North Korean businesses. It supports the Pyongyang Business School founded in 2004. European business activities include the PyongSu pharmaceutical joint venture (JV), producing generic medicines like aspirin for the domestic market, a Korean–Polish shipping JV, a partnership in IT services between the Korea Computer Centre and a German company, a Dutch commodity inspection company, DHL courier services and mining development. The most successful joint ventures to date are tobacco and beer. The British American Tobacco (BAT) plant near Pyongyang is reputedly making millions, even if few foreigners get to visit. Taedonggang's Brewery in Pyongyang, a redundant plant literally shipped lock, stock and barrel from Trowbridge in Wiltshire, is setting new standards of quality and reliability and has become the toast of Korean drinkers. In 2007 an attempt was made to formally establish a European Chamber of Commerce.

## Diverging interests

The six-party talks failed for five rounds and three years to overcome the deep mistrust between Pyongyang and Washington, and exposed the sharply divergent interests of other participants. For the United States the principal objective was CVID, for South Korea 'soft – or rather no – landing', for China non-proliferation and regional stability, for Japan the missing missiles and military rearmament, for Russia economic opportunities and for North Korea regime survival. The talks were important for China politically and diplomatically, but the paradigm chosen was wrong. In terms of the two recent non-proliferation initiatives, the Libyan model – in which North Korea would relinquish its nuclear weapons programme(s) in exchange for integration into the international community – will not work. Libya is rich and needs access not aid, while the North needs aid before access. The Ukrainian model, in which North Korea would give up its nuclear weapons programme(s) for a package deal of multilateral security guarantees and economic inducements, fits the bill but does not suit the US Administration.

A barrel from a Somerset town in Pyongyang

Washington and Seoul are at odds. Since German unification, or at least since future President Kim Dae Jung's study of it in 1993, South Korean politicians on both sides of the political divide – and more recently the general public – have come to realise that the costs of any unification by collapse were too high economically, socially and politically. The North is both larger and poorer than East Germany. Yet West Germany found the East a hard mouthful to swallow. If the *Ossis* (East Germans) have found it difficult to integrate, how much more so would millions of North Koreans? East Germans had an access to and knowledge of the West undreamt of on the peninsula. The Republic of Korea only became a fully fledged democracy with Kim Dae Jung's election as President in 1997. The influx of 20 million Communists and ex-Communists parachuted into a system they neither know nor understand nor support would be a shock for any democracy. The economic, social and political consequences of forced unification could see the South's fragile democracy collapse.

South Korea cannot afford the price of unity and its people will not pay. The Sunshine Policy was designed not so much for a 'soft landing', but for no landing at all. Once this is understood, South Korean attitudes towards investment, refugees, missile sales and the nuclear weapons become clear. For Seoul, North Korea is to remain a quarantined state until economic reform and the passage of time turn it into a new China or Vietnam. In the meantime the border will be semi-permeable. There will be a process of osmosis. Aid and investment will travel in, but people will not travel out. As the right-wing British newspaper *The Sun* said of a possible Labour victory in 1992, 'will the last person to leave Britain please turn out the lights!' In North Korea there are no lights. The South will make creeping territorial gains as the Kaesong industrial complex is incorporated into Seoul's industrial infrastructure, but its workers will remain North Korean. They travel North at the end of their shift, while the products of their labour will go South. Ten million North Koreans live within seven days walk of Seoul and 21 million only a railway journey away.

In total contradiction to Seoul, US policy is aimed at best at weakening and undermining the regime in the North, and at worst at regime change. The first forces a soft landing, while the second guarantees a hard one. Washington does not care about the consequences. (Allowing for the East German experience, what conceivable new regime save a military one is imaginable in Pyongyang that would not seek immediate unification? Hence from the South's perspective, appropriate actions must contribute to stabilising the regime.) Nevertheless Washington is in no great hurry; while 'regime change' is the goal, the North has other purposes to serve before it disappears into cold war history. If it collapses too soon the bottom falls out of shares in Star Wars technologies. Even with Cheney's '1 per cent doctrine' that the United States must defend itself against probabilities as low as one in a hundred, threats even at this level of probability emerge from too many UN member states. The number of countries with missiles and nukes is very limited. Pakistan is the only one that might fit the bill, but geography is even more difficult in its case than in North Korea's. The two nations are on diametrically opposite sides of the globe, Pakistan is stuck for the moment with cumbersome HEU technology, and its fundamentalists favour clandestine attacks rather than full frontal confrontation. Why spend $40 billion (€30 billion) on the prospects of Taliban technologists performing a miracle, even if they are stupid enough to try it?

Equally, if Japan's ruling Conservatives did not have the North their drive for constitutional reform and Japan's 'normalisation' would be that much more difficult. Japan's new self-confidence and nationalism need a 'weak' enemy. Previously, in the section on 'Sleeping with the enemy', we noted how Koizumi incited resentment among Japan's former victims with his visits to the Yasakumi Shrine even after it was revealed that Emperor Hirohito refused to go there.[2] His successor, Shinzo Abe, is if anything to the right of Koizumi. Yet while Koizumi was to an extent a maverick, Abe is mainstream, illustrating how far and how fast Japan's conservatives have travelled in a short time.

In contrast, Beijing does not wish North Korea's nuclear weapons or missiles to distract and divert China from its own economic transformation. North Korea's missiles have already given Japan the excuse of developing and deploying TMD and THAAD in tandem with the United States. As described before, this will provide Japan, and to an extent the United States, with the ability to neutralise and trump not only North Korea's missiles but China's limited number of ICBMs as well. This threatens to force China to divert spending from the civilian economy and managing the crisis in the countryside to the military. It will have to multiply its ICBMs from the current 20 to several hundred and to MIRV and mobilise them to be confident of either overwhelming the Missile Defence shields or withstanding a pre-emptive counterforce strike. Such a diversion of funds will in turn provoke a response from Taiwan and trigger an arms race in the region. If the current agreement fails and the North at the second time of asking successfully tests a nuclear weapon, the consequences would almost certainly see China and North Korea joined in short order by Taiwan, South Korea and Japan as nuclear powers, despite Abe's protestations to the contrary. Russia would prefer stability to sell its goods and expertise. The North and Kim Jong Il want regime survival.

The six-party talks in February 2007 seemingly made the breakthrough to take us back to the world of 1994's Agreed Framework. HFO was to finally flow again after more than four years, in exchange for the

North sharing its missile secrets while – in what the United States unconvincingly claimed was an independent decision – the North's Macao bank accounts were freed to do their worst. Five independent working groups, were established to deal with the details, as referred to in Chapter 7, alongside a joint energy needs survey of the North, in the hope that they would lead to the resolution of all outstanding issues. Yet with the six parties united only in their diversity, different interests and mutual distrust and it will be a long and painful march to any final resolution. But at least the agreement has stopped the bleeding of further plutonium into a weapons programme. It may well be that if progress is slow or non-existent, then some participants will choose to cut to the chase to short-circuit US or Japanese intransigence.

## Possible solutions

There are three possible novel scenarios, all of which can either stand alone or serve as add-ons to other elements of any settlement. There is a desire by China to avoid any further deterioration of the North's situation. But that requires first a comprehensive resolution of the nuclear crisis – that is a necessary but not sufficient condition for long-term stability – and second, major economic and systemic reform. The return to the 1994–2002 standoff, when Pyongyang was given enough to halt but not remove its nuclear weapons programme, is only a stopgap solution. The Washington–Pyongyang confrontation requires a conclusion, not a time-out.

Should China make the judgement that it is the North's intransigence blocking such a settlement, then trouble orchestrated or even imagined in border areas of Korea's North Pyongyang province would allow sympathetic army commanders to call for Chinese assistance under the terms of the 1961 Treaty of Friendship, Cooperation and Mutual Assistance. China's military would intervene to 'save the revolution', as they did in 1950 when the Chinese People's Volunteers intervened during the Korean War. It would be a 'hit and run' intervention – in and out. The Chinese would tinker with the North Korean leadership to make it sufficiently pliable for its purposes then swiftly withdraw, with Kim Jong Il left in charge and conservative anti-reformists sidelined. Job done.

The KPA is deployed heavily towards the state's southern borders, and any military intervention from the South would therefore result in a blood-bath, with Seoul enveloped in a 'sea of fire'. In contrast North Korea has few, if any, units deployed on the Chinese border and the circumstances of any intervention would be sufficiently confusing and disorientating that local military commanders in the North would probably be slow to react. China and North Korea may no longer be 'lips and teeth', but they are allies not enemies.

A second solution to sidestep US intransigence would be to utilise the common self-interests of South Korea, China and Russia. South Korea's President Roh Moo Hyun wants peaceful coexistence with a stable evolving regime in the North. *In extremis* he or his successor might be willing to face down the United States. Despite its conservative image, the opposition Grand National Party (GNP) may well embrace a nuanced pro-engagement position in the late 2007 presidential election, given the evidence that this commands strong public support. The GNP is divided into an 'old guard' who hark back to the past and a 'young guard' who are trying to come to terms with a transformation of politics as generational change, a decade so behind Japan, promoting a similar increasingly self-aware and self-confident Korean nationalism. Emerging from left-wing opposition to the South's authoritarian rulers and US complicity, this sea-change led to victory for Kim Dae Jung in 1997 and Roh Moo Hyun in 2002. Now, with the GNP's 'young guard', the same self-confident nationalism is emerging on the right. Whatever their other failings, Kim Dae Jung and Roh Moo Hyun inaugurated a new era of South Korean politics. Current GNP leader, Park Gun Hye, the daughter of the former president and military dictator Park Chung Hee, is one of the 'young guard'. She was invited in May 2002 by Kim Jong Il to visit Pyongyang, where Kim praised the South's economic growth during her father's era when the ROK learnt the lessons of Japan's economic success. In private, she approves of North Korea moving towards Market-Leninism. Currently more popular amongst Party members than her challengers, she may yet make it to Korea's Blue House.

The use of US nuclear technology to satisfy North Korea's demand for electricity and nuclear power is not an option. The legalities of a South Korean-designed reactor being built in the North would prove too intractable as ultimately all the technology would originate in the United States. Yet there is a third way. South Korea and China could turn to Russia, who would be only too delighted to sell a proliferation-resistant nuclear reactor to the North, paid for by the South Koreans and politically sanctioned and endorsed by China.

North Korea might be persuaded to accept the unacceptable with such a behind-the-scenes deal on offer to construct a nuclear reactor in the North. A parallel announcement that the North would make further progress on denuclearisation, backed by China, South Korea and Russia, would give the United States little wriggle room. It might be an offer impossible to refuse. World opinion would not favour US unilateralism in rejecting such a solution.

The third solution would be, instead of narrowing the number of players, to widen them. The North needs to give up its nuclear weapons and eventually its missile development, exports and over-sized military.

But it faces the prisoners' dilemma. It does not trust the United States and the United States is unwilling, and almost certainly politically unable, to deliver the economic assistance required to create that trust. Yet there is no final solution without US acquiescence. Squaring the circle might be achieved by widening the range of participants to include those willing to pay if given a say. The prime candidate would be the EU, bigger than the United States, richer than the United States, and the world's largest donor of international aid. The EU with the recent consolidation of its industrial, social and economic and monetary union is with the new Reform Treaty in the process of developing a full Common Foreign and Security Policy (CFSP). The EU has already taken distinctive positions on the Middle East, where it has shown more understanding of the Palestinian position than evidenced by the US administration; Iran, where the troika of France, Germany and the United Kingdom tried to engage with the regime and its nuclear ambitions in an effort to find a peaceful resolution; and North Korea, where the EU has pursued its line of 'critical engagement'.

In practical terms the EU has seen the inauguration of a 60,000 strong Rapid Reaction Force designed for intervention in its own 'near abroad'. Subsequently, there have been EU military deployments in Macedonia and Afghanistan, the Democratic Republic of the Congo and Kosovo. It also helped to negotiate the peace settlement in Aceh between the government of Indonesia and the separatist Gerakan Aceh Merdeka (GAM – the Free Aceh Movement) that had been engaged in a civil war for more than a quarter of a century. The Aceh Monitoring Mission was deployed from summer 2005, jointly with ASEAN, to oversee the surrender of arms, the withdrawal of the Indonesian 'non-organic' troops and the resettlement of combatants. The process culminated in fresh province-wide elections in December 2006 and March 2007 and Irwandi Yusuf, representing GAM, went from prisoner to governor in less than two years.

There is also a wider strategic argument for an enlarged EU to strengthen its political and economic presence in East Asia as a whole. The EU has close relations and shared economic and political interests with Japan and South Korea, while dynamic relations are developing with China. Thus developments in the northeast Asian region are of growing importance to the EU. In terms of North Korea, the EU provided a total of almost half a billion euros between 1995 and 2007 for KEDO, humanitarian aid and economic development. Retrospectively EU officials and politicians complain the United States left Europe to pick up its unpaid bills while denying it more than token involvement in the decision-making processes. After February's deal in Beijing, the spokesperson of Javier Solana, the High Official for the CFSP, speaking to the EP's Foreign Affair's Committee made it clear that this time around the EU wanted to be a player not a payer in any final accounting.

Would the North Koreans respond positively to EU participation in resolving the nuclear crisis? The evidence is encouraging. There have been pro-EU articles appearing in *Rodong Sinmun* since the 2001 visit of the EU President in Office Göran Persson.[3] Their emphasis is on the EU's increasing global influence, autonomy and economic power, a welcome for the EU's independent positions and its opposition to US military action, its growing economic status with the rising euro, and progress towards an independent CFSP. *Rodong Sinmun* portrays the EU as the only superpower it believes can check and balance US hegemony and unilateral exercise of military power. Pyongyang's perception is reflected in editorials headed; 'The EU becomes a new challenge to the US unilateralism', 'Escalating frictions between Europe and the US', 'The European economy (euro) dominating that of the US', 'Europe, strongly opposed to US unilateral power plays'.

Since the EU reluctantly backed the US position on the nuclear crisis, the quantity of favourable mentions has fallen, but the tone and quality remains. The EU's advantage is that it is neither the United States nor Japan. North Korea has pursued an active engagement with the EU, establishing diplomatic relations with 26 out of 27 EU member states. North Korea adopted the euro as its official foreign currency of choice, replacing the US dollar, in December 2002. It turned out it was an astute financial move, as between then and July 2007 the euro rose sharply against the US dollar.

Head of State Kim Young Nam is on record as welcoming EU involvement. South Korea's President Roh Moo Hyun has also been supportive, effectively overruling the agnosticism of the Ministry of Foreign Affairs and Trade. China's position is that it welcomes the EU's increasing role in global politics and wants to do what it can to strengthen it, with the need for the emergence of a multilateral new global economic and political order. Russia has said nothing, while Japan's former Prime Minister Koizumi did say 'at the right time'. His successor Abe, who has appointed his successor solely responsible for dealing with the Japanese abductees issue, might prove less amenable, particularly as Japan – despite signing off on February's agreement and participating in the energy assessment – is refusing to commit to financing any settlement without full closure of its own intractable issues. Only the United States has consistently shown little or no enthusiasm for EU participation.

In many respects, the approach recommended here mirrors, albeit in a different context, earlier engagement strategies, most notably West Germany's *Ostpolitik* and the idea of 'Change through Rapprochement'. This approach has a long-term focus, and stresses engagement as a motor for change, with bottom-up economic reform driving change rather than blunt attempts to advance humanitarian and security objectives, coercive diplomacy and conditional aid.

Kim Jong Il has started – 'in his own style' – to bring the country into the international community of nations and to open it up to the realities of the twenty-first century. It will be a long, slow and painful journey for North Korea and its people – but not as painful as all the alternatives.* It will require international cooperation on a massive scale. Participating in a partnership to improve the situation may appear financially costly, but politically it will be a bargain. Considering the consequences of chaos in Korea for the world, it is a price worth paying, not only for those suffering in the North but for everyone. 'Changing regime' trumps 'regime change' as Korea struggles to survive.

---

* Footnote: As the book went to press the breakthrough second North–South Korea summit between Kim Jong Il and Roh Moo-hyun, initially scheduled for 28–30 August in Pyongyang, was postponed until 2–4 October because of catastrophic floods in the North.

# Notes

## 1. North Korea in context

1. 'North Korea prepares to come in from the economic cold', *Financial Times*, 13 March 2006.
2. 'Diary' from Kaesong *FT.com* site, 13 November 2006.
3. 'Beijing's rising influence in Pyongyang raises fears in Seoul', *Financial Times*, 3 February 2006.
4. 'Mammon rears its head in Kim Jong Il's socialist paradise', *Financial Times*, 25 January 2006.

## 2. Drawing the Iron Curtain

1. George Orwell, *The Complete Works of George Orwell*, Vol. 13, London: Secker & Warburg, 1998, p. 317.
2. Kim, Ha Young, *Kukche chuui sigak eso pon hanbando* [The Korean Peninsula from an internationalist perspective], Seoul: Chaekbulae, 2002, pp. 234–5.
3. Andrew C. Nahm, *Korea: Tradition & Transformation*, Elizabeth, N.J.: Hollym International Corp, 1988.
4. Quoted in Adrian Buzo, *The Making of Modern Korea*, London: Routledge, 2002, p. 63.
5. Quoting Bruce Cumings in Sonya Ryang, *North Koreans in Japan*, Boulder, Colo.: Westview, 1997, p. 87.
6. Taiwan is where Chiang Kai-Shek retreated from mainland Communist China. It was then called by its Portuguese name Formosa (*ilha formosa*), meaning 'beautiful island'.
7. Documents in the South Korean government archives from 1949 and 1950, including letters and memorandum by Rhee and Chang Myun (then, South Korean Ambassador in Washington), military reports, and even a strategic map for an attack on North Korea illustrate the military adventurism of Rhee's Administration. *Facts Tell: Secret Documents Seized by North Korea from the South Korean Government Archives*, Hawaii: University Press of the Pacific Honolulu, 2001.
8. Joseph S. Bermudez, *North Korean Special Forces*, 2nd edition, Annapolis, Md.: Naval Institute Press, 1988, pp. 36–7.
9. Quoting Chen Jian in Chuck Downs, *Over the Line: North Korea's Negotiating Strategy*, Washington D.C.: AEI Press, 1999, p. 24.
10. This Pulitzer-award-winning book by three investigative journalists details the July 1950 incident at No Gun Ri. Charles J Hanley, Sang-Hun Choe and Martha Mendoza, *The Bridge at No Gun Ri: A Hidden*

*Nightmare from the Korean War*, New York: Henry Holt and Company, 2002.

11. *ibid*, 2002, p. 223–4.
12. Quoting Robert Leckie in Chuck Downs, *Over the Line*, p. 29.
13. C. Turner Joy, *How Communists Negotiate*, New York: Macmillan, 1955, p. 18.
14. Ha Jin, *War Trash*, New York: Pantheon, 2004.
15. Kongdan Oh and Ralph C. Hassig, *North Korea Through the Looking Glass*, Washington D.C.: Brookings Institution Press, 2002, p. 7.
16. John Halliday and Bruce Cumings, *Korea: The Unknown War*, London: Viking, 1988.
17. Chuck Downs, *Over the Line*, p. 34.
18. Churchill's remark was quoted in *Monthly Review*, April 1997.

## 3. Kim's Korea

1. Kim Il Sung, 'Our People's Army is an army of the working class, an army of the revolution; class and political education should be continuously strengthened', speech delivered to People's Army cadres on 8 February 1963, in Kim Il Sung, *Selected Works*, Vol. III, p. 519.
2. Il Pyong Kim, *Communist Politics in North Korea*, New York: Praeger, 1975, pp. 65–76.
3. The conspiracy is detailed in Chapter 4 in Andrei Lankov, *Crisis in North Korea: The Failure of De-Stalinization 1956*, Honolulu: University of Hawaii, 2005.
4. Kim Il Sung, 'On some problems of our party's *Juche* idea and the government of the republic's internal and external policies, answers to a Japanese journalist for *Mainichi Shimbun* on September 17, 1972', in Kim Il Sung, *On Juche in Our Revolution*, Vol. 2, Pyongyang: Foreign Languages Publishing House, 1975, pp. 425–36.
5. Kim Il Sung's speech at the Fourth Supreme People's Assembly, December 16, 1967. See *Kim Il Sung Works*, Vol. 21, Pyongyang: Foreign Languages Publishing House, 1985, p. 414.
6. These issues echo today. In December 1998, with snow on the ground, the construction of the Pyongyang-Nampo motorway was underway, using tens of thousands of workers seconded from Pyongyang's offices. Construction was by hand with almost no mechanical assistance. There were a couple of lorries and two mechanical diggers to be seen in 20 kilometres of driving. On that evening, North Korean Central Broadcasting showed heroic workers labouring under waving red banners with stirring martial music and juddering earth-moving equipment. The road was finished ahead of time. But as early as summer 2003 it was showing signs of flawed construction, with patches of subsidence that the vehicular traffic zigzagged around.
7. A disappointing performance during this plan forced the planners to extend the plan three more years.

8.  Kim Il Sung 'Every effort for the country's reunification and independence and for socialist construction in the northern half of the Republic', *Selected Works of Kim Il Sung*, Vol. 1, Pyongyang: Foreign Languages Publishing House, 1965, p. 510.

9.  N. Vreeland and R. S. Shinn, *Area Handbook for North Korea*, Washington D.C.: Library of Congress, 1976, p. 225.

10. Andrea M. Savada, *North Korea: A Country Study*, 4th edition, Washington D.C.: Library of Congress, 1994, p. 126; also see N. Vreeland and R. S. Shinn, *Area Handbook for North Korea*, p. 224.

11. Andrea M. Savada, *North Korea*, pp. 114–15.

12. Kim Il Sung, 'Let us embody the revolutionary spirit of independence, self-sustenance and self-defence more thoroughly in all state activities', speech at the first session of the fourth Supreme People's Assembly December 16, 1967 in *Selected Works of Kim Il Sung*, Vol. 4, Pyongyang: Foreign Languages Publishing House, 1971, p. 557.

13. Kim Il Sung, 'On the immediate tasks of the government of the Democratic People's Republic of Korea', *Selected Works of Kim Il Sung*, Vol. 3, Pyongyang: Foreign Languages Publishing House, 1971, p. 399.

14. Kim Il Sung, in fact, boasted that the number of technical personnel increased from 497,000 in 1970 to 1 million in 1976. Kim Il Sung, *New Year Address*, Pyongyang: Foreign Languages Publishing House, p. 3. Also see Kim Il Sung's New Year address in *Rodong Sinmun*, 1 January 1976.

15. The GDP growth rate in North Korea was 5.4 per cent in 1975, 3.8 per cent in 1980, –3.7 per cent in 1990, –7.6 per cent in 1992, –4.6 per cent in 1995, –3.7 per cent in 1996, –6.8 per cent in 1997, –1.1 per cent in 1998. Estimated by the Bank of Korea. See the publication of the Ministry of Unification of the Republic of Korea, *2000 Understanding North Korea* [in Korean – *Pukhanihae*], Seoul: Ministry of Unification, 2001, p. 153.

16. Andrea M. Savada, *North Korea*, p. 91.

17. See 'Changes in occupational structure among North Korean people', in T. H. Ok and H. Y. Lee, *Prospects for Change in North Korea*, Berkeley: University of California, 1994, p. 267, Table 5.3.

18. Andrea M. Savada, *North Korea*, p. 59; Vreeland and Shinn, *Area Handbook for North Korea*, p. 54.

19. T. H. Ok and H. Y. Lee, *Prospects for Change in North Korea*, p. 228 and p. 267.

20. Kim Il Sung, 'Let us defend the socialist camp', *Rodong Shinmun*, 28 October 1963.

21. Adrian Buzo, *The Guerilla Dynasty: Politics and Leadership in North Korea*, Boulder, Colo.: Westview, 1999, pp. 57–79.

22. Kim Il Sung, 'The present situation and the tasks of our Party', report to the 5 October 1966 Conference of the Korean Workers' Party, *Selected Works of Kim Il Sung*, Vol. 4.

23. Koo, Bon-Hak, *Political Economy of Self-Reliance: Juche and Economic*

*Development in North Korea, 1961–1990*, Seoul: Research Center for Peace and Unification of Korea, 1992, p. 123.

24. Kim Jong Il expressed his concern about the US–China rapprochement and the real intention of the US behind Nixon's visit to China. See Kim Jong Il, 'Let us inspire the young people with the spirit of continuous revolution', talk to the senior officials of the Youth-Work Department of the Central Committee of the Workers' Party of Korea, and of the Central Committee of the LSWY on 1 October 1971, in *Kim Jong Il Selected Works* (1995) Vol. 2, Pyongyang: Foreign Languages Publishing House, 1971, p. 282.

25. A chronology of North Korea's stamps across the years show alternations between pro-Soviet and pro-Chinese issues that may give a better reflection of relations than official announcements.

26. Website of the Non-Aligned Movement, http://www.nam.gov.za/background/history.htm.

27. See a section on 'Incidents and infiltrations: targeting South Korea', in Andrea M. Savada, *North Korea*, pp. 261–2.

28. Kim Il Sung, 'For the independent unification of Korea', report at the celebrations of the 15th Anniversary of the August 15 Liberation, 1960.

29. Kim Il Sung (1960), 'For the independent unification of Korea'.

30. The list of people who were purged for opposition to the hereditary succession plan is shown in the 'Chronology of purges by Kim Il Sung', in I.S. Lee, *North Korea: The Land that Never Changes*, Seoul: Naewoe Press, 1995, p. 19.

31. For a detailed study of the leadership in North Korea, see Soyoung Kwon, 'Changes in the composition and structures of the North Korean elite', *International Journal of Korean Unification Studies*, Vol. 12, No. 2, Seoul: Korea Institute for National Unification, 2003.

## 4. A life in Wonderland

1. The promises can often found in the Party newspaper, *Rodong Sinmun*, even in the early 1990s.

2. Kim Il Sung, 'Thesis on socialist education', in *Kim Il Sung: Selected Works*, Vol. 7, Pyongyang: Foreign Languages Publishing House, 1979 (originally published in 1977).

3. Sonia Ryang, *North Korean in Japan: Language, Ideology, and Identity*, Boulder, Colo.: Westview, 1997.

4. For details of political study sessions in the workplace, see Helen-Louise Hunter, *Kim Il-Song's North Korea*, Westport: Greenwood, 1999, Chapter 13.

5. Kim Il Sung, 'On creating revolutionary literature and art', speech to workers in the field of literature and art, 7 November 1964, in *Selected Works of Kim Il Sung*, Vol. 4.

6. Guy Delisle, *Pyongyang: A Journey in North Korea*, Montreal: Drawn & Quarterly Books, 2005, p. 112.

7. Dr Quinones also served on the US team that negotiated the Agreed Framework of 1994.

8. Quinones's personal recollection in C. Kenneth Quinones and Joseph Tragert, *Understanding North Korea*, New York: Alpha Books, 2003, p. 320.

9. Patrick O'Brian is the author of a series of 21 historical novels set in the early nineteenth century, based around the exploits of a Royal Navy captain, Jack Aubrey, and a naval surgeon, Stephen Maturin. The first book was made into the highly successful film *Master and Commander: The Far Side of the World* in 2003.

10. Kim Jong Il, *The Cinema and Directing*, Pyongyang: Foreign Language Publishing House, 1987.

11. The defectors are American soldiers who crossed the border to North Korea while on patrol on the South Korean side of the DMZ and chose to remain in the North. At a press briefing in May 1997, the Pentagon officials confirmed that six American soldiers had defected to North Korea between the 1960s and the 1980s. They were named as Private Larry Abshier (May 1962), Pfc James Dresnock (August 1962), Army Spc Jerry Wayne Parrish (December 1963), Sgt Robert (Charles) Jenkins (January 1965), Pfc Roy Chung (June 1979), and Pfc Joseph White (August 1982). Jenkins and Dresnock are now in their 60s and were thought to be the last remaining American defectors. Jenkins attracted media attention when he travelled in 2004 to Japan to be with his wife, Hitomi Soga, who was returned to Japan as one of North Korea's abductees. Nick Bonner of the Koryo group interviewed Dresnock in June 2006 for his film *Crossing the Line*, which tells the stories of all six defectors based on Dresnock's account and those of the families of the deceased. Speaking to the film-maker, Dresnock said: 'I find it more convenient to live among peaceful people, living a simple life.' The former American servicemen worked in North Korea as English teachers and movie actors. They also made appearances in various propaganda publications and magazines over the years. See press briefing by Colonel Larry Greer of the Defense Department's POW/MIA Affairs Office (DPMO) in May 1997.

12. The following comic books, bought in bookstores in Pyongyang and Nampo, were chosen to exclude a second series of essentially historic comics illustrating Korea's deep history: A *Special Operation (2001); The Dark Shadow on a Full-moon Day (2001); The Snow Storm in a Tropical Forest (2001); They Have Returned! (2001); The Foggy Island (2002); Operation 'Ryu-sung' (2002); A Story of Three Bows (2002); The Bullet Shields (2003); Fights under the Water (2004); The True Identity of the 'Pear Blossom' (2004)*.

13. Nick Bonner has produced three films on North Korea: *Crossing the Line* (www.crossingthelinefilm.com), *A State of Mind* (www.astateofmind. co.uk), and *The Game of their Lives* (www.thegameoftheir lives.com).

14. In February 2004, the British Embassy sponsored an impressive collection of blooms.
15. Frank Bough, BBC commentary, 1966.
16. For detailed history, organisation and function of the Ministry of People's Security and its bureaus, see Jon Hyun-Jun, *A Study of the Social Control System in North Korea: Focusing on the Ministry of People's Security* [published originally in Korean and translated into English], Seoul: Korea Institute for National Unification, 2003.
17. Ali Lameda, *A Personal Account of a Prisoner of Conscience in the Democratic People's Republic of Korea*, London: Amnesty International, 1979.
18. Kang Chol Hwan with Pierre Rigoulot, *The Aquariums of Pyongyang: Ten years in the North Korean Gulag*, translated from French by Yair Reiner, New York: Basic Books, 2001, pp. 95–6.

## 5. Food, famine and fugitives

1. Andrew Natsios, *The Politics of Famine in North Korea: Special Report 51*, Washington D.C.: US Institute of Peace, 2 August 1999.
2. See the estimate on the WFP web: *http://www.wfp.org* – DPRK.
3. FAO/WFP, *Special Report: FAO/WFP Crop and Food Supply Assessment Mission to the Democratic People's Republic of Korea*, 22 December 1995.
4. European Parliament Resolution, 23 October 1997 (OJ C 339, 10.11.1997, p. 153) on the famine in North Korea.
5. European Parliament resolution, 12 March 1998 (OJ C 104, 6.4.1998, p. 236) on the food crisis in North Korea.
6. The report of the Parliament ad hoc delegation that visited the Democratic People's Republic of Korea in December 1998. PE 229.331.
7. Glyn Ford 'Through the looking glass: Alice in Asia', *Soundings*, No. 18, Summer/Autumn, 2001, pp. 75–6.
8. Resolution on the food crisis in North Korea, European Parliament, 3 December 1998; also see Resolution on relations between the European Union and the Democratic People's Republic of Korea, 23 March 1999.
9. UNICEF, 'Analysis of the situation of children and women in the Democratic People's Republic of Korea', October 2003. Available on the UNICEF website, http://www.unicef.org/dprk/situation analysis.pdf.
10. Kate Pound Dawson, 'DPRK seeks shift in aid to grow economy, prevent hunger', *Voice of America News*, 30 September 2004.
11. For detailed description of change inside North Korea, see special report of FAO/WFP, 11 November 2004.
12. 'Historical lesson in building socialism and the general line of our Party', Kim Jong Il, speech given on 3 January 1992, published in *Rodong Sinmun* on 4 February 1992, and broadcast on the same day by KCNA, transcribed by *FBIS*, East Asia, 92–024, 5 February 1992, pp. 11–24.

13. Kim Jong Il, 'Historical lesson in building socialism and the general line of our Party', *FBIS*, East Asia, p. 23.
14. Kongdan Oh and Ralph Hassig, *North Korea Through the Looking Glass*, Washington DC: Brookings Institution Press, 2000, p. 30.
15. Speech given by Kim Jong Il on the occasion of the 50th Anniversary of Kim Il Sung University; text can be found on the web at http://www.kimsoft.com/korea/kji-kisu.htm.
16. *Rodong Sinmun* editorial, 'Let us see and solve all problems from a new perspective and a new height', 9 January 2001. The so-called 'innovation in thinking and work attitude' in building an economically prosperous country, however, first appeared in a *Rodong Sinmun* editorial on 4 January 2001.
17. See the data on http://www.unikorea.go.kr – Inter-Korean cooperation.
18. Soon Ok Lee, *Eyes of the Tailless Animals: Prison Memoirs of a North Korean Woman*, Bartlesville, Okla.: Living Sacrifice Book Company, 1999.
19. The EU commitment is based on the Vienna Declaration of the European Union of 10 December 1998.
20. EP Resolution on Humanitarian Crisis in North Korea, 16 January 2003; EP report on Human Rights in the World (article 58), 5 April 2005, p. 11; EP Resolution on Violations of Human Rights in North Korea, 15 June 2006.
21. 'Western "standards of human rights" cannot work', *KCNA*, 5 August 1993.
22. For reference, see the following articles: 'Shop till you drop', *Hong Kong Far Eastern Economic Review*, 13 May 2004; 'Hermit kingdom peeps cautiously out of its shell', *Financial Times*, 12 February 2004; 'How N. Korea is embracing capitalism by any other name', *Guardian*, 3 December 2003; 'A crack in the door in N. Korea', *Washington Post*, 24 November 2003; 'Quietly, North Korea opens markets', *New York Times*, 21 November 2003; 'N. Korea shifts toward capitalism', *Washington Post*, 14 September 2003.
23. 'North Korea: status report on nuclear program, humanitarian issues, and economic reforms', US Congress, 23 February 2004.

## 6. WMD paranoia rules

1. Excerpt from Central Intelligence Agency, 'Estimate of North Korea missile force trends', in *Department of Defense, Proliferation and Response*, Washington, D.C.: US Government Printing Office, 2002.
2. This report by Olenka Frankiel, which later turned out to be a confidence trick, is detailed in Chapter 5 under the section 'Defectors' world tour'.
3. For the US claims, see the *New York Times*, 27 February 2004; *International Herald Tribune*, 28–29 February 2004 'North Korea and Pakistan: a joint nuclear test'; and *International Herald Tribune*, 29

August 2006, 'North is capable of a nuclear test'. The October test was signalled by the North Korean Foreign Ministry, which made a public statement on 3 October 2006 of its intent to carry out a nuclear test: 'the field of scientific research of the DPRK will in the future conduct a nuclear test under the condition where safety is firmly guaranteed.' 'DPRK Foreign Ministry clarifies stand on new measure to bolster war deterrent', *KCNA*, 3 October 2006.

4. This point was made both by William Perry, the former Defense Secretary at the State Department, and Philip W. Yun who served as a US Department of State official from 1994 to 2001. Quoted from my meeting with Perry and Yun at the Asia Pacific Research Center, Stanford University, on 3 February 2005.

5. HFO is the refuse of refining. It is the tar-like remnant after gasoline, diesel fuel, kerosene, lubricants and other products have been distilled and separated out. The offer of HFO was acceptable to both sides: to the United States because it cannot be processed for jet fuel etc., and to North Korea because the Soviet had years before sold them a power station that was designed to run on this environmental horror, high in carbon, sulphur and other impurities that make it a polluter's dream and a corrosion expert's nightmare.

6. Robert A. Wampler (ed.) *North Korea's Collapse? The End is Near – Maybe*, National Security Archive Electronic Briefing Book No. 205, posted on 26 October 2006.

7. *Rodong Sinmun*, 4 April; 11 May; 20 June 2001 .

8. CNN News 'US: North Korea admits nuke program', 17 October 2002.

9. In the report of the official Korean Central News Agency (KCNA), the North Korean Foreign Ministry stated that 'the DPRK was entitled to possess not only nuclear weapons but any type of weapon more powerful than that so as to defend its sovereignty and right to existence from the ever-growing nuclear threat by the US', KCNA, 25 October 2002. www.kcna.co.jp For details of the controversial 'confession', see 'N. Korean nuclear "admission" in doubt', *BBC Asia Pacific*, 18 November 2002.

10. William Langewiesche, 'The point of no return', *The Atlantic*, January/February 2006, p. 111.

11. A cargo ship with aluminium destined for the North Korean firm *Nam Chon Gang*. See 'Germans shipping nuke parts to N. Korea?' in *World Net Daily*, 19 August 2003. http://www.wnd.com.

12. *New York Times*, 28 February 2007, 'US concede uncertainty on North Korean uranium effort'; *Washington Post*, 1 March 2007, 'New doubts on nuclear effort by North Korea'.

13. The US is building a three-tier antiballistic missile defence system. The lower tier is the TMD, which is designed to defend against short-range missiles. This system was jointly developed and deployed by the US and Japan. They are working on developing the second-level THAAD, which is designed to destroy intermediate large missiles. The third tier

is NMD, which consists of long-range antiballistic missiles based in the United States.

14. Chris Mooney, *The Republican War on Science*, New York: Basic Books, 2005.

15. Andrea M. Savada (ed) *North Korea*. See section on 'Relations with the Third World', pp. 259–60.

## 7. Negotiating its place

1. See *The Cold War In Asia*, Cold War International History Project Bulletin, Nos. 6–7, Washington DC: Woodrow Wilson International Center for Scholars, winter 1995/1996, pp. 30–123. Also see *The Cold War in the Third World and the Collapse of Detente in the 1970s*, Cold War International History Project, Nos. 8–9, Washington DC: Woodrow Wilson International Center for Scholars, winter 1996/1997, pp. 220–243.

2. *Rodong Sinmun*, 23 January 2001.

3. In response to criticisms raised by North Koreans of the term 'Sunshine Policy', the name was later changed to a 'reconciliation and cooperation policy' towards North Korea.

4. For the contents and achievements of the Kim Dae Jung administration's 'Sunshine Policy' towards North Korea, see Ministry of Unification, *Promoting Peace and Cooperation*, Seoul: Ministry of Unification, Republic of Korea, 2003. Also visit the website: www.unikorea.go.kr.

5. When asked about the DPRK's government's perspective on the abductees issue, the deputy director of the Foreign Affairs Ministry for Japan, Song Il Ho, acknowledged that North Korean secret agents did wrongly abduct 13 Japanese nationals, of whom he claims eight had died due to accidents or illness. He said that those responsible for the abduction had been charged and punished. 'North Korea: status report on nuclear program, humanitarian issues, and economic reforms', a staff trip report to the Committee on Foreign Relations of the United States Senate, 108th Congress, 2nd session, 23 February 2004.

6. *New York Times*, 21 July 2006.

7. Myong-Chol Hwang, 'Tok Islet is Korea's islet historically and by international law', *Democratic People's Republic of Korea*, No. 589, July 2005, pp. 38–9.

8. See Selig S. Harrison, *Korean Endgame: A Strategy for Reunification and US Disengagement*, Princeton: Princeton University Press, 2002.

9. The European Parliament questioned the US claim in the Resolution on the Non-Proliferation Treaty 2005 Review Conference – Nuclear arms in North Korea and Iran of 10 March 2005: '[It] is aware that central to the ongoing crisis are the claims that North Korea has a full fledged highly enriched uranium programme and has supplied

uranium to Libya; considering, however, that neither of these claims has been substantiated, asks for a public hearing in the European Parliament to evaluate the claims'.

10. Korean Peninsula Energy Development Organization Annual Report 2004, p. 6.

11. The full text of the six-nation statement on North Korea can be found in Nautilus Institute Special Report 05–77A: September 20th 2005. http://www.nautilus.org/napsnet/sr/2005/0577.

12. United Nations Security Council Resolution 1695 adopted by the Security Council at its 5490th meeting on 15 July 2006, S/RES/1695 (2006).

13. European Parliament, Resolution on the Non-Proliferation Treaty 2005 Review Conference – Nuclear arms in North Korea and Iran: 'Calls on the Council and the Commission to offer financial support for heavy fuel oil supplies to remedy North Korea's primary energy needs, and asks the Commission and the Council to make the necessary approaches regarding EU participation in future six-party talks while at the same time making it clear that "No Say, No Pay" is a principle which the EU will follow in its dealings with the Korean Peninsula'.

14. EU member states that sent troops to fight with the UNC in the Korean War were the UK, France, Greece, Netherlands, Belgium and Luxembourg. Denmark, Sweden and Italy sent medical assistance.

15. European Parliament, Resolution 'on the Community's Trade with North Korea', Document A2 169/85.

16. Technical assistance projects for institutional support and capacity building for North Korea's sustainable economic development were on hold because of the current nuclear crisis. The data for the EU contribution can be found on the European Commission website on the EU's relations with the DPRK: http://europa.eu.int/comm/external_relations/north_korea/intro/index.htm.

17. Resolution on the Food Crisis in North Korea, European Parliament, 3 December 1998; Resolution on Relations between the European Union and the Democratic People's Republic of Korea, 23 March 1999.

18. Author's interview with Commissioner Patten, Strasbourg, 20 July 2004. Also see his recollection of the meeting with the North Korean Leader in Chris Patten, *Not Quite The Diplomat*, London: Penguin, 2006, pp. 177–8.

19. Excerpt from speech of President Kim Dae Jung at the European Parliament, 11 December 2001 in Strasbourg.

## 8.   Changing regime or regime change?

1. *Rodong Sinmun*, 23 January 2001.

2. *New York Times*, 21 July 2006.

3. An analysis of the Party newspaper, *Rodong Sinmun*, (2001–03) finds over 20 positive articles related to Europe and the EU per year from

2001. Most of them praise its autonomy and independent position, the expansion of its influence, regional integration and rising economic power. Soyoung Kwon (2004), 'Change in North Korea reflected in *Rodong Sinmun* 1980–2002', in *BAKS journal*, Vol. 9, and *British Museum Occasional Paper No. 106*. The analysis is later expanded to add EU-related articles in 2004, and published in 'Pyongyang under EU's wing', *The Japan Times*, 17 March 2005.

# Recommended reading and viewing

Beal, Tim (2004) *North Korea: The Struggle Against American Power*, London: Pluto Press. A sympathetic view of the North Korean regime.

Bermudez, Joseph S. (1988) *North Korean Special Forces*, 2nd edition, Annapolis, Md.: Naval Institute Press. The North's real threat.

Bradley, K. Martin (2004) *Under the Loving Care of the Fatherly Leader: North Korea and the Kim Dynasty,* New York: Thomas Dunne. A doorstop of a book, confused, muddled and sometimes enlightening.

Buzo, Adrian (1999) *The Guerilla Dynasty: Politics and Leadership in North Korea*, Colorado: Westview. The era of the Patriot Generals.

Buzo, Adrian (2002) *The Making of Modern Korea*, London, Routledge. A wider history.

Chang, Gordon, (2006) *Nuclear Showdown: North Korea Takes on the World,* New York: Random House. Neo-Cons wanting action.

Cha, Victor and David Kang (2003) *Nuclear North Korea: A Debate on Engagement Strategies*, New York: Columbia University Press.

Cummings, Bruce (1981) *Origins of the Korean War*, Vol. I and Vol. II, Princeton N.J.: Princeton University Press. The definitive work in English.

Cummings, Abrahamian, Maoz, (2004) *Inventing the Axis of Evil: The Truth about North Korea, Iran and Syria.* Left-wing academic dismantling the case against North Korea.

Delisle, Guy (2005) *Pyongyang: A Journey in North Korea*, Montreal: Drawn & Quarterly Books. Cartoon criticism.

Dorfman, Ariel and Armand Mattelart (1984) *How to Read Donald Duck*, New York: International General. Cartoon capitalism.

Downs, Chuck (1999) *Over the Line: North Korea's Negotiating Strategy*, Washington D.C.: AEI Press. Neo-Con worries.

Ha Jin (2002) *War Trash*, London: Penguin. Biography as fiction in South Korean POW camp told from the perspective of a Chinese soldier.

Harrison, Selig S. (2002) *Korean Endgame: A Strategy for Reunification and US Disengagement*, Princeton: Princeton University Press. Left leaning US academic.

Hoare, Jim and Susan Pares (2005) *North Korea in the 21st Century*, Kent: Global Oriental. Story of Britain's first chargé d'affaires in Pyongyang.

Kang Chol Hwan (2000) *The Aquariums of Pyongyang: Ten Years in the North Korean Gulag*, New York: Basic Books. The defectors' memoirs for George W. Bush.

Kongdan Oh and Ralph C. Hassig (2000) *North Korea: Through the Looking Glass*, Washington D.C.: Brookings Institution Press. Korean–American View.

Lankov, Andrei (2005) *Crisis in North Korea: The Failure of De-Stalinization*

*1956*, Honolulu: University of Hawaii. Russian Academic using Soviet Archives.

Quinones, Kenneth and Joseph Tragert (2003) *Understanding North Korea*, New York: Alpha. On how Americans don't!

Richard, Jeffery T. (2006) *Spying on the Bomb*, London: Norton.

Scalapino, Robert and Chong Sik Lee (1972) *Communism in Korea*, Vol. I and Vol. II, Berkeley: University of California Press. Definitive writings.

Snyder, Scott (1999) *Negotiation on the Edge*, Washington D.C.: US Institute of Peace. Engage not enrage.

Suh Dae Sook (1988) *Kim Il Sung: The North Korean Leader*, New York: Columbia University Press. Best biography of Kim Il Sung.

Suskind, Ron (2006) *The One Per Cent Doctrine*, New York: Simon & Schuster. If it might possibly happen it will.

Szalontai, Balazs (2006) *Kim Il Sung in the Khrushchev Era: Soviet-DPRK Relations and the Roots of North Korean Despotism, 1953–1964*. Hungarian Using Hungarian archives.

Willoughby, Robert (2003) *North Korea: The Bradt Travel Guide*, Bucks: Bradt Travel Guides. Where to go and what to see.

## Films

*Heaven's Soldiers* (2005) directed by Min Joon Ki, Korea. Koreans vs Japan.

*Team America: World Police* (2004) directed by Trey Parker, USA. Puppet politics.

*Silmido* (2003) directed by Kang Woo-suk, Korea. Korean version of *The Dirty Dozen*.

*Joint Security Area* (2000) directed by Park Chan Wook, Korea. Fraternisation across the Line.

*One Minute to Zero* (1952) directed by Tay Garnett, USA. No Gun Ri incident as fiction.

*The Manchurian Candidate* (1962) directed by John Frankenheimer, USA. Soviet sleeper sent from Korea.

*Deterrence* (1999) directed by Rod Lurie.

## Documentaries

*The Game of Their Lives* (2002) by Koryogroup, China.
   The North Korean football team and their return to the UK.
*A State of Mind* (2004) by Koryogroup, China.
   Two school girls training for the Mass Games.
*Crossing the Line* (2006) by Koryogroup, China.
   US military defectors in North Korea.

# Index

9/11, policy following, xix, 5, 174,
    182
38th Parallel, 1, 16, 25, 29

abductions
    by DPRK of Japanese, 7, 8,
        178–9, 192, 217, 223n4-11,
        227n7-5
    by Japanese of Koreans, 7, 24
Abe, Prime Minister Shinzo, 7, 146,
    179, 180, 213, 217
Aceh Monitoring Mission (AMM),
    100, 216
Acheson, Dean, 30–1, 32, 45
advertisements (in Pyongyang),
    206
Afghanistan, 10, 68, 158, 168, 216
Agreed Framework, xix, 5, 11, 150,
    151–3, 181, 201–3
    US abandonment of, 6, 148, 182,
        202
    US reneging on commitments
        under, 5, 187
agriculture, 24, 58, 59, 63, 113, 123
    assistance for, 118
    collectivisation of, 57
    lack of investment in, 60
    marketisation of, 204–5
    modernisation of, 209
    problems in 1990s, 113
    productivity increases in, 123,
        204
aid
    Chinese military to DPRK, 32,
        34
    food aid in 1950s, 51
    food aid after the famine,
        114–21
    from DPRK to South Korea, 75
    organisations, xix
    Soviet military to DPRK, 31–2,
        34, 66
    to DPRK by China, 57–8, 120
    to DPRK by Eastern Europe,
        57–8

    to DPRK by the EU, 11, 114, 117,
        216
    to DPRK by Japan, 117–18
    to DPRK by South Korea, 11,
        114, 120, 175
    to DPRK by the Soviet Union,
        57, 58, 66
    to DPRK by the US, 114
    to South Korea by the US, 31,
        35–7, 57, 70
    under the Agreed Framework,
        11
Air Koryo, 13, 14, 71, 100
air
    space, US violation of, 71
    terrorist incidents, 75, 177
    traffic to DPRK, 13–14, 71
Al Qaeda, 158
Albright, Madeleine, 90, 93, 181
Amnesty International, 109, 136,
    140
Amnok (Yalu) River, 14, 32, 36
*An Jung Gun Shoots Ito Hirobumi*, 94
Andropov, President Yuri, 68
Anti-Japanese People's Guerrilla
    Army, 22
*Arirang* festival, 12, 96
armistice (for Korean War), xviii
arms trade, 7, 158–9, 165–7, 192,
    2007
art, 93–4
ASEAN, 10
Asher, David, 185
assassinations, real and attempted,
    73, 75, 89, 94, 130, 205
Attlee, Prime Minister Clement, 39
autarky, economic, 60–2
'axe murder', 72–3
'axis of evil', xv, xix, 5, 145

badge, Kim Il Sung, 53, 54
Ban Ki-Moon, 144
Bandung Conference (1955), 69
bank accounts frozen, 189, 191, 214
bars and clubs, 100

BBC, 138–9, 148
beer, 100, 101, 210
bicycles, 83
bird flu, 14
Blair, Prime Minister Tony, 153, 195, 197
Blake, George, 43, 44
bombs
   'bunker busters', 37
   nuclear *see* nuclear plant/weapons
   terrorist, 5, 75, 100
   used in Korean War, 38
Bonner, Nick, 97, 223n4-11, 223n4-13
books, 93–4
   comic, 95–6, 223n4-12
   crime novels, 108
borders of DPRK, 16–17
   with China, 16–17, 119, 132–5
   closing of southern, 29
   incidents along southern, 73
   transport across, 13–15, 17
   *see also 38th Parallel;* Korea, division of; demilitarised zone
borrowings, DPRK's from West, 3
Bosch, Orlando, 6
brewing/breweries, 100, 101, 210
Brezhnev, President Leonid, 68
*Bridge at No Gun Ri, The*, 38
Brinkhorst, Jan, 116
British Free Corps, 41
Bush, President George Sr. (as director of CIA), 6
Bush, President George W., 5, 6, 138, 140, 145, 154, 162, 164, 174, 182, 186, 187, 188, 195, 199, 202
   'Axis of Evil' speech, xix, 182
Bush, Jeb, 6
business cards, 93
buying goods in DPRK, 13
   *see also* markets, shops

Cairo Conference (1943), 25
Cambodia, 36, 71, 109
Carter, President Jimmy, 76, 151, 180, 201

Ceausescu, Nicolae, 48, 55, 109
*Chaebol*, 3
Chalabi, Ahmad, 29
Chang, Gordon, 159
Chang Ung, 100
Cheju Island, 30, 33
chemical weapons, 38, 147–8
Chemulpo, Treaty of, 19, 20
Cheney, Dick, 9, 213
Chernenko, Konstantin, 170
Chiang Kai-Shek, 32
children
   education of *see* education
   malnourished, 114, 116–17, 119, 120
   orphaned, 85
   'palaces' for, 88
China, xv, xvii, xviii, 3, 25, 69, 144
   1894–5 invasion of Korea and Sino-Japanese War
   attitudes to DPRK, 8, 67–8, 171, 213, 214, 217
   border with DPRK, 16–17, 119, 132–5
   civil war, 32
   Communist Party, 22, 32, 49, 68
   economic partner of/aid to DPRK, 2–3, 4, 57, 58, 66, 114, 120, 170
   economic success, 62, 144, 171
   fact-finding visits to, 172, 208
   founding of People's Republic, 32
   'Great Leap Forward' (1958–60), 59
   human rights dialogue with EU, 10
   and Japanese invasion of Manchuria, 22
   Korean refugees in, xix, 51, 112, 119, 132–9
   Maritime Territories ceded to Russia, 16
   military aid to DPRK, 32, 34, 159
   military spending, 164, 171, 213
   nuclear programme, 6
   and Opium War, 18

physical communications with DPRK, 13–14

relations with DPRK, 191

relations with United States, 68, 222n3-24

role in Korean War, 34, 36, 46

Sino-Indian border war (1962), 67

Sino-Japanese Treaty (1978), 68

Sino-Soviet rift, 52, 59, 66–7

treaty with Soviet Union (1950), 32

US perceived threat from, 10

Chinese People's Volunteers, 34, 36, 45

Chirac, Jacques, 197

Cho Man Sik, 27, 28, 49, 50

Choe Chang Sik, 105

Choe Kwang, General, 110

Choi Chang, 51

Choi Chang Ik, 51

Choi Su Hon, 116, 117, 118

Choi Tae Bok, 138

*Chollima* Campaign, 58

Chondoism, 107

Chondoist Chungu Party, 49, 50, 107

Chongsanri campaign, 58–9

Chosen Soren, 70, 84, 86–7, 138, 186

Choson dynasty, 18, 20

*Chosun Daily News*, 175

Christianity in Korea, 18–19, 106–7, 138

opposition to, 20

Chun Doo Hwan, President, 75

Churchill, Prime Minister Winston, 46–7

CIA, 6, 15, 110, 120, 170

assessment of DPRK's weapons capability, 147–8

predicts collapse of DPRK, 152

predicts Korean War, 33

prevents Japan–DPRK rapprochement, 176, 182

circuses, 96–8

civil war *see* war, Korean

classification of citizens, 63–6

cleanliness of DPRK, 83

Clinton, President Bill, 5, 151, 153, 160, 164, 174, 180–1, 195

Coca-Cola, 152

cold war, 26, 32, 33, 47

collective mentality, xix

colonial
   crimes, 11
   experiences in Korea, xvii, 16, 17, 20–4, 57, 176

COMECON, 61

'comfort women', 7, 24

comics, 95–6

Communism
   crusade against by US, 1, 35, 36
   early in Korea, 21, 25
   Kim Il Sung's version of, 54–6, 152
   New Communist Party (UK), 12
   repression in 1920s, 22
   repression in United States, 46
   suppressed in South Korea post-war, 29

*Communist Manifesto*, 23

Communist Party
   of China, 22, 32, 49, 68
   in Japan, 35
   of Korea, 27, 49, 50
   of Soviet Union (CPSU), 27, 55
   and the Spanish Civil War, 34

Confucianism, xviii

Constitution (1972), 106

Constitution (1992), 56, 106

consumer goods, 3

Cook, Robin, 195

cost
   of aid *see* aid
   of KEDO project, 184, 186
   of the Korean War, 44
   of military *see* military expenditure
   of potential Korean war, 1, 5
   to rehabilitate DPRK, 11

crime, 107–8

Cuba, 3
   exiles from, 6
   Missile Crisis, 67

Cumings, Bruce, 45

currency
   acceptable for payment in DPRK, 13, 81

DPRK's foreign of choice, 217
exchange rates, 122

Dai Bingguo, 172
*Dawn of a New Age*, 93
deaths
    on Cheju Island, 30
    death penalty, 107
    by execution, 127, 128
    from famine, 3, 79, 112–14
    in the Korean War, 36–8, 44
    in riots, 42
    by suicide, 75, 137
    in terrorist attacks, 6
    in the Vietnam War, 71
debt, DPRK's, 62
    to European banks, 11, 194
    inability to pay, 62
    to Soviet Union, 27
debt, US to China, 171
Declaration of Independence
    (1919), 21
defectors
    from the DPRK, 9, 134–7
    US to DPRK, 43, 94, 223n4–11
    world tour of, 137–40
    *see also* refugees
defence industry, 59, 67, 127
    *see also* arms trade, military
        expenditure
Delisle, Guy, 93
demilitarised zone (DMZ), 1, 16, 71
democracy, concepts of, 2
Democratic People's Republic of
    Korea
    anticipated collapse of, 152
    formation of, 29
    negotiations with South Korea,
        75, 174
    soldiers fighting in Vietnam, 71
    size and geography, 16
    withdrawal from Non-
        Proliferation Treaty, 150
    *see also* other aspects indexed
        separately
Democratic Republic of the Congo
    (DRC), 10
Deng Xiao Ping, xv, 68

Diana, Princess, 56
diplomatic relations with DPRK,
    11, 112, 117, 169–98
    of EU countries, 194–7, 217
disabled, rights for the, 105
division of Korean peninsula *see*
    Korea, division of
dogs, as food, 98–9
Doi, Takako, 177
Dorfman, Ariel, 96
Down with Imperialism League, 22
Downs, Chuck, 46
Dresnock, James, 223n4–11
drought, 113

*East Wind 61*, 159
Eberstadt, Nick, 183
economy of DPRK
    based on heavy industry post-
        war, 3, 23, 27, 48, 51, 56–7,
        112
    breakdown in 1990s, 48, 79, 112,
        113
    debate on, 89
    GDP, 221n3-15
    growth in 1950s, xviii, 58–9
    options for reform, 124–5
    problems from 1960s, 3, 48, 60,
        62
    problems with reform in 2000s,
        124
    reform and impact of, xix, 3,
        122, 200
    similar to Eastern Europe, 209
    skewed to defence, 59, 67, 127
education, 63, 82, 84–8, 221n3–14
    'social', 87–8
Eisenhower, President Dwight D.,
    42
elections
    (1948), 28, 30
    subverted in South (1952), 46
emigrants from Korea, 49, 70, 134
    *see also* defectors, refugees
employment of Koreans, 4
enemy, the West's need for DPRK
    as, 7–8
energy issues, 11–12, 181, 188–9

electricity supplied by South
Korea to DPRK 175, 188
fuel/electricity shortages, 13,
84, 92, 151, 187
Heavy Fuel Oil Agreement,
151–5, 181, 185, 191, 202–3,
213–14
hydro power failures, 113
see also nuclear power
Equal Emphasis policy, 67
equal opportunities, 105–7
Euro, 122, 217
Europe, Eastern
aid to DPRK, 57–8
brittle communism in, 152
European attitudes to DPRK, 9
see also European Parliament,
European Union
European Business Association
Pyongyang, 210
European Commission, 121, 124–5
Humanitarian Aid Office
(ECHO), 117
European Parliament, xv, 116, 138,
227n7-9, 228n7-13
addressed by Kim Dae Jung,
195–7
delegation to assess aid
requirements, 116–17
delegation to DPRK (2007), 144
delegation for relations with
Korean peninsula, 11
External Economic Relations
Committee, xv, 194
Foreign Affairs Committee, 117,
193, 216–17
European Union
Action Plan for DPRK, 210
aid to DPRK, 114, 116–18, 193–5,
209–10, 216, 228n7-16
attitudes to DPRK, 9–10, 141–3,
193, 199–200, 216–17
Common Foreign and Security
Policy (CFSP), 9, 194
and DPRK Workshop on
Economic Reform, 131, 205,
208–9
foreign policy of, 9–11, 216

as 'honest broker', 11
and KEDO, 153, 184–5
mission to DPRK, 10–11
as payer not player, 11, 209-10
power of, 9
Rapid Reaction Force, 10, 216
Reform Treaty (2007), 9
relations with United States,
11–12
executions
during the Korean War, 37
opponents of Kim Il Sung, 50
opponents of Kim Jong Il, 128

factionalism in 2000s, 129–30
family break-up after Korean War,
44, 175
famine, xviii–xix, 51, 79, 110, 112–24
deaths from, 3, 79, 112–14
Fatherland Liberation, 30
Fifield, Anna, 3
Five-Year Plan (1957–60), 57
Flood Damage Rehabilitation
Committee, 116
floods, 113, 218
flowers, 98
national, 70, 98
food, 98–100
shortages, 113, 204, 206 (see also
famine)
football, xv, 100–3
footballers imprisoned, 110
Ford, President Gerald R., 72–3
foreign investment in DPRK,
209–10
foreign policy/relations of DPRK,
66–73
see also China, European Union,
Japan, Soviet Union, United
States, etc
France, 197-8
Franco, General Francisco, 34
Free Trade Agreements (FTA),
208
Freedom House, 141
French, Sid, 12
Frenkiel, Olenka, 139
funfair, 12–13, 98

Gallucci, Robert, 152
*Game of their Lives, The*, 102, 110, 224n4-13
Geneva Convention, 41, 136
geography of DPRK, 16–18
Germany, reunification of, 74, 173, 212
Gorbachev, President Mikhail, 68–9, 152, 169
Gore, Al, 162
Greater East Asia Co-Prosperity Sphere, 24
gross national product (GNP), 27
Gruimchaek *see* comics
guerrilla warfare, 22, 26, 30, 49
    *see also* revolts and rebellions
Guevara, Ernesto ('Che'), 53

Ha Jin, 42
Halliday, John, 45
Hamgyong Province, 113
Hamhung, 105
Hashimoto, Ryutaro, 179
Hayes, Peter, 190
health services, 63, 103–5
Heavy Fuel Oil (HFO), 226n6-5
    promised deliveries, 151–5, 187, 191, 202–3, 213–14
Hecker, Siegfried, 155
Heritage Foundation, 139, 142, 162
Hill, Christopher, 199
Hirobumi, Ito, 21
Hirohito, Emperor, 180, 213
Hiroshima Peace Park, 24
Ho Kai, 32, 51
Hodge, General John R., 29
holidays, public, 96
housing, 84
Hu Jintao, President, 172, 191
Huichon, 12
human rights, 92, 138–44
    abuses in DPRK, 70, 107–10, 132, 138–9, 200–1
    allegations by defectors, 138–9
    EU–DPRK dialogue, 10
    UN resolutions condemning DPRK, 120, 142
hurricanes, 113

Hussain, Saddam, xv
Hwang Jang Yop, 127, 137

Inchon, 36
India, 6, 157, 158
    war with China, 67
Indonesia, 10, 70, 144, 216
industry in Korea/DPRK, 3, 23, 205
    nationalisation of, 27
    under Japanese colonisation, 24
    *see also under* economy
inflation, 206
information technology, 89, 92, 206–7
Inter-Korea Summit 2000, 173, 174, 178, 182, 185, 195, 202
Inter-Korea Summit 2007, 218
International Atomic Energy Agency (IAEA), 150, 191, 201
International Covenant on Civil and Political Rights, 143
Internet, the, 89, 92–3, 200
investment (foreign) in DPRK, 4, 125
Iran, 4, 153, 156, 158, 159, 192, 199
    defence against threat from 10, 162
Iraq, xv, 4, 199
    foreign attitudes to, 11
    wars, 5, 154, 159, 192
Ishii, Shiro, 39
isolation of DPRK, 12, 48
Israel, 6, 71, 157, 158
Iwo Jima, 38

Jang Song Taek, 130, 132, 172, 204, 205
Japan, 16, 19, 30, 142, 213
    1894–5 invasion of Korea and Sino-Japanese War
    19th-century opening up, 18
    aid/repayments to DPRK, 11–12, 114, 117–18, 176
    attitudes to/by DPRK, 8, 95, 217
    as coloniser/occupier of Korea, xvii, 16, 17, 20–4, 57, 176
    Communist Party, 35

defence against perceived
    Korean threat, 161–2, 164
economic performance of, 3
and KEDO, 185
gained from Korean War, 47
invasion of Manchuria, 22
Koreans resident in, 24, 70,
    86–7, 138
military expenditure, 145, 146,
    161–5
post-war policies of, 7
Red Army Faction, 5–6
relationship with DPRK, 7, 70,
    176–80, 188, 190
relationship with US, 179
repayments to South Korea, 11
and Russo-Japanese War, 20, 26
in the six-party talks, xix
Sino-Japanese Treaty (1978), 68
Soviet-Japanese Neutrality Pact,
    23
surrender after Second World
    War, 25
*Taisho* democracy period, 21
transport links with DPRK, 15
US view of, 38
wartime atrocities, 180
Japan-Korea Annexation Treaty, 21
Japanese, numbers in Korea, 24
Jenkins, Charles Robert, 179,
    223n4-11
Jiang Zemin, 172
Jo Myung Rok, 181
Johnson, President Lyndon B., 157
*Joint Security Area*, 43
joint ventures, 210
    *see also* Kaesong industrial
        complex,
Jon Sung Hun, 3
Jospin, Lionel, 197
journalists, 12, 90
    *see also* media
Joy, Vice Admiral C. Turner, 40, 41
*Juche*, xviii, 2, 48, 52, 54–6, 66, 81, 113
    culture, 93–4
    gives way to pragmatism, 125–7

Kaesong, 40

industrial complex, 4, 175,
    207–8, 212
Kang Ban Sok, 52
Kang Byong Sop, 139
Kang Chol Hwan, 109–10, 137–8
Kang Song Guk, 139
Kang Song Hak, 139
Kang Suk Ju, 154, 185, 202
Kanggye, 37, 148
Kanghwa (island), 29–30
Kanghwa, Treaty of, 19, 24
*Kangsong Daeguk*, 128, 206
Kansong Steel Works, 58
*Kapsan* faction, 49
Kartman, Charles, 149
Katsura, Prime Minister Taro, 20
Kaysone Phomvihane, 53
Kelly, James, 154, 185, 202
Kerry, John, 188
Khabarovsk Infantry Services
    School, 23
Khan, A. Q., 155, 158
Khrushchev, President Nikita, xviii,
    2, 51, 52, 55, 66, 67, 74
Kidron, Michael, 89
Kim Chin Myung, 175
Kim Dae Jung, 75, 76, 110, 169,
    172–4, 181, 182, 185, 195–7, 212,
    215
    addresses European Parliament,
        195–7
Kim Hyong Jik, 52
Kim Il Sung
    as anti-Japanese fighter, xvii, 22
    autobiography, 53
    birth, 22, 86
    chairman of KWP, 28
    commander of Red Army 88th
        Brigade, 26
    commemorative tower, 81
    death, xviii, 3, 53, 56, 76, 78, 126
    desecration of pictures, 183
    devises monitoring system,
        108
    as 'Eternal President', 128
    exiled to Soviet Union, 23
    family, 76–8 (*see also* individual
        members by name)

formative influences, 23
focus of history teaching, 86
gains control of North Korea,
    xviii, 14, 23, 27–8
gifts to, 82
as 'Great Leader', 23, 53, 82
Higher Party School, 85
imprisoned, 22
interviews with, 55
Korean War role, 32–3, 37, 41–2,
    45
led June 1937 attack on
    Pochonbo, 22–3
marriage, 23
meeting with Jimmy Carter, 151,
    201
original name, 22
parents, 52, 86, 107
period of control, 48–78
personality cult, xviii, 51, 52–3, 70
post Second World War role,
    26–7, 30–1
purge of opponents, 2, 50, 51,
    55, 89, 222n3-30
quotes from, 50–1, 60–1, 67–8,
    74, 84–5, 91–2
Square, 82
statues of, 4, 80
University, 85, 87, 111
visits Beijing, 68
visits Moscow, 68
*Kimilsungin*, 70, 98
Kim Jong Chol, 132
Kim Jong Il, xix, 7, 52–3, 112, 125,
    127, 215
assessment of regime, 200–1
attempted assassination, 89,
    130
birth, 23, 96
confesses to Japanese
    abductions, 178
as 'Dear Leader', 53, 86
as economic reformer, 199
health of, 192
likely succession to, 132
loathed by George W. Bush, 187
in Malta, 76, 77, 166
meets Kim Dae Jung, 174

meets Madeleine Albright, 181
meets Roh Moo Hyun, 218
promotion of, 14
quotes from, 55, 94, 122, 125,
    127, 204
schooling, 85
stops smoking, 105
succeeds Kim Il Sung, 3, 76–8,
    127–8
threats to leadership, 130–2
in US movie, 145–6
weapons programme of, 5
visits to China, 8, 172, 204, 205
visit to Russia, 170
*Kimjongilin*, 98, 99
Kim Jong Nam, 132, 182
Kim Jong Suk, 23, 52
Kim Jong Un, 132
Kim Pyong Il, 77
Kim Song Ae, 77, 106
Kim Tu Bong, 49, 51
Kim Ung U, 52
Kim Young Ju, 76–7
Kim Young Nam, 128, 155, 192, 217
Kim Young Sam, President, 76, 181
'kiosk capitalists', 3
Ko Young Hee, 130, 132
Koguryo kingdom, 17
Koizumi, Prime Minister Junichiro,
    7, 178, 179, 213, 217
Kojong, King, 18, 20
Korea (peninsula)
    colonised/occupied by Japan,
        xvii, 16, 17, 20–4
    cost of reunification, 173
    division of, xvii–xviii, 1, 16, 21,
        25–6, 28
    early history of, 17
    nineteenth-century history of,
        18–21
    'One Korea' nationalism, 175
    proposed Trusteeship of, 25
    reunification aims/proposals,
        36, 38, 43, 73–6
Korea Electric Power Corporation
    (KEPCO), 186
Korean Air, bombing of flight, 5,
    75, 100

Korean Central Broadcast Agency, 130
Korean Central Intelligence Agency, 75–6
Korean Central News Agency (KCNA), 90
Korean Computer Centre, 92, 210
Korean Democratic Party, 21, 49
Korean Expedition (US), 18–19
Korean Film Studio, 94
Korean National Police, 30
Korean Peninsula Energy Development Organisation (KEDO), 11–12, 149, 153, 183–6, 195, 196, 197
Korean People's Army (KPA), 31, 146
Korean People's Revolutionary Army, 22
Korean–US (KORUS) Free Trade Agreement, 208
Korean war *see* war, Korean
Korean Workers' Party, 13, 27, 28, 49, 88
 Central Committee, 51, 178
 Congress, 51, 75, 77
 losses during the war, 50
 reshuffle in 2000s, 130, 204
Korean Youth League, 22
Koreans
 fighting in Second World War, 24
 Japanese treatment of, 23–4
 numbers in Japan, 24, 70, 86–7, 138
Koryo Hotel, 81
Koryo Tours, 12
Kouchner, Bernard, 198
*Kulloja*, 51, 59, 88, 89, 105
Kumchangri, 153, 181
Kumsusan Memorial Palace, 53
Kung Sok Ung, 125, 131
Kwangju massacre, 75
*Kwangmyonsong*, 181
Kwon Hyok, 138–9
*Kyongje Yongu*, 89

labour protection laws, 27

Lameda, Ali, 109
land reform, 27, 57
language, use of, 86
Laos, 3, 36, 53
laws, 27
Lee Hu Rak, 75
Lee Hyon Ik, 18
Lee Soon Ok, 109, 138
Lee Sung Ki, 149
Leiber, Keir, 165
Lenin, V. I., 21
Libya, 159, 167
Lie, Trygve, 40
Lim Dong-Won, 75–6
Lin Bao, 32
literacy rate, 63, 85
living standards, 79–111
Lon Nol, 71
Lüshun, 20
Luxembourg, 35–6

MacArthur, General Douglas, 33, 35–7
*Mainichi Shimbun*, 55
malaria, 103–4
Malik, Jacob, 40
Malta, 76, 77, 166
Manchuria, 20, 32, 49
 Japanese invasion of, 22
 Korean speakers in, 18
*Manchurian Candidate, The*, 43
*Manga*, 95–6
Mangyongdae
 Funfair, 13, 98
 Revolutionary School, 85
Mao Anying, 45
Mao Zedong, xvii, 31, 32, 39, 48, 51, 66, 149, 151
March First Movement, 21
March North, 30
Mariam, Haile, 111
Maritime Territories, 16
market economy, emerging in DPRK, 123–5, 204–5
Market Leninism, 9, 62, 208, 215
markets in DPRK, 13, 82, 107, 205
 farmers', 122, 204
 growth in 2000s, 122, 205

Tong-Il, 13, 107, 122, 123, 205–6
Marxism-Leninism, 54–6
Mass Games, 96–8
Mattelart, Armand, 96
Maurois, Pierre, 197
McCarthyism, 1, 46
Médecins sans Frontières, 118–19
media, 89–96
    state control of, 89, 93–4, 200
    *see also Kulloja, Rodong Sinmun*
Megawati, President Sukarnoputri,
    70
Military Armistice Commission, 43
military assistance by DPRK, 166
military, role of in DPRK, 89, 127,
    146
military expenditure
    of China, 164, 171, 213
    of DPRK, 7, 67–8, 89, 146, 201
    of Japan, 7
    of South Korea, 67, 146
    of United States, 7–8, 146, 161–5,
        226n6-13
Military Four Lines Policy, 68
Mindan, 70
Ministry of People's Security,
    224n4-16
*Minju Choson*, 89
Mintoff, Prime Minister Dom, 76
missiles, 148–9, 158–65, 176, 226n6-
    13
    defences against, 161–5
    range of, 148, 160–1
    sales of, 167, 192
    testing of, 160, 190
missionaries, 18–19, 107
Mitterrand, Francois, 197
mobile phones, 89
modernisation of Korea, 62, 63
    by Japan, 24–5
    resistance to, 25
Molotov, Vyacheslav, 42
monetary reform (2002), 122
Morris, James, 119
movies
    on Japanese abductions to
        DPRK, 179
    made in DPRK, 94

    made in South Korea, 175
    US about Korean threat, 145
multinational corporations, 3, 111,
    210
Mun Song Sul, 108
Muntarbhorn, Vitit, 118, 140
Murayama, Prime Minister
    Tomiichi, 153
Murphy, J. T., 54–5
music, 91–2
mutiny of South Korean army, 30

Naktong River, 38
Nam Il, General, 40
names, Korean, xi
Nampo, 83
napalm, 38, 39
nationalisation of industry, 27, 57
National Missile Defence (NMD),
    7, 161–5, 185, 202
NATO, 47
Needle, Clive, 116
New Communist Party (UK), 12
Nicaragua, 166
Nicholas II, Tsar, 16
Nixon, President Richard M., 68,
    74, 222n3-24
No Gun Ri, 38
Non-Aligned Movement (NAM),
    69–70
non-government organisations
    (NGOs), 119, 121
    *see also* individual NGOs by
        name
Non-Proliferation Treaty (NPT), 6,
    150, 157, 227n7-9
Nordpolitik, 75
North East Anti-Japanese Allied
    Army, 22, 32
North Korea *see* Democratic
    People's Republic of Korea
North Korean Communist Party, 49
North Korean Human Rights Act
    2003 (US), 140
North Korean Human Rights Act
    2004 (US), 92, 139, 140–1
North Korean Workers Party, 27,
    28, 49

*see also* Korean Workers Party
Northern Limit Line, 40–1
nuclear plant/weapons, xix, 5, 6,
    12, 39, 67, 147–51
    alleged/real DPRK
        programmes, 145–68, 181,
        185–8, 191, 201–3
    alleged confession about, 154
    Chinese programme, 6, 39
    crises over DPRK's, 1, 201–3
    Hiroshima bomb, 24
    inspections of, 150–1, 153, 156
    not provided to DPRK by
        China/Soviet Union, 67
    in potential new Korean war, 1,
        148–51
    Russian protection of DPRK by, 3
    and six-party agreement, 188
    testing of by DPRK, 6, 7, 149,
        157, 191, 25n6–3
    testing of by Soviet Union, 35
    threatened use by US, 39
    US, 6, 7–8
nuclear power, 11–12, 149, 151, 170,
    183–7, 215
    and the Agreed Framework,
        151–2, 183, 187
nurseries, 85

oil crisis (1973), 3, 194
oil tanker, 192
Olympic Games, 100, 169, 171,
    174
*One Minute to Zero*, 38
operas, 98
Operation Iceberg, 25
Operation Team Spirit, 75–6
Opium War (1839–42), 18
Orwell, George, 24, 34
Osgood, Cornelius, 29–30
Ozawa, Ichiro, 179

Paetku, Mt, 16, 23, 52, 86, 175
Pacific War *see under* Second World
    War
Pak Gil Yon, 191
Pak Hon Young, 21, 29, 32, 33, 50
Pak Pong Ju, 130, 204

Pakistan, 6, 148, 149, 155, 157–8,
    159, 163, 200, 203, 213
Palestine/Palestine Liberation
    Organisation (PLO), 69, 167, 216
Panmunjom, 40, 43, 72
Park Chung Hee, President, 30, 67,
    73, 215
Park Gun Hye, 215
Park Seung Jin, 101, 110
Partido Obrero de Unificación
    Marxista (POUM), 34
partition of Korea, *see* 38th Parallel,
    Korea (peninsula)
Patten, Chris, 182, 195, 228n7-18
Pearl Harbor, 33
Perry, William (Bill) (report by),
    151, 173, 181, 182, 226n6-4
Perry, Commodore Matthew, 18
Persson, Prime Minister Göran, 10,
    182, 195, 217
Peru, 166
Philippines, 20, 21, 30
plans, economic, 57–62
    abandonment of, 124, 205
Pochonbo, 22–3
Pol Pot, 71
political system of DPRK, 2
Port Arthur, 20 (see also Lüshun)
portraits
    desecreation of, 183
    of the two Kims, 53, 133
    removal of Kim Jong Il's, 131–3
Posada, Luis, 6
postage stamps, 69, 180, 222n3-25
Potsdam Conference/Agreement,
    16, 25, 26
Preparation Committee for Korean
    Independence (PCKI), 27, 28
Press, Daryl, 165
Preston, W. B., 18
Priestly, Julian, 118
Prince, Dorian, 197
prisoners
    allegedly used in chemical
        weapons experiments, 38–9,
        138–9, 148
    political, 30, 65, 105, 107–10, 138
    of war, 40, 41–3, 44

protests, public, 27, 45
    brutal suppression in South
        Korea, 29–30
    *see also* revolts and rebellions
Provisional People's Committee, 28
Public Distribution System, 63, 79,
    113, 116, 118, 121, 124, 204
Pugang, 3, 14
*Pukachev*, 26
purges *see* executions; *under* Kim
    Il-Sung
Pusan, 18
Pusan Perimeter, 33, 36
Putin, President Vladimir, 170
Pyongyang,
    bars and clubs, 100
    Business School, 210
    Grand People's Study House,
        82, 91
    growth of, 63
    fall in Korean War, 36
    foreign visitors to, 12–13
    golf course, 12
    International Cinema, 94
    Kim Il Sung Square, 82
    Kim Il Sung University, 85, 97,
        111
    Marathon, 103
    Maternity Hospital, 103
    May Day Stadium, 96
    metro, 83
    rebuilding after Korean War,
        81–3
    restaurants, 98, 206
    Station, 84
    Tong-il Market, 13, 107, 122,
        123, 205–6
    Tower of the *Juche* Idea, 81
    Zoo, 98

Quinones, Kenneth, 93

racism, US, 38
radio, 83, 90–1, 92
railways, 12–14, 24, 83–4, 170
    accidents on, 84
    Trans–Siberian, 20
    *see also* trains, transport

Railway University of
    Communism, 87
rainbow imagery, 52
Rajin-Songbong, 207
Rangoon bombing (1983), 5
Rao, Benegal, 36
Reagan, President Ronald, 119, 162,
    180
Red Army, 26
Red Army faction, 5–6, 177
'Red Banner', 127–8
Red Cross, 74
Red Peasant International, 21–2
refugees
    from China to Korea, 134
    from North to South Korea, 57,
        134–9
    Korean to China, xix, 51, 112,
        119, 132–9
    Korean to Japan (1948), 30, 70
    in the Korean War, 38
regime change, 5, 145, 190, 199–218
regime survival, 1, 3, 130
religion, attitudes to, 105–6
repatriation of prisoners of war,
    41–2
Republic of Korea *see* South Korea
resources, natural of DPRK, 17
restaurants, 98
Rhee, Syngman *see* Syngman Rhee
Ridgway, General Matthew, 37
Righteous Army, 21
*Rodong Sinmun*, 51, 52, 88, 89–90,
    92, 100, 105, 126, 128–9, 172, 204,
    205, 217, 222n4–1, 228n8–3
Roh Moo Hyun, President, 174,
    185, 208, 215, 217, 218
Roh Tae Woo, President, 75–6
Roosevelt, President Franklin D.,
    25, 27, 33
Roosevelt, President Theodore,
    20
Russia, xv
    attitude to DPRK, 217
    acquires Maritime Territories, 16
    border with DPRK, 16–17
    defence against threat from 10
    flights to/from DPRK, 14

marginalisation by US, 170
Russo-Japanese War, 20, 26
tourists to DPRK, 12
and Trans-Siberian railway, 20
Ryang, Sonya, 86–7
Ryonbong General Corporation, 3
Ryongchon explosion, 130, 205

Sa, Julie, 207
safety of Korean flights, 14
Sakchu, 148
San Francisco Peace Treaty, 47
sanctions against DPRK, 190
Santer, Jacques, 184
Sarkozy, Nicholas, 198
satellites, 176
    see also missiles, Star Wars
Second World War, xvii, 38
Japanese surrender, 25
Koreans fighting in, 24
Pacific war, xvii, 1, 7, 25
security
of DPRK's regime, 1, 3, 130
threat, xix
self-sufficiency see autarky
Seoul, 20, 25
changes hands in Korean War,
36, 37
Seven-Year Plan (1961–70), 59, 60,
220n3–7
Seven-Year Plan (1978–84), 61–2
Seven-Year Plan (1987–93), 62
sex trade during Pacific War, 7, 24
Shevardnadze, Eduard, 68
shops, 79–80, 82–3, 206
Sihanouk, Prince Norodom, 71, 111
Silmido, 73–4
Sinmindang, 49
Singanhoe, 22
Sinuiju, 14, 16, 152, 207
six-party talks (2003), xix, 156, 170,
172, 186–93, 199
in 2007, 213–14
failure of agreement, 189, 210–11
terms of agreement, 188–9
Six-Year Plan (1971–76), 60
size of DPRK, 16
smoking, 105, 111

So Hwang Hui, 127
social security, 27
Social Democratic Party, 50
Socialist International (SI), 50, 177
Socialist Working Youth League, 88
Soga, Hitomi, 179, 223n4–11
Sokcho ferry, 14
Solana, Javier, 182, 193, 195, 216
Song Il Ho, 227n7–5
South Korea
1948 government, 28
aid to DPRK, 11, 114, 120, 175
assassination squad, 73–5
attitudes to DPRK, 8, 141, 172–5,
215
avoidance of reunification, 212
communications with DPRK,
14–15
Democratic Labour Party, 50
diplomatic relations with,
169–70
economic cooperation with
DPRK, 144, 206
economic performance of, 3, 4,
144, 169
floods (1984), 75
military budget, 7, 146, 165
negotiations with DPRK, 75
and Non-Aligned Movement,
69–70
Olympic Games, 169
Park Chung Hee's coup, 67
and six-party agreement, 188
soldiers in Vietnam, 71
Soviet attitudes to, 8, 169
trade with China/Soviet Union,
169
US occupation of/support for,
xviii, 16, 27–31, 57, 70, 71, 74,
174
South Korean Workers' Party, 29,
49
South-North Coordinating
Committee, 74–5
Soviet-Japanese Neutrality Pact, 23
Soviet Union, 25, 66–7
architectural influence of, 79–80
attitudes to DPRK, 8, 68–9

collapse of, 3, 62, 112, 169–70
and COMECON, 61
departure from DPRK, 29
economic aid to DPRK, 57, 58, 66
former *see* Russia
invasion of Afghanistan, 68
Kim Il Sung in, 23
military aid to DPRK, 31, 34, 66, 158–9
nuclear weapons, 35, 67
occupation of North Korea after Second World War, 26–8
rearmament of, 46
Sino-Soviet rift, 52, 59, 66–7
Stakhanovite movement, 59
as supporter/patron of North Korea, xviii, 2–3, 16, 170
treaty with China (1950), 32
war against Japan, 26
Spanish Civil War, 34
special economic zones, 207
spies/agents, 1, 75, 109
Chinese paranoia about, 23
Pak Hon Young as alleged, 50
POWs as, 43
spy ships, 71, 177
as theme for comics, 95
*see also* CIA
sport, 100–3
Stalin, Josef, xvii, xviii, 16, 25, 26, 31, 34, 42, 66
denunciation of, 2, 52, 66
*History of the Communist Party*, 56
Stalinism, xvii, 23
*Star Wars*, xix, 7–8, 160, 161–5, 171, 212
*State of Mind, A*, 97
State Price Control Bureau, 122, 204
State Security Department (SSD), 108
Stone, I. F., 33
submarine incident (1996), 181
Suh Gwan Hee, 128
Suharto, President, 70
Sunjong, King, 20

Sunshine Policy, 76, 110, 169, 172–4, 195, 212, 227n7-3, 227n7-4
Supreme People's Assembly, 50, 105
Suskind, Ron, 9
sustainable development, 10
Sutherland, Peter, 194
Syngman Rhee, 21, 28–9, 30, 31, 43, 45, 46, 49, 50, 219n2-7
Syria, 159

*Taean* work system, 59
Taechon, 150
Taedong, 16
River, 18, 98
Taepodong missiles, 159–61, 176, 190, 192
*Taewongun*, 18
Taft, William H., 20
Taft–Katsura Agreement, 20, 21
Taiwan, 30, 32, 43, 144, 165, 213, 219n2-6
Takeshita, Prime Minister Noburu, 176
*Team Spirit*, 75, 76
television, 90
terrorism
DPRK as alleged state sponsor of, 5–6, 75, 100
DPRK harbouring terrorists, 177
DPRK as victim of, 6
specific acts of, 5, 75, 100 (*see also* 9/11)
supporters of, 6
textile industry, 62, 149
Thailand, 135
Theatre Missile Defence, 10, 145, 161, 202
theocracy, DPRK as, 56
Thomas, David, 116
Three Revolutions Campaign, 60–1
Three-Year Plan (1954–56), 57
Tibet, 32, 37
Tindemans, Leo, 116
Tito, Marshal Josip, 34, 48, 55
Tonghak Uprising (1894), 20–2, 49
movement, 107

rebellion, 20
torture, 9, 109, 138
tourism, 12, 175
trade
    19th-century attempts to
        establish, 18–19
    in arms, 7, 158–9, 165–7, 192, 200
    with China, 206
    DPRK's volume of interna-
        tional, 4, 124, 165–6, 170, 194
    Free Trade Agreement (FTA),
        208
    in IT, 207
    rejected in favour of autarky, 61
    reluctance to trade with DPRK,
        11
trains
    Kim's personal, 54
    steam, 12, 84
    *see also* railways
transport
    links with rest of world, 13–15,
        71, 84, 170, 190
    links with South Korea, 14–15,
        136, 175, 208
    network, 24, 83–4, 175, 220n3–6
    public, 12–13, 83
    shortage of private, 82, 84
travel
    restrictions for foreigners in
        DPRK, 12, 15
    restrictions/permits for
        Koreans, 89, 200
treaties
    between China and Japan, 68
    between China and Soviet
        Union, 32
    San Francisco, 47
    signed by Korean governments,
        19, 20, 21, 32, 66
triplets, status of, 103
Truman, President Harry S, 16, 35,
    36, 37, 39
Tumen River, 16, 132–4
tunnel warfare, 71
Turkmenistan, 200–1

*Uibyong*, 21, 22

United Kingdom, 25, 161
    and the Korean War, 34, 35
United Nations, 33–4, 36, 119, 188
    1947 proposals, 28
    Command in Korea, 35–6, 40
    Food and Agriculture
        Organization, 114
    Human Rights Commission,
        140, 142
    resolutions condemning DPRK,
        10, 34–5, 120, 167, 190–1
    Security Council, 34–5, 36, 190
    Soviet Union boycott of, 35
    Special Rapporteur, 118, 141
    UNDP, 114
    UNICEF, 114, 119
    World Food Programme, 114,
        119–21, 195
United States
    1882 treaty with Korea, 19, 20
    aid to DPRK, 114
    as supporter/occupier of South
        Korea, xviii, 16, 27–31, 57, 70,
        71, 74, 75
    attitude by/to DPRK, xix, 8,
        70–1, 95, 145–68, 212–13
    at war with DPRK, xviii, 1, 43
    and the 'axe murder', 72–3
    citizens shipwrecked, 18
    citizens visiting DPRK, 15
    control of United Nations, 35
    debts to China, 171
    defectors to DPRK, 43, 94,
        223n4-11
    defences against DPRK's threat,
        161–5
    fear of Communism, 35
    House Committee on Foreign
        Relations, 119, 137
    keen to attack Soviet Union post
        Second World War, 31
    lack of aid to DPRK, 11
    military expenditure of, 7–8,
        145, 146, 161–5, 226n6-13
    Military Government in Korea
        (USMGIK), 27, 28, 29
    need for strategic 'enemy',
        7–8

North Korean Human Rights
  Acts, 92, 139, 140–1
nuclear weapons of, 6
Office of Technology
  Assessment (OTA), 163
perimeter of defence in Asia, 30
policy after 9/11, xix, 5, 174, 182
post-Second World War
  proposals for Korea, 25
pre-emptive attack by feared, 5
propaganda to DPRK, 92
racism of, 38
relations with China, 68,
  222n3–24
relations with DPRK, 180–6,
  188, 190
relations with Japan, 20
role in the Korean War, 35–7
talks with DPRK, 180
terrorist acts sponsored by, 6
seen as threat to security, 175
USS General Sherman, 18–19, 52
USS Liberty, 71
USS Pueblo, 71–2
USS South America, 18
withdraws from South Korea
  (1949), 29
university
  Kim Il Sung, 85, 87, 111
  and lifelong learning, 88
  others in DPRK, 87
  study at foreign, 87, 173
Unsung Heroes, 94
urbanisation, 63

Vietnam, 3, 46, 62, 69, 87, 208
  war, 59, 71
Vinalon, 149

wages, 84, 124, 183, 204
war, Korean, xviii, 1–2, 16, 30,
  32–41, 71, 194, 228n7-14
  armistice/truce talks, 40, 43
  battles of, 40
  biological weapons used in, 148
  countries participating, 35–6
  of 1871, 18
  situation after, 50

start of, 33
war
  First World, 21
  Iran-Iraq, 159, 192
  Iraq, 154
  potential of new Korean, 1, 5
  Russo-Japanese, 20
  Second World see Second World
    War
  Sino-Japanese (1894–5), 20
  Spanish Civil, 34
  Vietnam, 59, 71
  Yom Kippur, 166
weapons
  developed/acquired by DPRK,
    147–8, 159–60, 163
  sold abroad by DPRK, 165–7
  used in Korean War, 38
  see also arms trade, bombs,
    military expenditure,
    missiles, nuclear
    plant/weapons
welfare state, 62–5
West Sea Barrage, 127
Westerners in DPRK, 110–11
Willoughby, Maj.-Gen. Charles, 33
Wilson, President Woodrow, 21
With the Century, 53, 54
women, status/treatment of, 83,
  105–6, 134
Wonson, 71–2, 190
Woolsey, James, 110
workers
  education for, 88
  pattern of employment, 63
  productivity of, 58–60
World Health Organization, 114
World Trade Organization, 4
  observer status, 4
Wu Banguo, 172
Wu Yi, 172

Yalu River see Amnok River
Yanan faction, 49, 51
Yang Bin, 207
Yang Jiechi, 192
Yanji, 132
Yeltsin, President Boris, 170

Yemen, 167
Yokota, Megumi, 11, 178
Yongbyon nuclear plant/research centre, 6, 93, 148, 149–51, 154–5, 183, 191, 193
Yosu-Sunchon, 30, 33
Young Friends of the Celestial Way, Party of *see* Chondoist Chungu Party

Yudhoyono, President Susilio Bambang, 70
Yun Hong Kum, 51
Yun, Philip W., 226n6-4
Yusuf, Irwandi, 216

Zhou Enlai, 42, 68